OBJECTS OF DESIRE

OBJECTS OF DESIRE

Design and Society since 1750

ADRIAN FORTY

with 272 illustrations

THAMES AND HUDSON

Edited and designed by Ian Cameron
Produced by Cameron Books, PO Box 1, Moffat, Dumfriesshire DG10 9SU

First published in Great Britain in 1986 by Thames and Hudson Limited, London
This paperback edition 1992
Published in paperback in the USA in 1992 by Thames and Hudson Inc.,
500 Fifth Avenue, New York, New York 10110

Library of Congress Catalog Card Number: 91-67302

Printed and bound in Great Britain.

In writing this book, I have been fortunate in the help that many people have given me so freely. In particular, I would like to thank Hazel Clarke, Francis Duffy, Anthony D. King, Caradoc King, Pat Kirkham, Rodney Mace, John North, Dorothy Ogden, Rozsika Parker, Michèle Roberts, Helen Smith, Robert Thorne, Clive Wainwright and Deborah Weiner for their help, advice, suggestions, information and criticism.

My greatest debts are to my colleague Mark Swenarton and to my wife Briony Fer, both of whom read much of the book in draft and were frank and constructive in their criticisms. While I was writing, both gave more encouragement than I could ever have asked for, and although I must take the responsibility for the book's arguments and ideas, it owes more to them than they may know.

The arduous task of assembling the illustrations for the book was made much easier through the helpfulness of a number of archives, firms and museums: in particular, I would like to thank Lynn Miller of the Wedgwood Museum at Barlaston, Jim Gibson of Twyfords Ltd, Stoke-on-Trent, Ivan Sparkes of High Wycombe Museum and Tony Coulson of the Open University.

The manuscript of this book was completed in 1980 and uses research published up to that date. Despite the interval that has elapsed, I believe that the arguments and ideas of the book remain valid and sustainable.

Contents

Introduction

*Anthony J. Coulson, *A Bibliography of Design in Britain 1851-1970*, London, 1979, gives a good indication of the range of British design literature available.

Nearly every object we use, most of the clothes we wear and many of the things we eat have been designed. Since design seems to be so much a part of everyday life, we are justified in asking exactly what it is, what it does, and how it came into existence. In spite of all that has been written on the subject, it is not easy to find the answers to these apparently simple questions.* Most of the literature from the last fifty years would have us suppose that the main function of design is to make things beautiful. A few studies suggest that it is a special method of solving problems, but only occasionally has design been shown to have something to do with profit, and even more rarely has it been seen as being concerned with the transmission of ideas. This book developed out of my realisation that, especially in its economic and ideological aspects, design is a more significant activity than has usually been acknowledged.

Particularly in Britain, the study of design and its history has suffered from a form of cultural lobotomy which has left design connected only to the eye, and severed its connections to the brain and to the pocket. It is commonly assumed that design would somehow be soiled if it were associated too closely with commerce, a misconceived attempt at intellectual hygiene that has done no good at all. It has obscured the fact that design came into being at a particular stage in the history of capitalism and played a vital part in the creation of industrial wealth. Limiting it to a purely artistic activity has made it seem trivial and relegated it to the status of a mere cultural appendix.

Just as little attention has been given to design's influence on how we think. Those who complain about the effects of television, journalism, advertising and fiction on our minds remain oblivious to the similar influence of design. Far from being a neutral, inoffensive artistic activity, design, by its very nature, has much more enduring effects than the ephemeral products of the media because it can cast ideas about who we are and how we should behave into permanent and tangible forms.

Since 'design' is a word that will figure large in this book, it is as well to state at the outset what it means. In everyday speech, the word has two common meanings when applied to artefacts. In one sense, it refers to the look of things: saying 'I like the design' usually involves notions of beauty, and such judgements are generally made on that basis. As will already be clear, this book is not about the aesthetics of design. Its purpose is not to discuss whether, say, William Morris's furniture designs were more beautiful than those displayed at the Great Exhibition of 1851, but rather to try to discover why such differences existed at all.

The second, more exact use of the word 'design' refers to the preparation of instructions for the production of manufactured goods, and this is the sense meant when, for example, someone says 'I am working on the design of a car.' It might be tempting to separate the two meanings and deal with them independently, but this would be a great mistake, for the special quality of the word 'design' is that it conveys both senses, and their conjunction in a single word rightly expresses the fact that they are inseparable: the way things look is, in the broadest sense, a result of the conditions of their making.

History, as I use it here, is concerned with the explanation of change, and the subject of this book is therefore the causes of change in the design of industrially-made goods. In other aspects of human existence that have been studied by historians – politics, society, the economy and some forms of culture – the theories that have been developed to explain change appear highly sophisticated compared to those employed in the history of design. Such a poor showing has come about largely through the confusion of design with art, and the consequent idea that manufactured artefacts are works of art. This view has been fostered by the collection and display of manufactured goods in the same museums as painting and sculpture, and by much that has been written about design. Thus, in a recent book, the statement 'Industrial design is the art of the twentieth century', seems calculated to obscure all the differences between art and design.*

*S. Bayley, *In Good Shape. Style in Industrial Products 1900 to 1960*, London, 1979, p.10.

The crucial distinction is that, under present conditions, art objects are usually both conceived and made by (or under the direction of) one person, the artist, whereas this is not so with manufactured goods. Both conceiving and fabricating their work allows artists considerable autonomy, which has led to the common belief that one of art's main functions is to give free expression to creativity and imagination. Whether or not this is an accurate view of art, it is most certainly not true of design. In capitalist societies, the primary purpose of the manufacture of artefacts, a process of which design is a part, has to be to make a profit for the manufacturer. Whatever degree of artistic imagination is lavished upon the design of objects, it is done not to give expression to the designer's creativity and imagination, but to make the products saleable and profitable. Calling industrial design 'art' suggests that designers occupy the principal role in production, a misconception which effectively severs most of the connections between design and the processes of society.

When it comes to explaining change, the confusion of design with art has led to a theory of causation which is as common as it is unsatisfactory. In many histories of design, change is accounted for by referring to the characters and careers of individual artists and designers – Chippendale's furniture designs might be said to differ from Sheraton's because Chippendale and Sheraton were different people, each with his own artistic ideas. It is when we try to identify the reasons for these differences that we run into difficulties, which become more acute when we consider not simply the work of individuals but the appearance of whole classes of goods involving a multitude of designers: why, for example, was office equipment designed in the 1900s universally different in appearance from that produced in the 1960s? Putting this down to differences in artistic temperament would be ridiculous.

Historians of design have often tried to get around the problem by attributing the changes to some sort of evolutionary process, as if manufactured goods were plants or animals. Changes in design are described as if they were mutations in the development of products, stages in a progressive evolution towards their most perfect form. But artefacts do not have a life of their own, and there is no evidence for a law of natural or mechanical selection to propel them in the direction of progress. The design of manufactured goods is determined not by some internal genetic structure but by the people and the industries that make them and the relationships of these people and industries to the society in which the products are to be sold.*

*P. Steadman, *The Evolution of Designs*, Cambridge, 1979, discusses the problems of biological analogies at length.

Yet while it is easy enough to say that design is related to society, the precise way in which the connection occurs has rarely been dealt with satisfactorily by historians. Most histories of design and of art and architecture have treated their subjects as largely independent of the social circumstances in which they were produced. Recently, though, it has become fashionable to refer to the 'social context' or the 'social background'. For example, Mark Girouard, in *Sweetness and Light*, a book about the nineteenth-century 'Queen Anne' style of architecture, begins by describing the critics' reception of the style, and continues:

'Both the fury and the rapture seem surprising until one examines its background, out of which it appeared with something approaching inevitability. "Queen Anne" flourished because it satisfied all the latest aspirations of the English middle classes.'*

*M. Girouard, *Sweetness and Light*, Oxford, 1977, p.1.

These remarks are followed by a few pages of generalisation about nineteenth-century society, after which Girouard proceeds to describe the work of the 'Queen Anne' architects almost entirely in architectural terms. Such cursory references to the social context are like the weeds and gravel around a stuffed fish in a glass case: however realistic these may be, they are only furnishings, and taking them away would have little effect on our perception of the fish. The use of 'social context' is rarely more than an ornament, allowing the objects themselves still to be regarded as if they had an autonomous existence where all but purely artistic considerations are trivial. To historians, the great attraction of the 'social context' has been to save them the trouble of having to think about how objects are related to their historical circumstances, and statements as imprecise as Girouard's 'something approaching inevitability' abound in other histories. The casual use of 'social context' is particularly deplorable in the study of design, which by its very nature, brings ideas and beliefs up against the material realities of production.

In this book, therefore, the history of design is also the history of societies: any account of change must rest upon an understanding of how design affects, and is affected by, the processes of modern economies.

One of the more elusive aspects of these processes is the part played by ideas, by what people think about the world they live in. Design, I believe, features large in this particular realm, and its role can be clarified, albeit in a somewhat mechanical way, by reference to Structuralist theory. The Structuralists argue that in all societies the troublesome contradictions that arise between people's beliefs and their everyday experiences are resolved by the invention of myths. These conflicts arise just as often in advanced societies as in primitive ones, and myths flourish equally in both. In our own culture, for example, the paradox of the existence of rich and poor and of the great inequality between them in a society that maintains a belief in the Christian concept of the equality of all is overcome in the story of Cinderella who is sought out and married by the prince, proving that despite her poverty she can be his equal. Cinderella is a fairy story and thus remote from everyday life, but there are plenty of latter-day variants (e.g. secretary marries boss) which enable people to think that the paradox is unimportant or non-existent. Stories have been the traditional means of conveying myths, but in this century they have been supplemented by films, journalism, television and advertising.

In his book, *Mythologies*, the French structuralist critic Roland Barthes set out to explain the way myths work, and the power they have over the way we think. Taking a wide variety of examples, ranging from the language of guidebooks to the imagery of cooking in women's magazines and the reporting of weddings by the press, Barthes showed how these apparently familiar things signify all kinds of ideas about the world. Unlike the more or less ephemeral media, design has the capacity to cast myths into an enduring, solid and tangible form, so that they seem to be reality itself. We can take as an example the common assumption that modern office work is more friendly, more fun, more varied and generally better than office work was in 'the old days'. The myth serves to reconcile most people's experience of the boredom and monotony of office work with their wish to think that it carries more status than alternatives, such as factory work, where there is no pretence about the monotony. Although advertisements for office jobs, magazine stories and television serials have been responsible for implanting in people's minds the myth that office work is fun, sociable and exciting, it is given daily sustenance and credibility by modern equipment in bright colours and slightly humorous shapes, designs that help make the office match up to the myth.

For entrepreneurs, the utilisation of these myths is necessary to commercial success. Every product, to be successful, must incorporate the ideas that will make it marketable, and the particular task of design is to bring about the conjunction between such ideas and the available means of production. The result of this process is that manufactured goods embody innumerable myths about the world, myths which in time come to seem as real as the products in which they are embedded.

Design's extensive influence and complex nature make it far from easy to deal with historically. The number of industrially made artefacts is infinite, and even the most insignificant seeming design can prove on analysis to be extraordinarily complicated. Rather than making a vain attempt to be comprehensive, I have set out to suggest how the history of the design of any manufactured article might be approached, the kinds of question that could be asked and the answers that the study of its design might yield. Although I have discussed a great variety of articles in the course of this book, many of them in some detail, my choice has inevitably been somewhat arbitrary, and there are many cases where another article would have illustrated the argument equally well. Indeed, it would be true to say that the book could have contained a different set of designs and yet retained its argument intact.

Instead of discussing every aspect of each design introduced, an approach that might quickly become tedious, I have chosen to treat design in a series of essays, with each chapter developing one theme. As no object is dealt with exhaustively, I must leave it to the reader to pursue the other themes that arise from any particular design. Although the chapters should each stand on their own, they are intended, taken together, to suggest the significance of design in our culture and the extent of its influence on our lives and minds.

Pye 'Unit System' receiver, 1922. The earliest radio sets were unashamed assemblies of technical apparatus.

1. Images of Progress

For all its benefits, progress can be a painful and disturbing experience. Our reactions to it are often ambivalent: we want the improvements and comforts that progress provides, but when it forces upon us the loss of things we value, compels us to change our basic assumptions and makes us adjust to the new and unfamiliar, we are inclined to resist it.

What is described as progress in modern societies is in fact largely synonymous with the range of changes brought about by industrial capital. Among the benefits are more food, better transport and a greater abundance of goods. But it is a peculiarity of capitalism that each beneficial innovation also brings a sequence of other changes, not all of which are desired by all people so that, in the name of progress, we are compelled to accept a great many distantly related and possibly unwanted changes. The steam engine, for example, brought greater efficiency to manufacturing and greater speed to transport, but the making of it helped turn master craftsmen into wage labourers and caused towns to grow in size and unhealthiness. The idea of progress, though, includes all the changes, desirable as well as undesirable.

The success of capitalism has always depended upon its capacity to innovate and to sell new products. Yet, paradoxically, most societies in which capitalism has taken hold have expressed resistance to the newness of things, a newness that was as evident in eighteenth-century England as it is in developing countries today. What is it, then, that has made people in Western societies prepared to accept new products, in spite of the changes they threaten? Since any successful product must have overcome resistance to novelty, it appears to be an axiom that the products of industrial capital aim to create acceptance of the changes they bring about. Among the ways in which this acceptance is won, design, through its capacity to make things seem other than they are, has been most important.

Design alters the ways people see commodities. To take an example of this process, we can consider the design of early radio cabinets. When broadcasting began in the 1920s, the first wireless sets were crude assemblies of resistors, wires and valves. Manufacturers quickly realised that if they were to sell radios for people to put in their living rooms, they had to develop a more sophisticated approach to design. In the late 1920s and early 1930s, three basic types of solution were evolved, each one of which presented the same commodity, the wireless, in an entirely different way. The first was to house the radio in a cabinet which imitated a piece of antique furniture, and so referred to the past. The second was to conceal the radio within a piece of furniture

The 'Beaufort' radiogram, 1932. Most early radio cabinets used the forms of traditional furniture. From *The Cabinet Maker*, 27th August 1932.

11

*These developments are described more fully in A. Forty, 'Wireless Style. Symbolic Design and the English Radio Cabinet 1928-1933', *Architectural Association Quarterly*, vol.4, no.2, Spring 1972, pp.23-31.

*Some ideas about Utopian imagery were suggested by W. Benjamin in 'Paris—the Capital of the Nineteenth Century', reprinted in W. Benjamin, *Charles Baudelaire: A Lyric Poet in the Era of High Capitalism*, London, 1973, pp.155-177. Manfredo Tafuri has discussed the significance of Utopia in modern design in his *Architecture and Utopia*, Cambridge, Mass., 1979, and in his essay 'Design and Technological Utopia' in *Italy, The New Domestic Landscape*, edited by E. Ambasz, New York, 1972, pp.388-404, and referred to it in numerous other writings.

The Radio 'Easy Chair', 1933. A few manufacturers went for outright disguise by incorporating their sets in other kinds of furniture. From *The Cabinet Maker*, 25th February 1933, p.417.

that served some entirely different purpose, like an armchair. The third, which became more common as people became familiar with radio and found it less disturbing, was to place it within a cabinet designed to suggest that it belonged to a future and better world.* Each design transformed the original, 'primitive' wireless out of all recognition. The three approaches evident in these radio cabinets, the archaic, the suppressive and the Utopian, have recurred so often in industrial design that they might be said to form a basic grammar or repertory of design imagery.*

Where twentieth-century design happens to have been dominated by the Utopian images, eighteenth-century manufacturers relied heavily upon the archaic model in their efforts to overcome resistance to innovation*. To describe design as an activity that invariably disguises or changes the shape of what we take to be reality runs contrary to many present-day platitudes about design, in particular the belief that the appearance of a product should be a direct expression of the purpose for which it is used, a view embodied in the aphorism 'Form Follows Function'. The logic of this argument is that all objects with the same use should look the same, but this is patently not the case, as a glance at, say, the history of ceramics will show: cups have been produced in an endless variety of designs. If the only purpose of a cup was to drink from, there might well be only one design, but cups do have other uses: as articles of commerce, they serve to create wealth and to satisfy consumers' craving to express their sense of individuality, and it is from the conjunction of such purposes that the variety of designs results.

Many writers have argued that it is wrong for artefacts to be given forms that do not belong strictly to themselves or their period. Such a judgement is not a particularly useful contribution to the history of design. Right or wrong, it is nevertheless the case that in the artefacts of industrial societies, design has been employed habitually to disguise or change their true nature and to play tricks on our sense of chronology. It is the task of the historian to lift those disguises off, to compare them and to explain the choice of one appearance rather than another, but not to dismiss the process.

Manufactured goods have varied in appearance, not because of the immorality or wilfulness of their makers, but because of the circumstances of their production and consumption. In order to make sense of design, we must recognise that its disguising, concealing and transforming powers have been essential to the progress of modern industrial societies.

Neo-Classicism: an Antidote to Progress

Reactions to progress are most revealing when a society first experiences its effects. In Britain, the development of capital and industry reached a noticeable scale for the first time in the latter part of the eighteenth century. Most of the people who recorded their views about the changes that were taking place were those most closely involved, and, not surprisingly, they were generally enthusiastic and only rarely mentioned their misgivings about the negative effects. Scientists like Joseph Priestley, political economists like Adam Smith and entrepreneurs like Matthew Boulton, James Watt and Josiah Wedgwood shared the view that progress was a beneficial process that would continue indefinitely.

However, such people formed only a very small part of the middle and upper classes of eighteenth-century Britain, and their point of view was distinctly radical. There is also evidence of strong contrary views. Thus Dr Johnson, recognising that men were no longer savages, acknowledged that progress had occurred in the past, but believed mankind had already reached its most advanced state and saw no place for further progress in the present or the future.

Nevertheless, Dr Johnson, and others who shared his view, showed much curiosity about the changes taking place around them, about the new factories and about the men who ran them. The main industrial districts of the late eighteenth century – Birmingham, Manchester, the Coalbrookdale iron works and the Staffordshire potteries – were visited regularly by travellers, regarded as being among the greatest sights in the land and frequently depicted by artists.* Yet despite their curiosity, not all were enthusiastic about what they saw.

*The reactions of some eighteenth-century artists and writers to industrialisation are described by F.D. Klingender, *Art and the Industrial Revolution*, revised edition, London, 1968.

One eighteenth-century traveller who recorded his opinions was the Hon. John Byng, later Viscount Torrington, who undertook a series of tours through England and Wales between 1781 and 1794. He never intended his journals, which have been published as *The Torrington Diaries*, to appear in print, and the honesty of the opinions makes them very valuable to the historian. Although Byng was an extremely conservative, indeed reactionary character, he went out of his way to visit the new industrial centres, invariably disliking them when he arrived. In 1792, he wrote of Aysgarth in the Yorkshire Dales:

'But what has completed the destruction of every rural thought, has been the erection of a cotton mill on one side, whereby prospect, and quiet, are destroy'd: I now speak as a tourist (as a policeman, a citizen, or a statesman, I enter not the field); the people, indeed, are employ'd; but they are all abandon'd to vice from the throng... At the times when people work not in the mill, they issue out to poaching, profligacy and plunder – Sr. Rd. Arkwright may have introduced much wealth into his family, and into the country; but, as a tourist, I execrate his schemes, which, having crept into every pastoral vale, have destroy'd the course, and beauty of Nature;

Opposite:
Radio Cabinet Design, 1932. The alternative, and eventually most popular, solution to radio set design was to use 'modern' forms, suggesting a product belonging to the future. From *The Cabinet Maker*, 17th September 1932, p.522.

The Torrington Diaries, edited by C. Bruyn Andrews, London, 1934, vol.III, pp.81-82.

The Torrington Diaries, vol.III, p.92.

why, here now is a great flaring mill, whose back stream has drawn off half the water of the falls above the bridge.

'With the bell ringing and the clamour of the mill, all the vale is disturb'd; treason and levelling systems are the discourse; and rebellion may be near at hand.'*

A few days later, he was gratified that when he asked a man 'if the cotton trade did not benefit the poor?' the man replied, 'The worst thing in the world in my opinion, Sr., for it leaves us neither stout husbandmen, nor modest girls; for the children bred in a cotton mill, never get exercise or air, and all are impudent and saucy.'*

Since Byng found manufacturing industry so abominable, one cannot but ask why he repeatedly visited industrial towns. Yet his curiosity seems to have been as strong as his dislike, an attitude that was very common in his time.

Byng's real interest was in antiquities. He toured the country looking for relics of the past and wishing that he had lived before the country had been covered with fast turnpike roads and the land enclosed. Byng's taste for antiquities was shared by many of his contemporaries, but while Byng, true to his Toryism and patriotism, preferred English antiquities, others hunted avidly for Greek and Roman remains.

The interest in classical antiquities was part of the neo-classical movement, which had developed in the 1750s and 1760s, and which dominated European taste in the late eighteenth century. Neo-classicism aimed to regain for art and design the purity of form and expression which was felt lacking in the rococo style of the first half of the eighteenth century, but which was identified in the products of Greece and Rome. Much of the inspiration of neo-classicism came from the discovery of Herculaneum in 1738 and of Pompeii in 1748, and Italian tours to study classical remains at first hand became part of artistic education. It also became

P.J. de Loutherbourg: detail from *Coalbrookdale by Night*, oil painting, 1801. The great industrial enterprises, like the Coalbrookdale iron works in Shropshire, were a source of fascination and wonder to eighteenth-century travellers and artists.

Benjamin West: *Etruria*, oil painting, 1791. West's painting of Wedgwood's factory transforms it into a scene in the ancient world.

*Hugh Honour, *Neo-Classicism*, Harmondsworth, 1968.

fashionable for cultured aristocrats from all over Europe to travel to Rome to view, purchase and, in cases of extreme enthusiasm, excavate classical antiquities.*

Whether the objects of the search were classical or English antiquities, the motives were similar. The study of the remains of the past provided inspiration for how the present could be. The paradox of eighteenth-century taste – that an age which was so fascinated by progress was at the same time devoted to the study of the far distant past – was expressed in all the artistic products of neo-classicism. These were not slavish reproductions of antiquity: they used imagery and forms from the past but were intended to express modern sentiments. Sometimes the effects seem perverse and contradictory. Dr Johnson described contemporary life in poems which closely imitated those of the Roman poet Juvenal in form. New buildings, such as the country houses of the late eighteenth century, made use of the forms and motifs of antique architecture but had internal planning and organisation designed to serve decidedly modern purposes. To popularise the scientific knowledge of the day, the physician and scientist Erasmus Darwin did not use the plain language of science, but wrote a classical epic poem, *The Botanic Garden*, which was published in two parts in 1789 and 1791, and was a great popular success. Darwin deliberately described science in classical metaphors and images: the power of the steam engine, for example, was described in a long and elaborate metaphor as equivalent to the strength of Hercules. The result now seems perverse and artificial, but the popularity of the poem

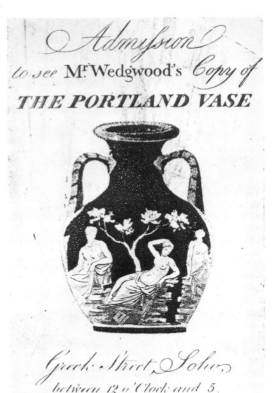

at the time shows that this was an acceptable way of communicating progressive ideas and knowledge.

Just as unrealistic was Benjamin West's painting of Josiah Wedgwood's factory at Etruria: women decorators clad as Roman matrons, in languid classical poses against scenes of artistic craftwork, could hardly have been less representative of the actual conditions in the factory, which was renowned throughout Europe for its progressive methods of manufacture and its high degree of separation between the different processes.

It was typical of the eighteenth-century approach to novelty that when Wedgwood sought to advertise his technical abilities as a ceramist, he set himself the task of reproducing the Portland Vase, the celebrated piece of Roman cameo glass acquired by the Duke of Portland in 1786. The point of the reproductions was not just that they were as good as the original, but that they demonstrated the sophistication of contemporary manufacturing techniques better than any new and original designs could have done.

Unease about progress and a compulsive interest in the past were connected phenomena. In *The Decline and Fall of the Roman Empire* (1776-88), Edward Gibbon described Rome of the second century AD, the Golden Age, as a place of perfect peace and harmony, which was only subsequently disturbed by the introduction of Christianity from elsewhere. Not until recently have historians questioned this idealised picture of the Golden Age and argued that, far from being static, Rome was going through a period of considerable internal change, a view which would not have been well received in the eighteenth century, as it would have deprived antiquity of one of its greatest attractions. To the leisured classes of the eighteenth century, much of the pleasure of studying ancient

Rome and collecting relics from it was the contact it gave them with a civilisation that had seemingly been stable. Their desire to see classical principles, and classical designs, applied to contemporary life arose partly out of a wish to suppress from their consciousness its disturbing tendency to change.

Of course, it can be argued with justification that when, for example, Wedgwood introduced neo-classicism into the design of his pottery, he did so because that style was in fashion. Yet such an explanation is incomplete in that it does not tell us why neo-classicism rather than some other style was the fashion: to answer this and know why eighteenth century consumers preferred neo-classicism to the alternatives, we need to know what it meant to them. Unfortunately, the reconstruction of consumer preferences in the past is a historical enterprise fraught with difficulties and generally leading to unsatisfactory results. Even the evidence of the few consumers who took the trouble to articulate and record the reasons for their choices cannot be wholly relied upon, since they may not have been fully conscious of their motives, or have failed to record them completely. Moreover, we cannot assume that the preferences recorded by one consumer were shared by others, even others of the same class, age or sex. In these circumstances, the best we can do is to indicate the predisposing factors that might have led consumers to act in one way or another at a particular time. In general, the best historical evidence about consumer preferences, at least for the purposes of understanding design, comes from manufacturers, who can, after all, be expected to have had their fingers on the pulse of the market, and we should value their testimony above that of any individual consumer. Josiah Wedgwood's experiences with neo-classicism largely confirm that, among other things, it was the style that made the late eighteenth-century middle and upper classes feel most at ease with progress.

*The account of the history of the Staffordshire pottery industry, and of Wedgwood, is based on the following sources: J. Thomas, *The Rise of the Staffordshire Potteries*, Bath, 1971; L. Weatherill, *The Pottery Trade and North Staffordshire 1660-1760*, Manchester, 1971; Wolf Mankowitz, *Wedgwood*, London, 1953; D. Towner, *Creamware*, London and Boston, 1978; N. McKendrick, 'Josiah Wedgwood: an Eighteenth Century Entrepreneur in Salesmanship and Marketing Techniques', *Economic History Review*, 2nd series, vol.XII, no. 3, 1960, pp.408-433. See also N. McKendrick, J. Brewer and J.H. Plumb, *The Birth of Consumer Society. The Commercialization of Eighteenth Century England*, London, 1982.

Wedgwood: Neo-Classicism in Industrial Production

*See note above.

In 1759, when Josiah Wedgwood ended five years of partnership with the potter Thomas Whieldon in Stoke-on-Trent in Staffordshire, considerable changes were taking place in the English potteries. At the beginning of the century, few workshops had employed more than half a dozen men, and most of their output had been sold locally. By 1750, some potters had increased their sales by extending their markets to more distant parts of the country and so were employing more men in their workshops. By 1769, the average potworks in Staffordshire was thought to employ about twenty men.*

At the end of his partnership with Whieldon, Wedgwood rented a potworks nearby at Burslem and began production on his own, shrewdly recognising the business possibilities open to him. As he later wrote at the beginning of the Experiment Book he started at this date, 'I saw the field was spacious, and the soil so good as to promise ample recompense to anyone who should labour diligently in its cultivation.'*

*Quoted in Mankowitz, p.27.

How Wedgwood went about this cultivation is known to us through the exceptional series of letters that Wedgwood wrote to his friend Thomas Bentley. These letters provide a unique picture of the mind of an entrepreneur during the early stages of industrialisation, revealing the problems he faced and the solutions he

*The letters have never been published in full. There are two published selections: *The Letters of Josiah Wedgwood*, edited by K.E. Farrer, 2 vols, 1903 (subsequently referred to as Farrer), with a supplementary volume, *Correspondence of Josiah Wedgwood 1781-1794*, 1906; the second is *The Selected Letters of Josiah Wedgwood*, edited by A. Finer and G. Savage, London, 1965 (subsequently referred to as Finer and Savage).

developed.* In particular, they show the unprecedented importance that design was to have in the production of his wares.

The demand for pottery increased steadily in the eighteenth century, but not simply because of the growth in population. The new popularity of tea required ceramic cups (since hot liquids cannot comfortably be drunk from pewter), while colonial expansion created a market overseas. These developments stood to benefit the industry as a whole, and the majority of manufacturers did increase their trade. Wedgwood, however, was more successful than most.

Among the reasons for Wedgwood's exceptional success were the rationalisation of production methods in his factory, his imaginative marketing techniques and, of particular significance here, his attention to his products. Not only was he determined to produce wares of consistently higher quality than other potters, but he also attached great importance to the appearance of his pots.

The main products of Wedgwood and Whieldon in the 1750s, in common with other Staffordshire potters, had been a salt-glazed stoneware, a white earthenware with various coloured glazes, and a red earthenware. In his experiment book, Wedgwood described the problems presented by these products as follows:

'White stoneware (viz. with salt glaze) was the principal article of our manufacture; but this had been made a long time, and the prices were now reduced so low that the potters could not afford to bestow much expense upon it, or make it so good in any respect as the ware they would otherwise admit of; and with regard to elegance of form, that was an object very little attended to.

'The article next in consequence to stoneware was an imitation of tortoise-shell, but as no improvement had been made in this branch for several years, the consumer had grown nearly tired of it; and though the price had been lowered from time to time in

Salt-glazed shell teapot, mug and jug, Staffordshire, c.1750. Typical products of the Staffordshire potteries in the mid eighteenth century.

Moulded teapot, green tortoiseshell glaze, probably Wedgwood, c.1765. A teapot of the sort described by Wedgwood as typical of Staffordshire in the mid eighteenth century.

order to increase the sale, the expedient did not answer, and something new was wanted to give a little spirit to the business.

'I had already made an imitation of Agate which was esteemed beautiful, and made a considerable improvement, but people were surfeited with wares of these various colours. These considerations induced me to try for some more solid improvement, as well in the body as the glazes, the colours, and the forms of the articles of our manufacture.'*

*Quoted in Mankowitz, pp.27-28.

Agate jug in red earthenware with brown glazes, c.1750. Characteristic example of the type of agate ware described by Wedgwood.

Wedgwood moulded cauliflower teapot, green glaze, c.1759. These brightly coloured, exotic wares were a standard Wedgwood product in the early 1760s.

In his first years at Burslem, Wedgwood went about developing new products to replace the existing unsatisfactory ones. His first important innovation was a green glaze he invented. This glaze, in combination with a yellow one, was applied to white earthenware with moulded ornament, giving results that were vivid in colour and rather baroque in appearance. These wares were Wedgwood's staple product in the early 1760s.

At the same time, Wedgwood was also perfecting a cream glaze for white earthenware. Although cream-glazed ware had already been produced in Staffordshire for some time, Wedgwood was concerned to produce a glaze that was relatively white and gave constant results in the firing. He had perfected it by 1765, and around this date he began large-scale production of creamware, decorated with hand-painted enamel or with enamels applied on printed transfers – a more rapid process developed by the Liverpool firm of Sadler and Green, with whom Wedgwood did business. By 1766, the creamware had become sufficiently successful for

Wedgwood creamware teapot decorated with hand-painted enamels, late 1760s. One of the early creamware products, which superseded green-glazed ware.

Wedgwood creamware plate with transfer-printed enamel decoration, c.1775. Hand-painted enamels were slow to produce, and the introduction of transfer-printed enamels enormously speeded up the process of decoration.

Wedgwood to cease production of the green-glazed ware.

Wedgwood's remarks in the Experiment Book show that he was also concerned about the form of his pots, which he thought far from satisfactory. It was not until the mid-1760s that the designs began to change appreciably. The basic shapes of creamware were not very different from those of greenware, although moulded ornament was reduced and eventually eliminated altogether; the most striking change was in the enamelled decoration, which could be very intricate as it was applied by hand or transfer after the pot had been glazed.

Over the next ten years, up to 1774, when Wedgwood's first creamware catalogue was produced, the forms continued to become plainer and simpler, with decoration that became increasingly neo-classical. Creamware, or 'Queensware', as Wedgwood re-named it after Queen Charlotte commissioned a creamware service in 1765, became highly successful both nationally and internationally. As tableware, it filled a gap between the very poor quality of the ordinary ware made in other countries and the very expensive, high quality products of the royal porcelain factories like Sèvres, Meissen and Copenhagen. It also owed much of its success to the essentially neo-classical qualities of purity and simplicity of form. Wedgwood did not originally seem to be aware of this, but, when it was pointed out to him in 1769 that simplicity was esteemed, he sought to improve Queensware in that direction.* The popularity of Queensware continued to increase until the late 1770s, when the market seems to have become temporarily surfeited. Wedgwood wrote in 1778 that it was 'no longer the choice thing it used to be, since every shop, house and cottage is full of it.'* Nevertheless, with further refinement and more deliberate neo-classicising, it continued to be produced into the nineteenth century.

*Finer and Savage, p.78.

*Finer and Savage, pp.220-221.

*See N. McKendrick, 'Josiah Wedgwood and Thomas Bentley: an Inventor-Entrepreneur Partnership in the Industrial Revolution', *Transactions of the Royal Historical Society*, 5th series, vol.XIV, 1964, pp.1-34.

James Stuart: detail from a design for an interior, drawing, c.1757. The architect James 'Athenian' Stuart, a pioneer of neo-classical design in Britain, designed interiors furnished with antique ornaments. Urns and vases of the kind he incorporates would have had to be either genuine antiquities, or wood or plaster dummies.

Wedgwood Queensware catalogue, 1774. The shapes show some simplification from the earlier, more baroque products, and the quality of the engravings heightens the neo-classical effect of the products still further.

Wedgwood's main source of knowledge about the classical revival was his associate, friend and later partner, Thomas Bentley, a Liverpool merchant who exported his wares to the American colonies and the West Indies. Bentley was a cultured man, knowledgeable about the changes in artistic fashion that were taking place in Europe, and with wide social connections. In 1769, he and Wedgwood went into partnership to produce 'ornamental wares' (as distinct from the creamware products, which were known as 'useful wares') from Wedgwood's new factory at Etruria. Bentley moved to London and became responsible for marketing there.* He also brought his knowledge of art to bear on the design of the ornamental wares. Apparently it was under his influence that Wedgwood revised his designs: he began to produce conspicuously neo-classical ornamental objects and to make the useful ware more obviously neo-classical as well.

It was in the designs of the ornamental wares – vases, urns, statuettes, cameos and ceramic tablets – that Wedgwood and Bentley went to the greatest lengths to make use of neo-classicism. When they entered this market, ornamental pottery in England was still baroque and heavy. Bentley's inspired realisation that there might be a market for neo-classical ornamental pottery presumably arose from his knowledge of what was happening to contemporary furnishing. Neo-classicism, among its many other effects on domestic architecture, introduced the practice of decorating interiors in a unified style, so that all the details, mouldings, furniture and furnishings of a room appeared to convey a consistent set of references to the antique. While genuinely antique sculptures and vases were the ideal ornaments for a neo-classical interior, they were in short supply, and architects and decorators had to find substitutes. For example, the interior designs of the architect James Stuart, one of the pioneers of neo-classicism in Britain, incorporated urns, ewers and bowls, which would have had to be either genuine antiquities, or wood or plaster dummies.

Robert Adam: design for a sideboard at Kenwood, 1768-69. Adam's interior designs often included accurately drawn antique ornaments, which were generally executed in wood, the smaller ones in silver. The demand for antique ornaments presented an opportunity for Wedgwood & Bentley. From *The Works in Architecture of R.& J. Adam*, 1778, vol.1, no. 2, pl.viii.

The architect Robert Adam, aware of the lack of suitable ornaments for the neo-classical interiors of the houses he designed in the 1760s, went further than Stuart and himself designed ornaments, such as those for the sideboard at Kenwood House, all of which had to be specially made, the large urns from wood painted to look like stone or pottery, and the smaller objects from silver.

Bentley's most imaginative insight was to see that the demand for neo-classical ornaments might be satisfied by ceramics produced in Wedgwood's factory; he was the first to see that pottery and neo-classicism, hitherto unassociated, might be suited to one another. The marriage of the two, brought about by Wedgwood and Bentley, not only led to new designs for familar objects, like vases, but also opened up the prospect of a whole new range of products, such as urns, tablets and cameos, suited to the embellishment of neo-classical interiors. His espousal of neo-classicism transformed Wedgwood from an ordinary, though successful, potter into a leader of *avant-garde* taste. Wedgwood and Bentley took some trouble to further this position by associating themselves with the neo-classical movement, partly through their social connections, but also through trading on their familiarity with the neo-classical theorists. For example, they were keen to publicise the fact that Count Caylus, the author of a well-known six volume study of classical antiquities, had lamented that there were no modern equivalents of ancient Etruscan vases, a gap they were able to announce that their own products filled.*

*Farrer, vol.I, pp.377-378.

Wedgwood and Bentley gained their knowledge of classical design partly from their aristocratic contacts, who showed and sometimes lent them antique pottery and sculpture to study. They had a large collection of the books on classical archaeology that had been published in the eighteenth century, and Wedgwood made extensive use of them.* He also considered employing an artist in Rome to study original antiquities at first hand and to communicate new developments in artistic taste to

*Farrer, p.358; and Finer and Savage, p.149.

*Farrer, vol.I, p.428; and Finer and Savage, p.114; Wedgwood's relations with Flaxman are discussed in *John Flaxman R.A.*, catalogue of an exhibition at the Royal Academy of Arts, London, 1979.

him, but this scheme came to nothing, though he did later subsidise John Flaxman's trip to Rome.* The way that Wedgwood made use of his knowledge of antiquities was either to set his craftsmen to produce exact copies, or alternatively to re-interpret the classical originals. This approach Wedgwood described as follows:

'. . . I only pretend to have attempted to copy the fine antique forms, but not with absolute servility. I have endeavoured to preserve the stile and spirit or if you please the elegant simplicity of the antique forms, and so doing to introduce all the variety I was able, and this Sir W. Hamilton assures me I may venture to do, and that is the true way of copying the antique.'*

*Finer and Savage, p.317.

Wedgwood's method, in the approved manner of neo-classicism, was to improve upon rather than copy the antique. The actual work of design was carried out either by his own modellers at Etruria, or by artists specially hired for the purpose, the most famous of whom was John Flaxman. While Wedgwood's own craftsmen could copy antiquities, Flaxman's value lay in his ap-preciation of the spirit of the classical revival and his ability to give a classical air to new products which had no precise antique equivalent.* Flaxman's services were important in the design of cameos and busts of living people, and the relief decoration on vases and tablets, subjects which required a knowledge of classicism to give them a convincingly antique appearance.

*Farrer, vol.I, p.240.

Contrary to what many books about design suggest, Wedgwood and Bentley's development of a neo-classical style for the orna-mental wares took place only gradually. Many of Wedgwood's early ornamental products were baroque in style, with much surface ornament and gilding, and the process of refining the designs and producing convincing neo-classical products took a number of years. The changes were the result of suggestions from Bentley and hints from the cognoscenti among his customers. For example, the leading antiquarian, Sir William Hamilton, advised Wedgwood and Bentley to abandon gilding on their products. Wedgwood himself found this advice, and the demands of neo-classicism, rather hard to take, as they were contrary to his own notions of fine pottery. He complained to Bentley:

'I do not find it an easy matter to make a Vase with the colouring so natural, vairied, pleasing & *unpot-like*, & the shape so delicate, as to make it seem worth a great deal of money, without the ad-ditional trappings of handles, ornaments, & Gilding.'*

*Farrer, vol.I, p.456.

Opposite:
John Flaxman Jr: *Blind Man's Buff*, wax relief on slate, 1782. One of a number of designs in the antique manner executed by Flaxman for the decoration of Wedgwood's ornamental wares.

*Farrer, vol.I, p.250.

Wedgwood & Bentley: three-handled ornamental vase in Queensware, early 1770s. Many of Wedgwood & Bentley's wares were more obviously rococo than neo-classical, and as such were closer to Wedgood's own idea of what was ornamental.

Wedgwood & Bentley: *Sacred to Bacchus, Sacred to Neptune*, pair of ewers for wine and water, black basalt, 1775. An example of ornamental ware in the black basalt body developed in the early 1770s.

Nevertheless, Wedgwood was well aware of the attractions that neo-classicism had for his customers, and did not hesitate to modify his designs according to the expert advice he was given. His understanding of the strength of demand for neo-classical design was revealed when he wrote to Bentley about the pots of one particular product range, 'They certainly are not Antique, and that is fault enough to Damn them for with most of our customers.'*

Much of Wedgwood's own interest in pottery lay in technical discoveries and innovation; to make these profitable, the partners had to find marketable applications for them, to which end neo-classicism proved invaluable. Throughout his life, Wedgwood experimented prolifically with glazes and bodies, and he was clearly fascinated by everything that went on in the kiln. His reputation in his own lifetime was not only as a manufacturer but also as a scientific experimenter, for which he was elected to the Royal Society. Experiment and innovation were, therefore, as important to him as entrepreneurial activity and commerce; what made him so exceptional was that he was talented in all of them.

In his experiments, Wedgwood developed and perfected two new bodies, black unglazed stoneware called 'black basaltes' and a fine white, slightly translucent stoneware called 'jasper', which

Above:
Josiah Wedgwood: *Sacrifice to Aesculapius*, test medallion in blue and white jasper, c.1773. The development of the jasper body was a technical achievement, the result of much experiment, as shown by this test. Having developed the body, Wedgwood had to find applications for it.

Right:
Josiah Wedgwood: ornamental vase with relief of Venus in her chariot drawn by swans, white jasper with black dip, c.1784. Vases and urns in antique forms bearing antique motifs supplied suitable ornaments for neo-classical interiors.

*Farrer, vol.II, pp.341-342.

in its unglazed form had a texture similar to marble. Wedgwood also developed coloured jaspers and later 'jasper dip', a surface colouring for white jasper. Although many of the earlier ornamental wares had been made in glazed earthenware from the mid-1770s, an increasing proportion were made with these two new bodies. Black basaltes, a less remarkable invention than jasper, was used principally for urns and statuettes, while jasper had originally been developed to provide a suitable body for making good reproductions of antique gems and cameos. Having perfected it, the partners wanted to find other marketable applications for it. The solution to this problem was provided by neo-classicism. Realising that jasper closely resembled marble, Wedgwood and Bentley saw its possibilities in the growing market for neo-classical ornaments. It lent itself to urns, ewers and tablets with moulded relief designs, all of which Wedgwood started to make in antique patterns.

On the whole, the products were a great success and exactly satisfied the demand for neo-classical ornaments. Among the few products that did not prove popular were large jasper relief tablets for setting in architectural features such as mantelpieces and friezes. Despite their usual skill at marketing, Wedgwood and Bentley were unable to sell these products although they tried repeatedly to interest architects and designers in them. One of those approached was Capability Brown, the architect and landscape designer, who advised Wedgwood that they were unacceptable beause they were made in coloured jasper; he recommended making them in plain white jasper, so that they would look like marble.* For once, Wedgwood's technical accomplishment, here the application of colour to jasper, had led to products that were too novel for men of taste to accept. Brown's advice was that only

Wedgwood & Bentley: *Bacchanalian Procession*, blue and white jasper plaque, c.1778. These plaques, designed as interior ornaments, proved unsuccessful.

Wedgwood & Bentley: white jasper plaque showing Five Muses, c.1778. Following Capability Brown's advice, Wedgwood & Bentley stopped making coloured jasper plaques and turned instead to plain white jasper plaques, which simulated marble and looked more antique.

making them more like real antiques would give them any chance of success.

In fact, this was the basis of the policy generally adopted by Wedgwood and Bentley in their marketing: antique designs clothed technical innovation, and the novelty of the product was described in publicity material in the most guarded terms. For one of the most progressive manufacturers in the country, Wedgwood was surprising reticent, at least in the early part of his career, about advertising his technical innovations. Not until the demand for his wares was well established, in the late 1780s, did he judge it wise to draw attention to the technical and industrial changes of which his products were the results; even then, he was very selective about what he let his customers know.

Although Wedgwood and Bentley referred in their catalogues to their progress and 'continual improvements', the purpose of these statements appears to have been to draw the attention of established customers to the existence of new products for them to buy. However, the main technical advances, the development of new bodies and processes, were never directly referred to in the early catalogues as innovations. The usual form was to describe something new, such as encaustic painting on basaltes ware, which gave an effect similar to Etruscan pottery, as the 'rediscovery' of a lost craft of antiquity. Likewise, with the design of the products, it was not their novelty that was emphasised, but their antique origins. In the 1779 catalogue, the cameos and intaglios were introduced with the statement 'These are exactly taken from the finest antique gems.'* Since they included portraits of Lord Chatham, the reigning Pope and George II, this was hardly possible, but it

*The catalogue is reprinted in Mankowitz.

had the effect of drawing attention to the classical quality of the designs. Antiquity, not novelty, was the marketable quality. Similar sentiments directed the choice of the self-consciously classical name of Etruria for Wedgwood's factory, which was far from Etruscan in both appearance and management. Wedgwood and Bentley adopted this apparently devious way of advertising their innovations when they wanted people to know about them. But when Wedgwood introduced methods that bore no relation to any known antique process, such as the substitution of printed transfers for hand-painted enamels, he was very concerned that these developments, which had important effects on his production and his profits, should remain a secret.* His unwillingness to publicise certain of his discoveries suggests that he understood his products were popular because they did not remind his customers of the aspects of progress which would be unacceptable to them.

*Farrer, vol.I, pp.445-446.

Josiah Wedgwood: black basalt jug decorated with encaustic design, c.1770. Wedgwood's new decorative technique was described as 'the rediscovery of an antique art, a notion reinforced by the Etruscan form of this jug.

*Honour, p.48.

Some of Wedgwood and Bentley's attempts to convince their customers of the antique qualities of their new products and processes now seem rather disingenuous. But if their advertising copy was crude, their use of design to the same ends was highly sophisticated, and the more exact they made their references to the antique, the more sought-after their products became. Their purpose was not to deceive people into believing that anything they manufactured was antique, but to convince them that the products, though made by modern processes, were as good as, or better than, the products of antiquity. The very special value attached to antiquity in the eighteenth century made this a most effective way of overcoming the reservations their customers might have felt about innovations.

In some ways, Wedgwood and Bentley's relationship to neo-classicism was pragmatic. The style was not integral to their production, for they could and did produce goods in other styles. As Hugh Honour has pointed out, they used antiquity for decorative ends and were really perpetuating the rococo taste for decoration in antique fancy dress.* Nevertheless, if neo-classicism was simply another decorative style to Wedgwood and Bentley, it was also most valuable to their success through the unique power that it had in the eighteenth century to make modern methods of manufacture fashionable.

Wedgwood & Bentley: cameo portrait busts of George III and Queen Charlotte, blue and white jasper, 1778. Many of Wedgwood & Bentley's portrait cameos were of living people, but represented in the manner of antique cameos.

2. The First Industrial Designers

In the history of every industry, design has become necessary as a separate activity in production once a single craftsman ceases to be responsible for every stage of manufacture from conception to sale. In many industries, this organisational change took place in the eighteenth century; in few of them can the emergence of the specialist designer, and the great importance attached to his work, be seen more clearly than in Josiah Wedgwood's pottery manufacture. Although Wedgwood was not the first pottery master to make a distinction between the tasks of designing pots and making them, he attached more value to the work of designers than other manufacturers had done.

The Need for a Consistent Product

Wedgwood and Byerley's London showroom, 1809. To avoid tying up capital in unsold stock, Wedgwood displayed only samples in the shop; customers ordered from these or catalogues. From Rudolph Ackermann, *Repository of Arts*, vol.I, no.2, 1809.

Josiah Wedgwood's original intention, as he stated at the outset, was to be successful in business, to obtain 'ample recompense' from diligent labour in what he saw as a spacious field. The fulfilment of this simple ambition depended upon being able to make more pots, sell more pots and also, if possible, increase the unit profit on them. All the extensive changes that he subsequently introduced into the sale and manufacture of pottery can be referred back to those three conditions of success.

When Wedgwood began his own production in 1759, potters normally sold their goods by sending batches of completed work

*Farrer vol.I, p.150. See also McKendrick, 1960.

either direct to markets, or to merchants. Although Wedgwood sold some of his wares this way, he also adopted the apparently novel technique of selling by advance orders. In London and elsewhere, he opened showrooms with samples of his wares on display, but no stocks for sale.* The customers' orders were passed to the factory, and the pots were made and delivered direct. Later, Wedgwood extended this system by sending out travellers with cases of samples in Britain and abroad, and by publishing illustrated catalogues of the wares, from which customers ordered. With these methods of selling, Wedgwood did not have to tie up capital in unsold stock or risk making large quantities of designs for which there might be no demand.

However, selling from samples and catalogues required the products to be completely uniform in quality. A customer who bought a complete service on the basis of a few samples would expect to receive wares that were indistinguishable from the samples he or she had seen. Maintaining absolute consistency was a major problem in pottery manufacture; Wedgwood's solutions to this problem were at the root of many of his production methods.

Wedgwood's main product of the early 1760s, his greenware, could not be reproduced reliably. The decoration was in the glazes

Wedgwood Queensware sample tile with transfer-printed and hand-painted enamel decorations, c.1800. Sample tiles were carried by travellers to enable customers to choose the decoration for the shapes they ordered from the printed catalogues.

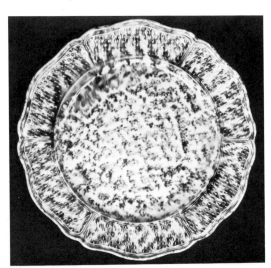

Above right:
Whieldon ware tortoiseshell glaze plate, c.1760. Tortoiseshell and greenware glazes varied unpredictably with the firing and the workmanship, and were too inconsistent for a business based on orders from samples and catalogues.

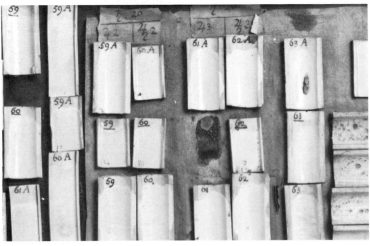

Tray of Josiah Wedgwood's creamware glaze tests, early 1760s. The white earthenware body of creamware was reliable, but much experiment went into finding a consistently flawless glaze.

applied over the moulded ornament, and the result depended on both the hand of the glazer and the conditions in the kiln, neither of them particularly dependable. Charming though the variations in the glazes may have been, they did not lead to a consistent product and so made greenware unsuited to the method of sale that Wedgwood was adopting.

The purpose of Wedgwood's experiments with creamware was to find a more reliable replacement for greenware. Cream-glazed earthenware had been produced in the Staffordshire potteries from the 1740s and would have been well known to Wedgwood.* The white earthenware body, which gave constant results under a fairly wide range of firing conditions, was well suited to Wedgwood's purpose. The problem lay in the glaze, which tended to vary in colour at different kiln temperatures, to run and become uneven in thickness, and to craze. Wedgwood needed to produce a glaze that was as reliable as the body, and, in 1765, he developed one that was reasonably satisfactory, although it tended to vary in colour and to run. It took several more years to perfect a creamware glaze that gave a completely uniform result.

Greenware had been unreliable because part of the decoration was in the colours of the glaze, which varied according to the firing conditions. To overcome this problem in creamware, Wedgwood did not use glaze colours, but glazed the pieces plain and decorated them with hand-painted enamels, which were applied after the glaze firing, and then baked on at a much lower temperature. Enamelling was a reliable process and gave constant results. It was not new, as it had been used on porcelain and, in Staffordshire, on salt-glazed stoneware, but because it was a laborious and expensive technique, it had not previously been used on the lower-valued earthenware products. Much of Wedgwood's early enamelling consisted of pictures and decoration in an attractive, though rather florid, freehand style. These designs, being often

*Towner; Mankowitz, chapter 2.

Detail of Wedgwood creamware *compotier*, mid 1760s. Crazing in the glaze, common in Wedgwood's early ceramics, was one of the faults he set himself to overcome.

Salt-glazed teapot with hand-painted enamel decoration, Staffordshire, c.1755. Enamelling was an accepted technique for decorating pots in the potteries, but was a laborious and unreliable way of producing anything but the simplest decoration.

Wedgwood Queensware coffee pot with transfer-printed enamel, late 1760s. Transfer-printed enamel offered a quick and reliably consistent way of decorating pots.

complicated and hard to reproduce accurately, were unsuited to Wedgwood's requirement for quantity production. To prevent variation and to make enamelling cheaper, Wedgwood experimented with enamel-printed transfers, which were applied to the pots and baked on. In time, the pictorial part of the enamel designs on creamware was generally applied by transfers, with the hand painters working only on edging and repeat patterns, which they could reproduce accurately. The only factor that still allowed room for variable results was the workmanship of Wedgwood's employees.

'Making Machines of the Men'

Wedgwood's intention to make Queensware a consistent, uniform product could not be achieved as long as his workmen were free to make idiosyncratic variations in the pots. To some extent, this freedom had already been curtailed by changes that had taken place in the potteries long before Josiah Wedgwood went into business. Although pottery had once been a craft industry, in the sense that a single individual was responsible for all the stages of making a pot, this form of production had ceased in Staffordshire before the beginning of the eighteenth century. From the 1730s, if not earlier, potters had specialised in one of the branches of the trade, such as throwing or handling, or making glaze and slip. A typical mid-eighteenth century pottery consisted of a number of workshops, each with employees engaged in a particular task. At Whieldon's pottery in the 1750s, the work was divided into at least seven different occupations, with each workman usually doing a single task.* As several craftsmen were responsible for the

*Weatherill, p.60.

32

Enamelling and modelling in a French porcelain factory, 1771. The division of tasks, and specialisation of workmen in each branch of work were recognised characteristics of the royal porcelain factories. In this, as in the technique of enamelling, Wedgwood was applying to cheaper goods methods previously reserved for high quality goods. From Le Comte de Milly, 'L'Art de Porcelaine', plate 8, in *Encyclopédie Méthodique des Arts et Métiers*, Académie des Sciences, Paris, 1771.

*Farrer, vol.II, pp.147-148.

*Finer and Savage, pp.82-83.

making of a single pot, no individual was able to make any major change to it.

Even so, men at each stage still had some control over the final results. For example, a workman employed at sprigging – the application of moulded ornaments to a pot – could make minor variations between pots, while a man working at glazing could cause major ones. Wedgwood frequently complained about his workmen's apparent inability to produce consistent results, especially with the ornamental wares. Wedgwood wrote once to Bentley of his problems:

'. . . the mixtures, & the colours too, after all the attention we can give them are liable to so many accidents, & alterations, from the Workmens *unhandiness and want of Ideas* . . .

'For Instance when the Clays are perfectly mixt to produce a *wildness, & extravaganza* in the Pebble, if the Workman gives the batts a twist *edgeways,* instead of keeping them *flatt* when he puts them into the mould, a little stringiness is produced which shews the Pott, instead of a *finely variegated Pebble.*'*

Wedgwood had already shown his concern with consistency a few years earlier when he had written to Bentley that he was 'preparing to make such *Machines* of the *Men* as cannot Err.'* For his creamware, just as much as his ornamental ware, this was indispensable to his success.

Wedgwood made the workmanship more reliable either by re-training the men or by dividing the labour into yet more stages, which could be supervised more closely. Teaching his men to work to higher standards than was customary in the potteries was both slow and unpopular with them. Breaking down the production process into more stages had the advantage that, for some of the tasks, he could make do with less skilled labour. The introduction of enamelling on creamware is an excellent example: in

*N. McKendrick, 'Josiah Wedgwood and Factory Discipline', *Historical Journal*, vol.IV, no.1, 1961, pp.30-55.

The Value of Modellers

*Mankowitz, p.34.

*A. Young, *A Six Months Tour through the North of England*, London, 1770, vol.III, p.308. Account book of Josiah Wedgwood, Wedgwood archives, E2-1339.

greenware, the two functions of glazing and decoration had been combined in the single process of glazing, but in creamware, glazing and enamelliing were carried out by entirely separate sets of people whose tasks were defined by exact sets of instructions and supervised by overseers.*

While pottery was a craft industry, as it was in Staffordshire until the end of the seventeenth century, the form of a pot was most likely decided upon by the man who was to make it. However, when the manufacture of pots was broken down into processes carried out by different workers, an additional stage was required, the preparation of instructions for the various workmen to follow: in fact, a design stage.

The work of designing, or modelling as it was known in the potteries, became a distinct and separate stage in the production of pots, although it was probably done by a craftsman or by the master potter working in the same factory. By the 1750s not only was modelliing recognised as a separate activity, but there were individuals described as modellers, whose sole task was to make prototypes for the other craftsmen to work from. For example, William Greatbatch, who subsequently set up on his own and supplied many of the earthenware pots which Wedgwood fired with his green glaze, worked in the 1750s as a modeller for Whieldon.*

The success of attempts 'to make machines of the men' depended on the exactness of the modellers' instructions, for, unless these were precise, it was impossible to restrain the men from introducing variations into their work. Good modellers became increasingly indispensable to Wedgwood as the craftsmen's freedom to control the form of the pot was curtailed; nowhere was this more so than in creamware, where the craftsmanship was directed entirely towards achieving uniformity. The modeller's value in preparing an exact design increased with the number of pots made from it, because he was, in a sense, taking over a fraction of the work that had once been done by each craftsman every time he made a pot. The monetary value of the modeller's work could actually be calculated as the sum of the value of all those fractions of the craftsmen's work. Because of the importance of their services, modellers were the most highly paid employees in the potteries. In 1769, Arthur Young reported that a modeller received a salary of £100 per annum, approximately twice the wage of skilled craftsmen, who were paid between seven and twelve shillings a week; the sculptor John Flaxman, who worked freelance for Wedgwood, was paid at the rate of one guinea per day for preparing designs.*

In spite of their apparently high earnings, modellers' wages did not necessarily correspond to the value of their work. If this exceeded what they were paid in wages, the difference would have been profit to the entrepreneur. Since the modellers were paid a flat rate and not a royalty for their designs, the employer's margin also increased with the number of pots produced from a single design, and the use of modellers opened up the way to greater profitability.

It was not just the division of labour in the potteries that made modellers indispensable to Wedgwood. Their value became even more apparent to him when he began to change the style of his pots. Since neo-classicism originated far from Staffordshire in the centres of fashion in London and abroad, modellers from the

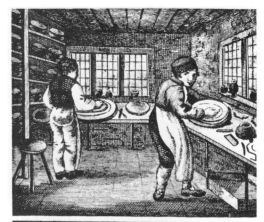

'Pressing" or "Squeezing", which is making jugs turenes &c. of the clay, ready for being fired.

Engraving designs on Copper Plates, for producing the much admired "blue printed pots" &c.

The division of labour in pottery in 1827. These illustrations, showing mould making, engraving for transfers, modelling and mould pressing, are from a book that illustrated eighteen distinct stages, carried out by different people, in the production of pots. By the early nineteenth century, a complete division of labour was accepted in the potteries. From *A Representation of the Manufacture of Earthenware*, published by Ambrose Cuddon, London, 1827.

*Farrer, vol.I, pp.190-191.

potteries had little idea of the sorts of effect that were required of them as well as being generally reluctant to abandon the traditional ideas that had been handed down to them about the proper form of pots. Wedgwood had constant difficulty in finding modellers who could design in the antique style, whether for his ornamental or his useful wares. A letter from Wedgwood in 1767 describes well the kind of problems he often had with his modellers:

'I have recd. the Terrine model & mould, the imperfections of which you describ'd so justly in your last letter that I need only say your acct. of them was not exagerated, & I fear Mr. Chubbard will not be of much use to us, which I am the more concern'd for, as he seems so well dispos'd to do his best for us . . .

'The Terrine is capitally defective in point of truth in the form of all the *ends & sides* which do not correspond at all with each other, there is the same fault in the ornamts. & likewise in the top of the dish, & the Cover. The carv'd ornaments are not finish'd, & the whole shews such a want of that *Masterliness* necessary in the execution of these works, as quite discourages me from thinking of employing him again as a modeler.'*

Ultimately Wedgwood solved the problem by employing artists from outside the pottery industry to do the modelling. Understanding the principles of neo-classicism, these artists could use them to give modern products the character of the antique. At first, Wedgwood employed artist modellers at his works, but he found them very troublesome. Their sense of artistic independence made them disinclined to follow the strict routine he expected of his other workmen, and they threatened the discipline and standards of work he was trying to enforce. Of this problem, Wedgwood wrote on one occasion:

'Oh! for a dozen good & *humble* modellers at Etruria for a couple of months. What creations, renovations, & generations shod. we make! Well – fair & softly, we must proceed with our own natural forces, for I will have no more *fine* modellers here, though I seem to wish for them, they would corrupt & ruin us all. I have been oblig'd to part with Radford. The hours he chose to work would, by the example, have ruin'd ten times better men than himself.'*

*Farrer, vol.II, p.171.

Wedgwood's experiences with artists in his factory convinced him that he should not employ them in the works, but commission or buy designs from them. It was on this basis that he dealt with John Flaxman, who worked in London and sent his designs to Etruria. The operation of designing thus became not just separate but also geographically removed from the manufacture of the pots.

Wedgwood evidently understood that there were commercial advantages in employing artists to design his wares. As the middle and upper classes established stronger self-identity, they sought to distinguish themselves by exclusive and fashionable tastes of their own. Provincial craftsmen from the working class could not help being ignorant of these fashions, and Wedgwood was compelled to find men who had connections with society and the ruling taste. In a letter to Bentley, he made it clear that he believed that customers would rate the work of Academicians more highly than that of ordinary plaster-cast makers, like John Flaxman's father, who is referred to here:

'I wrote to you in my last concerning Busts, I suppose those at the Academy are less hackneyed and better in General than the plaister shops can furnish us with: besides it will sound better to say this is from the Academy, taken from an original in the Gallery of etc. etc. than to say we had it from Flaxman.'*

*Wedgwood to Bentley, quoted in *John Flaxman R.A.*, catalogue of exhibition at the Royal Academy, London, 1979, p.47.

Although the demands of neo-classicism gave Wedgwood a particular reason for making use of artists to design his products, the introduction of designing as a specialist activity has been general to the development of all manufactures, going hand in hand with the division of labour. Otherwise, without a set of instructions to guide the craftsman, the manufacture of any article would have had all the unpredictability of a game of consequences as one man after another added his labour to it.

Whether the design was prepared by a craftsman who worked for the rest of his time at some other job in the factory, or whether it was prepared by an artist or professional designer living in a distant town and conversant with the latest fashionable tastes and ideas, the nature of the work was the same and owed its origins to the same cause. Though the professional designer might have been able to conceive a very much more stylish and marketable product, the fact that there was work for him to do was the result not of his inventive genius, but of the division of labour in the factory.

Design and the Labour Process: the Elimination of Chance

Once a manufacturer had had a design prepared for his products, it was natural that he should want it reproduced as exactly as possible. Much could be done by the designer himself to ensure that his work was of a kind that the craftsmen, with the skills and tools they had, would be able to reproduce accurately and consistently. In almost every industry, one of the first conditions a design had to fulfil was that it should give consistent results in its execution, for a product in which there were haphazard variations would rightly be judged a failure. Almost all designs have therefore had characteristics that were arrived at in order to use the available means of production – machines or workmen's hands – in such a way that chance and variation would be eliminated.

Most histories of design in which Wedgwood's Queensware has been discussed have stressed its neo-classicism. Certainly, Wedgwood was concerned that his pots should have a neo-classical appearance, but his particular type of neo-classicism was related to the way in which the pots were made and to the organisation of his factory. Some historians of design have suggested that the smooth, regular forms of Queensware were the result of mechanical methods of production: for instance, Herwin Schaefer stated in *The Roots of Modern Design* that Queensware was 'perfected and standardized in shapes to be easily produced by mechanical means'.* Obsessed though Schaefer and other historians have been by the notion that the introduction of machines must have been the main cause of changes in design, there is no evidence of any mechanical revolution in the pottery industry in Wedgwood's time to justify Schaefer's description. The techniques of throwing, moulding and turning Queensware were exactly the same as had been used for greenware and for that matter, throughout the pottery industry for at least thirty years before Wedgwood went into business.* Although he did introduce a mechanically driven turning lathe, which has been made much of by historians, turning was in

*Herwin Schaefer, *The Roots of Modern Design*, London, 1970,

*See J. Thomas.

Mould for cauliflower teapot, c.1760. Making moulds was expensive, and the range of pots was limited to the number of different moulds.

fact a traditional craft that the machine did no more than speed up.* Wedgwood's claim to fame as a producer rests not on the use of machines, but on the way he organised the workmen in his factory. It is therefore to his innovations in this quarter that we must look for connections between the design of the pots and the method of manufacture.

The particular problem that compelled Wedgwood to adopt new designs for his pots was the need to find a way of creating variety without increasing the costs of production, and without having to accept irregularities and inconsistencies in workmanship. Wedgwood's customers expected a choice of designs, and indeed clamoured constantly for new patterns. His original product, greenware, had been notable for the large number of moulded

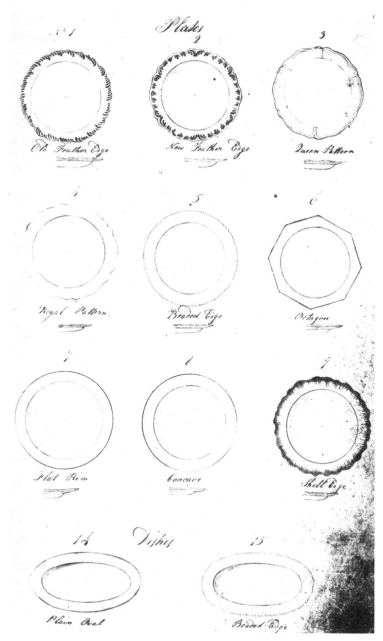

Josiah Wedgwood: shape book for plates, c.1770. Many of the shapes had rococo features, which restricted the range of enamel patterns that could be applied.

38

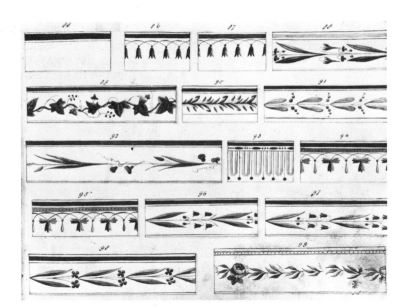

Josiah Wedgwood: page from pattern book of enamel decorations for Queensware, c.1780. Customers could choose from a wide range of decoration on a limited number of shapes.

designs and for the variety of glaze effects. However, the unpredictability of the glazes made the wares unsuitable for sale by samples and catalogues. The production of many moulded designs was costly because of the capital cost of all the moulds that were required and the time that was wasted by the workmen in shifting from one design to another. In a letter to Bentley, written when he was trying to lower his workmen's piece rates, Wedgwood referred to these problems:

'I have had several serious *Talks* with our Men at the Ornamental works lately about the price of our workmanship, and the necessity of lowering it, especially in Flowerpots, Bowpots, and Teapots, and as I find their chief reason against lowering their prices is the small quantitys made of each, which creates them as much trouble in *tuneing their fiddle* as *playing the tune*, I have promised them that they shall make dozens and Groces of Flower, and Teapots, and of the Vases and Bowpots too, as often as we dare venture at such quantitys . . . I have now got a book for my own use and speculation, with the prices of workmanship of every article, I shall proceed in the same way where I think there is room for it, and the infallible consequence of *lowering the price of workmanship* will be a *proportional increase of quantity* got up; and if you turn to the columns of Calculation and see how large a share *Modeling and Moulds* and the three next columns bear in the expence of Manufacturing our goods, and consider that these expences move on like clockwork, and are much the same whether the quantity of goods made be large or small, you will see the vast consequence in most manufactures of *making the greatest quantity possible in a given time.*'*

*Mankowitz, p.57.

In the ornamental wares, to which this letter referred, the quantities produced were nothing like as great as in the useful wares, where even larger economies could be made by reducing the number of designs. To achieve such a reduction, while still satisfying his customers' demands for variety, Wedgwood decided in the Queensware to limit the number of shapes but to offer a wide choice of enamelled decoration, which was applied to the pots after they had been fired, a relatively simple process.

Thomas Baxter: *Workshop of the Artist's Father, Gough Square, London,* watercolour, 1810. Enamellers decorating pottery, not in this case Wedgwood's.

When customers placed their orders, they had a wide range of decorative patterns to choose from: in 1774, there was a choice of thirty-one different enamel patterns on offer in addition to plain and gilt finishes. This meant that Wedgwood did not have to tie up capital in a large stock of different designs, for the enamelled ornament did not need to be applied until after receipt of the order. Once he had decided to concentrate all the work of decoration into the enamelling, the cost of decoration, whether by the cheap process of printed transfers or the more expensive one of hand painting, did not vary greatly if there was one design or a hundred. The only difficulty was that each pot had be equally suited to every design. Pots with a lot of relief pattern left few options in their decoration – though a feather-edged plate might be suited to a flower pattern, it would not take a geometric pattern. In order

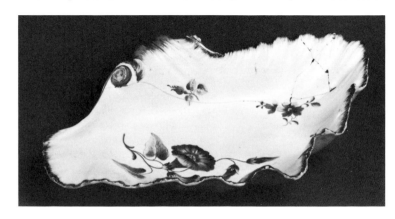

Wedgwood Queensware *compotier,* c.1770. Many of Wedgwood's earlier Queensware designs were far from neo-classical. Shapes like this did not lend themselves to different decorative patterns.

40

Josiah Wedgwood: Queensware plates, tureen, bowl and covered dish decorated in crimped ribbon and wreath design, c.1780. The same, or similar basic shapes, could be decorated in very different patterns.

to make the Queensware designs suitable for a wide variety of enamelled patterns, plain and simple shapes with large expanses of smooth surface were needed. It so happened that neo-classical forms satisfied this requirement very much better than the rococo ones that Wedgwood and other manufacturers had been producing.

The development of forms that both suited the methods of manufacture and satisfied the tastes of the market was the work of design. It would not have been enough for the designs just to have appealed to eighteenth-century middle and upper-class taste, or just to have been such that the craftsmen could be relied on to repeat them consistently: the achievement of Wedgwood's modellers was to arrive at forms which satisfactorily fused the requirements of both production and consumption. In this, the modellers were occupied in exactly the same task as every subsequent designer.

It is often said that industrial design is a new, specifically twentieth-century occupation. For instance Jeffrey Meikle states in his book about design in America between the two World Wars, *Twentieth Century Limited*, that industrial design came into existence as a result of the depression:

'Industrial design was born of a lucky conjunction of a saturated market, which forced manufacturers to distinguish their products from others, and a new machine style, which provided motifs easily applied by designers and recognized by a sensitized public as "modern".'*

*Jeffrey Meikle, *Twentieth Century Limited*, Philadelphia, 1979, p.39.

Certainly a group of professional industrial designers did emerge in America in the 1920s, but it is wrong to suppose (whatever they themselves claimed) that these were the first industrial designers. The activity that men like Raymond Loewy and Henry Dreyfuss were engaged in had existed in certain industries for well over a century, and the only novel things about their work were the ideas they brought to the job and the products they were called upon to design, from automobiles to radio sets and retractable ball-point pens. In all fundamental respects, the nature of their work, fusing ideas with manufacturing techniques, was identical to that of Wedgwood's humble modellers in the potteries.

3. Design and Mechanisation

Was Machinery Bad for Design?

It has long been the convention to see mid-Victorian design as degenerate and to blame this on the introduction of machine manufacture. In *Pioneers of Modern Design*, probably the single most widely read book on modern design, Nikolaus Pevsner described the state of mid-Victorian design as follows:

'It was not only that the machine had stamped out taste in industrial products; by 1850 it seems that it had irremediably poisoned the surviving craftsmen . . . Why was this bound to come? The usual answer – because of industrial growth and the invention of machines – is correct, but as a rule taken too superficially . . . The development from simple mechanical devices to modern wonders of machinery was logical and gradual. Why did the machine in the end become so disastrous to art? The transition from the mediaeval to the modern state of applied art was reached somewhere about the end of the eighteenth century.'*

*Nikolaus Pevsner, *Pioneers of Modern Design*, 3rd edition, Harmondsworth, 1960, pp.42-43.

Pevsner goes on to list the well-known sequence of mechanical inventions of the industrial revolution, encouraging us to believe that they were the cause of the deterioration in design. But could inanimate, senseless machines have had anything to do with the quality of design and were they really the cause of all the evils attributed to them? And is the historical process which Pevsner outlined in *Pioneers of Modern Design* an accurate account of the development of design in industry?

In his account of the degeneration of mid-Victorian design, Pevsner has followed closely the statements of those who saw the changes at first hand. The subject was much discussed in the nineteenth century, with repeated references to the evil influence of machines. A typical remark, though unusually early in its date (1835), is by the architect C.R. Cockerell: 'I believe that the attempt to supersede the work of the mind and hand by mechanical process for the sake of economy will always have the effect of degrading and ultimately ruining art.'*

*Select Committee on Arts and Manufactures, Minutes of Evidence, *Parliamentary Papers*, 1836, vol.IX, para. 1431.

Similar opinions were expressed by many others, among them John Ruskin, Richard Redgrave, editor of the *Journal of Design* which was published between 1848 and 1852, and William Morris. Within a short time, Cockerell's belief that machines led to inferior design had become widely accepted as incontrovertible truth. Thus Charles Eastlake could write with absolute conviction in his book *Hints on Household Taste*, which was published in 1868:

'Every lady recognises the superiority of hand-made lace and other textile fabrics over those which are produced by artificial means.

The same criterion of excellence may be applied to almost every branch of art-manufacture. The perfect finish and accurate uniformity of shape – the correct and even balance which distinguish European goods from those of Eastern nations, and English goods especially from those of other countries in Europe – indicate degrees not only of advanced civilization, but, inversely, of decline in taste.'*

*Charles Eastlake, *Hints on Household Taste*, reprinted Ontario, 1969, pp.104-105.

The arguments put forward by the nineteenth-century design reformers and followed by Pevsner rested upon an assumption that machines had usurped the craftsman's control over the form of the product: the effect of machines, they believed, had been to change the practice of design by separating responsibility for the appearance of a product from the tasks of fabricating it, with the consequence that the quality of design had deteriorated. So strongly was this idea held that one of the main purposes of the Great Exhibition of 1851 was to demonstrate the truth of it: the intention of Henry Cole, the principal organiser of the exhibition, was to display machine-made products alongside the hand-made goods of India and the Orient so that the simplicity and superiority of design of the latter would be there for all to see.*

*Siegfried Giedion, *Mechanization Takes Command*, New York, 1948, p.352.

Yet despite the wide acceptance of the ideas embodied in the Great Exhibition, machines could not possibly have been the cause of the much denigrated specialisation in the work of design, which was already established long before the development of mechanised production. At no point did machines alone have any independent influence upon design. It is the persistence of Victorian writers' misunderstanding and prejudices that, even today, brings us back to the hoary old theme of the effect of machines on the quality of design. The histories of three nineteenth-century British industries – calico printing, dress making and cabinet making – illustrate particularly well the actual relationship between the appearance of finished products and the machines used in their manufacture.

It is important to remember that the extent of mechanisation in mid-nineteenth-century industries was far less than was, and still is, often supposed. As Raphael Samuel has shown, the manufacture of a great many products relied for a long time on the manual skill and strength of workmen.* Even where machines were introduced, they were rarely applied to all the stages of production, and many processes continued to be carried out by hand: for instance in tailoring and dress making, until late in the century, machines were employed only for a few types of sewing. Of all British manufacturing industries in the middle of the nineteenth century, only textile production had been extensively mechanised.

*R. Samuel, 'The Workshop of the World', *History Workshop Journal*, no.3, Spring 1977, pp.5-72.

In the many industries that continued to be based on manual labour, products were still not necessarily made from start to finish by the same craftsmen: for example, the division of labour in the unmechanised pottery industry goes back as far as the early eighteenth century and it appeared in many other industries around the same time.* This pattern corresponds closely to the three stages of the development of capitalist manufacture described by Karl Marx in *Capital*.* After the initial condition of pre-capitalist societies, in which artefacts were made by individual craftsmen working on their own, Marx identified the first phase of capitalism as the simple co-operation of workers, who might, for example,

*L. Weatherill, *The Pottery Trade and North Staffordshire 1660-1760*, Manchester, 1971, chapter 5.

*Karl Marx, *Capital*, vol.I, Part 4. References are to the Pelican edition, Harmondsworth, 1976.

share a workshop and purchase their materials and sell their goods collectively. In the second stage, the different tasks of hand manufacture were divided among the workmen under the direction of a master; the third stage came about with the introduction of machinery and the establishment of the factory system. In many British industries, the second stage, the division of labour in handicraft manufacture, took place in the eighteenth century: it was as the individual craftsman lost control of the complete process that the new and separate activity of design became necessary. Marx was referring to this stage when he wrote:

'The knowledge, judgement and will which, even though to a small extent, are exercised by the independent peasant or handicraftsman, in the same way as the savage makes the whole art of war consist in the exercise of his personal cunning, are faculties now only required for the workshop as a whole.'*

*Marx, p.482.

Marx went on to quote the Scottish philosopher Adam Ferguson (1725-1826) on the advantages of ignorance for successful manufactures:

'Ignorance is the mother of industry as well as of superstition. Reflection and fancy are subject to err; but a habit of moving the hand or the foot is independent of either. Manufactures, accordingly, prosper most where the mind is least consulted, and where the workshop may . . . be considered as an engine, the parts of which are men.'*

*Marx, p.483.

Writing in 1767, Ferguson closely anticipated Josiah Wedgwood's remarks about 'making machines of the men'. It was at the second handicraft stage of industry that design, as the drawing up of instructions, became necessary in order to direct the ignorance of the workmen. The introduction of machines, Marx later explains, made further changes both in the kinds of labour used (women and children rather than skilled artisans) and in the way it was used (to mind and regulate machines rather than for skill in production), but it had no effect on the essential characteristics of the process of which design was already a part. According to Marx:

'Machine production drives the social division of labour immeasurably further than manufacture does, because it increases the productive power of the industries it seizes upon to a much greater degree.'*

*Marx, p.572.

Elsewhere he wrote:

'The separation of the intellectual faculties of the production process from manual labour, and the transformation of those faculties into powers exercised by capital over labour, is . . . finally completed by large-scale industry erected on the foundation of machinery.'*

*Marx, pp.548-549.

This excursion into theory can be illustrated and substantiated by events in the history of calico printing, an industry in which design was of the greatest importance, since the commercial success of printed cotton relied almost entirely upon the appeal of the pattern. As one manufacturer asked, '. . . what is it that makes the trade at all? Is it not the design upon the fabric, and the colour upon it, and the invention of art that is put upon it; if you put more and better of all these things, you will have more trade.'*

*Select Committee on the Copyight of Designs, Minutes of Evidence, *Parliamentary Papers*, 1840, vol.VI, para. 3062.

Because cotton was such a major industry in nineteenth-century Britain, the design of printed cottons received a great deal of public attention around the middle of the century.

The technique of printing cotton from engraved wooden blocks was developed in the late seventeenth century.* In the 1750s, a new technique was developed, using engraved copper plates, which were larger than the wooden blocks and could carry more detail. Whichever method was used, the printing itself was done by hand: the cloth was stretched out on a long table, and the printer worked along it, pressing the block or plate down upon the cloth, and inking it between each impression. Considerable skill was required in applying the correct quantity of ink, in registering the block accurately and in applying the right amount of pressure. The process was a slow one: it was said that one printer could not print more than six pieces of cloth a day (one piece equals 28 yards). By 1800, both the drawing of the designs and the cutting or engraving of the blocks had become entirely separate occupations from printing, and each craft had its own apprenticeship. In 1804, it was said that at Church Bank in Lancashire, 58 journeymen block cutters and 23 pattern drawers had entered the trade in the last 23 years.* Even while the printing was still done by hand, the designing of patterns had already become a separate occupation.

Although the introduction of engraved copper plates had made some difference to the appearance of calico prints, in permitting more detail and larger patterns with each impression, it had made no difference to the organisation of labour in the works. However, in 1796 came another technical development: the engraved plates were made into rollers, and it became possible to print an entire length of cotton continuously in a single mechanical process. The first roller printing machines were driven by water power,

*On the history of calico printing, see G. Turnbull, *A History of the Calico Printing Industry of Great Britain*, Altrincham, 1951; *English Printed Textiles 1720-1836*, catalogue, Victoria & Albert Museum, London, 1960 (text by P. Floud); and G. Dodd, *The Textile Manufactures of Great Britain*, London, 1844, pp.58-60.

*Minutes of Evidence on the Calico Printers' Petitition, *Parliamentary Papers*, 1806-07, vol.II, p.14.

Engraving wooden blocks for textile printing in eighteenth-century France. This was the original method of printing fabrics. From 'Arts et Métiers Méchaniques', *Encyclopédie Méthodique des Arts et Métiers*, n.d., vol.8, plate 5.

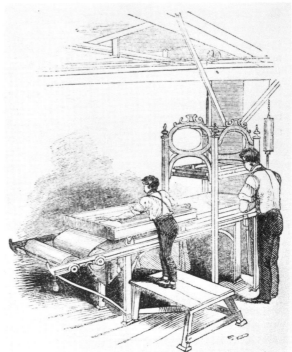

Above:
Printing calico with an engraved wooden block, early nineteenth century. A slow and skilled process. From *Book of English Trades*, published by R. Phillips, 1823.

Top right:
Printing cotton from an engraved plate in a flat press, early nineteenth century. As well as allowing more detail in the engraving, plates were larger than blocks and production was therefore faster. From G. Dodd, *The Textile Manufacturers of Great Britain*, London, 1844, p.66.

Design for printed fabric by Vivian Kilburn, England, c.1790. Designs of such detail were reproducible only with engraved plates printed on a press.

Roller printing press for printed cottons, England, early nineteenth century. Roller or cylinder printing accelerated the production of cotton prints enormously. Note the simplicity of the designs being printed. From E. Baines, *History of the Cotton Manufacture in Great Britain*, London, 1835.

*Turnbull, p.83.

*J. Emerson Tennent, *A Treatise on the Copyright of Designs for Printed Fabrics*, London, 1841, p.23.

*'The Rise and Progress of Great Manufactories by the Proprietors – Messrs. Hargreaves Calico Print Works at Broad Oak, Accrington', *Journal of Design*, vol.III, no.15, May 1850, p.79.

but it was not long before the introduction of steam made a much more rapid rate of production possible. Where it had been possible to print only six pieces a day on a single table, a steam-powered roller printing machine could print up to 500 pieces a day. Between 1796 and 1840, as a result of the introduction of these machines, the annual production of printed textiles in the United Kingdom increased from one million pieces to sixteen million pieces. Hand printing by blocks and plates continued and still survives, but only for specialised and highly detailed work. In 1840, there were 435 printing machines in the country and 8,234 printing tables; ten years later however, there were only 3,939 tables, while the number of machines had increased to 604.*

While hand printing declined, bringing considerable hardship among the craftsmen, the greatly increased output of printed cottons provided a growing demand for new designs, and the occupation of pattern drawing, already well established in the handicraft period of the industry, continued to flourish. In 1841, it was estimated that in Manchester alone 500 people were working as designers of printed cottons. Some were employed in-house by the cotton masters; others worked freelance and sold their patterns to printers.* A few designers, usually artists who had taken to drawing patterns, were retained by manufacturers on an annual salary, but it was more common for pattern designers to be employed on a weekly wage. Of all the employees in calico printing they received the highest average wages. At one factory in 1850, the top wage for a designer was 60 shillings a week, while the rate for the next most highly paid trade, engraving, was no more than 50 shillings.*

The practice of the print masters was to have large numbers of designs prepared but to engrave and print only a few. One large Manchester manufacturer said that in 1838 his pattern drawers

*Select Committee on the
Copyright of Designs, Minutes
of Evidence, *Parliamentary
Papers*, 1840, vol.VI, para.105.

*Select Committee on
Copyright of Designs, 1840,
paras 108, 2085, 2879.

*Select Committee on
Copyright of Designs, 1840,
paras 4646-47.

*Tennent, p.31.

had prepared between two and three thousand designs, of which only five hundred had been engraved and printed.* This apparent extravagance and wastefulness was possible because the designs cost so little in comparison to the cost of engraving the cylinders and printing the cloth. In the Report of the Select Committee on Design of 1840, different manufacturers gave estimates of the proportion that the cost of design bore to the total cost of production. Various manufacturers estimated the cost of preparing a design at between five pounds and fifteen pounds.* One large manufacturer reckoned that design cost him between ½d. and ¾d. per piece, while another said that it cost him $\frac{1}{192}$ (0.52%) of the cost of the cloth and represented $\frac{1}{352}$ (0.28%) of the selling price.*

It is worth pointing out that in spite of these infinitesimal costs, the value of the design to the manufacturer was very great. The cotton print masters relied for their profit on the volume of sales from the individual machine-printed designs, and the commercial success or failure of a particular print depended almost entirely on the popularity of the design. One manufacturer estimated that a single successful design had been worth between £200 and £300 in the receipts it had brought him.* On an initial outlay of not more than fifteen pounds, this was a handsome profit. Because machine printing greatly increased the quantity of cloth that could be printed from a single pattern, it made a successful design far more valuable to manufacturers than could ever have been the case with hand printing. It is not surprising that it was in the 1830s

Design for a cotton print, watercolour on paper, with a sample of the cotton printed from the design, English, early nineteenth century. The designs were drawn out to a large scale for engraving. Manufacturers had hundreds of such designs produced, only a few of which were engraved and printed.

and 1840s, when machine printing began to expand rapidly, that manufacturers first became concerned to protect ownership of their designs. The major print masters began to campaign in the early 1830s for the copyright laws to be extended to cover designs for printed cottons, and, although other justifications, such as the argument that it would lead to better design, were put forward for copyright, the main object of the print masters was to establish their proprietorship over designs as a source of wealth.

The debates over copyright gave rise to a great deal of discussion on other aspects of design. However, the new attention that was being paid to design did not mean that designing was a new activity or even that its essential nature had lately changed in any way because of the introduction of machines. Nevertheless, the view was sometimes expressed that the hand printed textiles of the early decades of the century were superior to the cylinder-printed designs of the 1830s and 1840s. Richard Redgrave put forward two reasons in the official report on design in the Great Exhibition of 1851 to account for what he saw as a deterioration in quality. His first point was that:

'Wherever ornament is wholly effected by machinery, it is certainly the most degraded in style and execution; and the best workmanship and the best taste are to be found in those manufactures and fabrics wherein handicraft is entirely or partially the means of producing the ornament . . .'*

*Great Exhibition of 1851, Jury Reports, vol IV, 'Supplementary Report on Design to Class XXX', pp.710-711.

Printed cotton, English, 1850. This complex, illusionistic design, of the kind criticised by Redgrave, would have been printed by roller for the flat areas of colour and by plate for the detail.

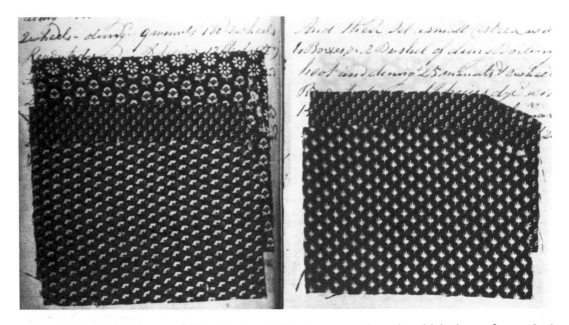

Cotton print samples in the record book of H. Fieldlong & Bros., dated 12th February 1824. This book records dye recipes and printing processes. These simple, repeat patterns of the kind admired by Redgrave were printed by roller.

What Redgrave liked were products in which the craftsmen had influenced the design, or been able to introduce variety; yet, if this had ever been the case in calico printing, it had ceased to be long before the nineteenth century, and certainly was not true of the patterns of the 1820s that he so admired. Redgrave's second reason for inferiority concerned the introduction of cylinder printing:

'The restrained use of means has often been adverted to . . . under the old and simple methods of cotton printing, when the resources were few and the means were limited, the style was in some respects better than at present obtains . . . Thus block printing by hand required flat forms and flat tints diapered regularly over the surface, and some simple flower or leaf so used had a pleasing and just effect . . . In the place, however, of the former limited means, printing from metal cylinders has put at the command of the designer all those powers of more perfect imitation enjoyed by the engraver, and, instead of using them as they should be used, consistently with the requirements of manufacture and the principles of ornamental art, they are wasted on the imitation of flowers, foliage and accidents of growth, quite out of ornamental character and opposed to just principles.'*

*Great Exhibition of 1851, Jury Reports, vol.IV, p.745.

Again Redgrave's analysis was at fault, for the 'restraint' he associated with block printing had been superseded, not by cylinder printing, but by the earlier invention of copper plate printing, which had been introduced in the handicraft stage of the industry. Far from offering 'more perfect imitation', cylinder printing, if anything, provided less, because the problems of register made it unsuited to designs with many colours. The evidence from calico printers' record books shows that during the 1820s it was the simpler patterns of the kind that Redgrave admired and thought to be handicraft products that were printed by cylinder, and the more complex, fussier ones of which he disapproved that were hand-printed.* Even by the 1850s, when Redgrave was expressing these opinions, most cylinder-printed designs were still fairly

*Manuscript record book of H. Fieldlong & Bros of dye recipes and printing processes, dated 12th February 1824, Victoria & Albert Museum, Department of Textiles, T12-1956.

Cotton print samples in the record book of H. Fieldlong & Bros., dated 12th February 1824. *Left:* A design printed by roller (for the large flat areas) and block (for the detail). *Right:* One of the most complex designs printed entirely by block, the hand process that Redgrave mistakenly believed produced simplicity in design.

The Mechanical Fallacy: Fashion and Furniture

*Many of Mayhew's original letters were reprinted in his *London Labour and the London Poor*, 4 vols, 1860; a further selection is contained in *The Unknown Mayhew*, E.P. Thompson and E. Yeo, Harmondsworth, 1973. The latter is particularly relevant to this chapter since it contains the bulk of the coverage of the needleworkers and the cabinet makers.

simple, with rarely more than two colours, while many of the more ornate designs that were castigated by the organisers of the Great Exhibition were printed either entirely by hand from blocks and plates, or by a combination of block and cylinder. If the deterioration in design that Redgrave and others perceived was not the result of mechanisation, we have to ask what caused the changes they saw and go on to consider why they insisted on attributing them to the introduction of machines.

To find explanations for changes in design, we have to look beyond the machines themselves to the social system in which they were used. In the effects both of the sewing machine upon costume design and of machine-cut veneers upon cabinet making, the crucial factor can be shown to be the particular characteristics of the relationship of labour to capital in the respective industries.

The system of garment manufacture on the eve of the introduction of the sewing machine was described by Henry Mayhew in his letters to the *Morning Chronicle* in 1849.* According to Mayhew, tailoring and dressmaking in London were divided into 'honourable' and 'dishonourable' sections. The 'honourable' section survived in establishments where only fully qualified journeymen were employed, mostly on a regular basis; they produced the highest quality of work, worked on the masters' premises, and were paid at piece rates on an agreement between masters and journeymen known as 'the log'. The forms of employment in the

Above:
Dressmaking workshop, 1850s.
The state of exhaustion of the
seamstresses suggests a
sweatshop. From *The British
Workman and Friend of the Sons
of Toil*, September 1858.

Right:
Sweated tailor, 1850s. The man
is working in his home, on
garments that have been put out
to him by a sweater. From *The
British Workman and Friend of
the Sons of Toil*, October 1855.

'dishonourable' section were very different. The 'dishonourable'
trade included tailors and dressmakers working casually for large
tailoring and dressmaking establishments that were short of hands,
but it consisted mainly of 'sweated' workers. Under the sweating
system, tailoring or dressmaking houses put work out to a 'sweater',
usually a journeyman, who contracted for the sewing of a quantity
of garments. The sweater in turn put the work out to needleworkers at rates of pay much below those of the 'log'. The work
was sometimes done in the workers' own homes, but increasingly
in a workshop provided by the sweater. Mayhew quoted one
sweated tailor's description of the system:

'The master here . . . gets work from the warehouse at the before-
mentioned prices; he gives it out to us at the same price, paying us
when he receives the money. We are never seen at the shop [i.e. the
warehouse]. Out of the prices the master here deducts 4s. per
week per head for our cup of tea or coffee in the morning, and tea
in the evening, and our bed.'*

The Unknown Mayhew, p.140.

In this case the sweater apparently made no profit out of the sewing
itself, but only out of the deductions for food and lodging. Most
sweaters, however, gave their workers a lower rate than they received on the completed goods; it was said that the sweater's
normal rate of profit was two shillings in the pound on completed
garments.* The sweaters were effectively small capitalists who
made their money out of the labour of the tailors and dressmakers
working for them. Their capital consisted of the security, usually
at least five pounds, which they had to give to the tailoring houses
or wholesale warehouses on receipt of the cloth.* It was the lack
of even this small amount of capital that prevented the majority of
needleworkers from getting work direct from the warehouses and
compelled them to work for the sweaters. By 1849, an estimated
six out of seven London garment workers were employed in the
dishonourable trade, either as casual or as sweated workers, making
ready-made shirts and outer wear for the large ready-to-wear men's
clothing shops, and uniforms and liveries.*

The Unknown Mayhew, p.265.

The Unknown Mayhew, p.141.

The Unknown Mayhew, p.218.

The introduction of the sewing machine caused no fundamental
change in the industry. Machines first became commercially available in 1851, and technical improvements over the next few years
made them relatively efficient by the end of the decade. The

*Royal Commission on Children's Employment, Second Report, *Parliamentary Papers*, 1864, vol.XXII, p.163.

*Royal Commission on Children's Employment, 1864, para.410.

*For further discussion of the impact of the sewing machine, see Marx, vol. I, pp.601-604.

*The Unknown Mayhew, p.232.

evidence to the Royal Commission on Childrens' Employment in 1864 shows that sewing machines were in widespread use by then.* Most were bought by sweatmasters and installed in their workshops, as few individual workers could afford them. Because the sewing machine greatly increased the needleworker's output, it was to his or her advantage to seek a place in a workshop where machines were provided, accelerating the trend towards the employment of workers in workshops rather than in their own homes.* Although manufacturers began to hire out sewing machines for one or two shillings a week, in theory allowing individual needleworkers to be their own masters and independent of the sweatshops, this was of little help to the workers, who still lacked the necessary capital to deal direct with the warehouses.* The sewing machine, then, made no structural difference to the relationship between workers, sweaters and masters, except in tending to make needleworkers more dependent on the sweaters who provided the sewing machines.

What the sewing machine did not do was further diminish the amount of control that individual garment workers had upon the form and appearance of garments. Evidence from the Royal Commission on Childrens' Employment and elsewhere shows that a division of labour between cutting and sewing, and between the sewing of various parts of garments was already well established before the introduction of sewing machines. A journeyman very rarely both designed and made a garment himself; it is because this was so unusual that Mayhew quotes one tailor as saying he had 'made a waistcoat of my own invention.'* In general, the pattern and cut of garments was still determined by the masters and retail shops, just as it had been before the introduction of the sewing machine.

However, it did appear to some contemporaries that the sewing machine had affected the design of clothes, but the reasoning here needs close examination. Because the sewing machine could not be used for the whole process of making clothes, some parts of the sewing of a garment became cheaper than others. The early sewing machines were good only for sewing flat seams and for sewing on trimmings. Machines for the blind stitching of hems, for buttonholing and for sewing on buttons were not developed until towards the end of the nineteenth century. Until then, these tasks had to be carried out by hand, even if the main seams of the garment could be machine sewn. It was only to be expected that garment manufacturers would want to exploit the parts of the process cheapened by the machine and to reduce as much as possible the more laborious and costly work of hand finishing. In women's dresses, the effect of the machines was greatly to increase the amount of trimming that could be applied to dresses for the same cost. A Cheltenham dressmaker giving evidence to the Royal Commission on Childrens' Employment stated:

'I have three machines. I should like every dressmaker to use them; they save much labour, and also enable you to pay at a higher rate those whom you employ, whether machinist or finisher. Much more work can be put in too; we should never put 100 yards of trimming in a summer dress, if it were all to be done by hand; the pleating up and finishing must still be hand-work; and we find it best to have different machines for different work,

*Royal Commission on Children's Employment, 1864, p.202, para.88.

just as with hand-workers, one will do the sleeves, another the skirts and a third the bodies.'*

The great increase in the quantity of trimmings had its effect upon women's fashions. Dresses of the 1860s and early 1870s were loaded with trimmings: it seems that a hundred yards per dress was no exaggeration. Contemporary writers on fashion noted this development, and by the early 1870s had begun to deplore it. One wrote:

'What . . . will characterize the present epoch in the History of Fashion . . . is the amount of trimming with which we have found it possible to load every separate article.'*

*Quoted by C.W. & P. Cunnington, *Handbook of English Costume in the Nineteenth Century*, London, 1959, p.486.

*Cunnington, p.487.

It was supposed that the fashion was due to the sewing machine: 'We owe much of the over-trimming now prevalent to the facilities afforded by the sewing machine.'*

Convincing though this explanation may seem, it was valid only because sewing machines had been introduced into a capitalist system of manufacture. One of the main objects of the sweat-masters and clothing wholesalers, who controlled their use, was to cheapen the price of sewing. In other circumstances, the speed of the machines could have allowed the machinists to earn more or to work for only a few hours a day instead of the twelve or more that were customary for hand sewers. To the customer, the cost of

Fashion plate, c.1860, showing the heavily trimmed dresses that were fashionable, and which contemporaries wrongly attributed to the introduction of the sewing machine.

the sewing could have continued the same, and all the advantages would have been to the worker. There would then have been no virtue in designing dresses with great lengths of elaborate trimmings, since they would only have been more expensive.

However, rather than paying the machinists at the same rate as the hand sewers, the sweaters actually paid them only a fraction of what the hand sewers received for an equivalent amount of sewing. In the United States, where circumstances were similar, a shirt factory in New Haven, Connecticut, paid its hand sewers in 1860 at the rate of 62½ cents per shirt, but when sewing machines were installed, the machinists received only 16⅔ cents for each shirt.[*] To earn as much as hand sewers or, as was usual, slightly more (in this particular factory, machinists were paid four dollars per week compared to the hand sewers' three dollars), the machinists had to work almost as long hours. Of the money that the sweater or dressmaker saved, part went to pay the cost of the machine, part went to increase profits, but most went to reduce the price of sewing to the customer, so that more sewing could be put into a dress at no additional cost. Thus the ultimate cause of the fashion for heavily trimmed dresses was not now the sewing machine itself, but its use within a capitalist system of manufacture.

Like the garment industry, the furniture industry in mid-nineteenth century London was divided into an 'honourable' section of men in regular employment, paid at agreed rates, and a 'dishonourable' section of self-employed men whose earnings were much lower and were determined by bargaining with the retailer for a price on each piece of furniture made.[*] The large majority of cabinet makers were self-employed men, working on their own, assisted (if they had any assistance) most often by their wives and children. Known as garretmasters, these men were indeed their own masters, but since they usually had no capital apart from their tools, and their livelihood depended upon selling each piece of furniture immediately they had made it, most of them were extremely poor. They generally made their furniture speculatively, carting it when it was finished to the West End to find a buyer among the furniture stores there. The stores were often accused of taking advantage of the garretmasters' desperate need for cash to beat them down to prices that hardly paid for their labour, for which the retailers earned themselves the name 'slaughterhouses'.

Until about 1830, it seems that most furniture was made by journeymen employed in the workshops from which it was sold, and in many places outside London this continued to be common until much later in the century.[*] There were also some masters, known as 'trade-working masters' who employed journeymen to make furniture which was sold wholesale to retail stores.[*] However, between 1830 and 1850, the regular employment of cabinet makers declined, and more and more became garretmasters, who by 1850 outnumbered the former by ten to one. The change appears to have been caused by the rise of the large furniture retailers who had sufficient capital to hold stocks of furniture for some time, and found that their expenses were much reduced by not having to employ directly the men who made the furniture.

Many of the slaughterhouses were said to be unconcerned about the quality of the furniture they sold, as long as it was superficially good enough to take in the customers. One garretmaster reported

[*]George Gifford, 'Argument of Gifford in Favor of the Howe Application for Extension of Patent', New York, United States Patent Office, 1860, referred to in Grace Rogers Cooper, *The Sewing Machine, Its Invention and Development*, 2nd edition, Washington D.C., 1976, p.58.

[*]See *The Unknown Mayhew*, pp.432-482.

[*]See, for example, the description of his shop in Liverpool by James Hopkinson, *Victorian Cabinet Maker*, edited by J.B. Goodman, London, 1968, p.96.

[*]*London Labour and the London Poor*, p.228.

to Mayhew that he had been told by a slaughterhouse: 'Make an inferior article so as it's cheap: if it comes to pieces in a month, what's that to you or me?' The garretmaster continued:

'There's no doubt of it that the linendrapers [furniture retailers] have brought bad work into the market, and have swamped the good. For work that ten or twelve years ago, I had £3 5s. to £3 10s. from them, I have now 30s. Of course it's inferior in quality in proportion . . .'*

London Labour and the London Poor, p.225.

Under the influence of the slaughterhouses, such 'scamping' became widespread. Garretmasters found themselves having to make twice as many pieces in the same time as men honourably employed in order to stay alive.

Nothing made scamping easier than machine-cut veneers, which became available cheaply with the introduction of steam-powered circular saws in the 1830s. Previously, veneers, cut by the most skilled branch of the hand sawyers, had been relatively expensive and used only in high class cabinet work. However, as one old hand sawyer explained to Mayhew, the circular saw changed all this by cutting veneers thinner and faster:

'They was cut more true than any sawyer could do them, but not half as well as they are now. The first that was done was eight to the inch, and now they can cut fourteen, as thin as a wafer, and that's impossible for the best sawyer in the world to do. I have cut as many as eight in the inch myself, but then the wood was very shallow – eight or nine inches deep. The general run of veneers cut by hand was about six in the inch.'*

Morning Chronicle, 4th July 1850, p.6.

By 1850, when Mayhew recorded this statement, all veneers were cut by steam power, and their price was much reduced as a result.

Machine-cut veneers were a boon to the garretmasters in their need to make superficially good furniture as cheaply as possible. Mayhew described how the garretmasters used them:

'The frequent use of rosewood veneers in the fancy cabinet, and their occasional use in the general cabinet trade, gives, I was told, great facilities for scamping. If, in his haste, the scamping hand injure the veneer, or if it has been originally faulty, he takes a mixture of gum shellac and "colour", (colour being a composition of Venetian red and lamp black) which he has already by him, rubs it over the damaged part, smooths it with a slightly heated iron, and so blends it with the colour of the rosewood that the warehouseman does not detect the flaw. Indeed, I was told that very few warehousemen are judges of the furniture they bought and they only require it to look well enough for sale to the public, who know even less than themselves.'*

London Labour and the London Poor, p.230.

Another garretmaster, talking about the production of ladies' sewing boxes said:

'Such boxes are nailed together; there's no dove-tailing, nothing of what I call *work* or workmanship, as you say about them, but the deal's nailed together, and the veneer's dabbed on, and if the deal's covered, why the thing passes.'*

The Unknown Mayhew, p.477.

The use of veneers was especially singled out by those to whom Mayhew spoke, and by others involved in the furniture industry, as one of the reasons for the quality of furniture. In the hands of

Garretmaster, 1860. The
garretmaster, who has just
made the chest-of-drawers on
the barrow behind, is
negotiating a price for it with a
furniture retailer. From H.
Mayhew, *London Labour and the
London Poor*, 1861, vol.3.

Hand sawyer. Veneers, like all
timber, were originally cut by
two sawyers, one above and one
below. The introduction of
steam-powered circular saws
made the craft redundant.
From *Book of English Trades*,
published by R. Phillips, 1823.

Morning Chronicle, 8th August
1850, Letter LXIV, 'Fancy
Cabinet Makers of London'.

the garretmasters, cheap, machine-cut veneers allowed an enormous change in the appearance of low-quality furniture which,
rather than being simply made of deal, could now have all the
appearance of superior products. As one garretmaster said to
Mayhew:

'I think that machinery has been a benefit to us: it increases the
material for our work. If there wasn't so much veneering, there
wouldn't be so much fancy cabinet work.'*

Although the veneer-cutting machinery facilitated the development of a new kind of furniture production, it would again be
wrong to suppose that machinery was responsible for any deterioration in quality. As the garretmasters themselves told Mayhew,
it was the growth of the slaughterhouses that had mainly caused
the decline in standards, because the low prices they offered the
cabinet makers encouraged scamping on a large scale. Machine-cut
veneers provided just another means of scamping but were not
themselves the cause of the practice. As with the sewing machine
and dress making, it was not the machine itself that brought about

changes in design, but the use of machinery under specific economic and social circumstances. Both garment manufacture and cabinet making involved a very simple level of technology and a relatively straightforward set of economic relations between capital and labour, but even when the technology is more complex, machinery alone has never determined the appearance of the goods. To attribute changes in design purely to technology is to misunderstand the nature both of machines and of design in industrial societies.

The Politics of Design

The idea that machines had ruined design represented only a small part of a much larger debate during the 1830s and 1840s, a period when design became an issue of national political importance in Britain. It was the subject of three Parliamentary Select Committees, in 1835-36, 1840 and 1849; there was pressure to set up, and subsequently to improve, government-subsidised schools of design, there was a campaign to establish copyright over designs, and there were numerous exhibitions of art and design, culminating in the Great Exhibition of 1851, all organised with the intention of improving public taste and educating artisans.*

*On these various matters, see Quentin Bell, *The Schools of Design*, London, 1963; T. Kusamitsu, 'Great Exhibitions before 1851', *History Workshop Journal*, no.9, Spring 1980, pp.70-89.

The underlying reason for this concern was that the development of machine production had made design very much more valuable to manufacturers. Maximising the sales from each design had not been so crucial in handicraft industries, where, although profit might depend on the volume of production, there was not necessarily any advantage in using a single design rather than a variety of different ones. In the hand printing of calico, for example, additional output required more tables, more printers and more blocks, but since each additional block had to be cut by hand, it made little difference if it was made to a new design or duplicated an existing one. The great advantage of machinery was its potential to manufacture a single design endlessly; the successful design became a very much more valuable possession, for it was what released the machine's capacity to make a profit. It was natural, therefore, that it was in the industries being mechanised in the second quarter of the nineteenth century that the greatest concern about design was shown, over both improving standards and protecting copyright.

The timing of all this in the late 1830s and early 1840s can also be explained by the severe economic conditions of those years. In what was the first trade depression ever to affect the newly industrialised economy, manufacturers and political economists were anxious to know whether capitalist industry would survive at all and, more immediately, to ensure that Britain did not lose her share of world markets to foreign competitors. Although Britain was better equipped to produce consumer goods, particularly textiles, more cheaply and in greater quantity than any other country, there were fears that Britain's trading position was threatened by foreign competitors who could manufacture goods of superior design. Whether the competitors' products were in fact better designed is an open question; what mattered was that their design was different and many English people believed it to be superior. In the circumstances, the improvement of design seemed vital for Britain's economic survival and caused people to advocate remedies that were wholly contrary to the principles of classical economics and *laissez faire* which dominated politics at

Small veneered box, c.1860. This box is a typical product of the garretmaster, taking advantage of cheap veneers. The box itself is of rough deal, as can be seen inside the lid; the veneer conceals the poor quality of the carcase.

the time. Copyright of design gave manufacturers a form of protection which interfered with free market competition, while the government subsidy of schools of design represented a form of state assistance to industry – another kind of interference with the 'natural laws' of the economy. Design was therefore a sufficiently important issue to cause even such strong advocates of *laissez faire* government as the political economist Nassau Senior

*N.W. Senior *et al.*, *On the Improvement of Designs and Patterns, and Extension of Copyright*, London, 1841.

to compromise their principles and recommend some legislative intervention in the interests of better design.* The events of these years in some ways anticipated the much more extensive state involvement with design in Britain in the 1930s and 1940s, when similarly adverse economic conditions threatened the exports of manufactured goods.

A major issue in the nineteenth-century debates was the cause of the apparent inferiority of British design. Two particular explanations appeared repeatedly and are worth looking at in order to understand the reasoning of those involved. One, the supposedly deleterious effect of mechanisation, has already been dealt with in this chapter; the second attributed the poor quality of design to the British workman's ignorance and lack of artistic ability. A great deal of weight was attached to this argument by some, who used it to justify setting up schools of design and organising exhibitions of art and design. Only, it was said, by educating artisans in the art of design, could any improvement in standards be looked for. This argument, too, needs to be approached with caution. There were people at the time who disagreed with it, and gave good grounds for doing so. In his evidence to the Select Committee on Arts and Manufactures in 1835, J.C. Robertson, the editor of the *Mechanics' Magazine*, pointed out that the argument was based on a misunderstanding of the nature of industry: in practice, it was unnecessary for artisans to have any design ability, since all that factory production required of them was the ability to execute the designs given to them. He added that he did not believe that there was any lack of ability among those concerned with design. When asked if designers were sufficiently instructed, he replied:

'I think they generally are sufficiently instructed. I have never met, in all my experience, any want of talent, in designing any branch of manufacture.'*

*Select Committee on Arts & Manufactures, *Parliamentary Papers*, 1836, vol.IX, para.1593.

His own explanation for the inferiority of British design directed blame in an entirely different direction. Any superiority of French goods, he said,

'is owing to the talents of our artisans being employed in a more profitable direction than to any inferiority of taste in them. The great object with every English manufacturer is quantity; with him, that is always the best article to manufacture of which the largest supply is required; he prefers much a large supply at a low rate to a small supply at a higher; and that even should the present profit be less from the former than from the latter, because, in the long run, the larger the demand, the steadier it is sure to be. I do not think this is a point which has been sufficiently considered. From the great command of capital possessed by the English manufacturer, the immense capabilities of his machinery, and the unrivalled skill and industry of his workmen, he is enabled to turn out a greater quantity of goods in a given time than the manufacturer of any other country whatever.'*

*Select Committee on Arts & Manufactures, 1836, vol.IX, para.1598.

Robertson was attributing bad design not to the workmen's lack of skill, but to the capitalist system of manufacture, which always put quantity and profit before quality. Although his explanation anticipated what William Morris later had to say about the causes of bad design, the argument was not to be found in the other evidence given to the Select Committee and hardly appears in the rest of the mid-century literature on the subject. In general, other writers and design reformers chose to concern themselves almost exclusively with such peripheral subjects as artisans' lack of artistic skill and the influence of machines.

What the critics of design were unable to see or refused to acknowledge, was that capitalist manufacture, itself the cause of the specialised work of design becoming necessary, was simultaneously responsible for the quality of design deteriorating. Yet the artists, architects and intellectuals who involved themselves in design reform in the mid-nineteenth century, were far too closely associated with industrial and commercial wealth to dare venture on such a radical line of criticism. While many of them disliked the effects of industry, they had no alternative conception of what an industrial society could be like, and it was thus extremely difficult for them to make any criticism of their own society that did not threaten the source of their own prosperity. Short of abandoning all the material progress of the previous century and a half and returning to a simple handicraft economy (which was very much what John Ruskin recommended), they could envisage no way of building a society with an abundance of wealth, but without the concomitant evils. Only a socialist like William Morris was in a position to see that criticism of industrial society need not necessarily be regressive and that there could be an alternative which did not preclude material progress. It was therefore open to Morris, through his socialism, to blame the poor quality of design upon the greed of capitalism when others hesitated, or were unable, to do so. Although Morris disliked mechanisation and thought its products ugly, he did not insist that it was the sole cause of inferior design. As he said in one lecture:

'It is not this or that tangible steel and brass machine which we want to get rid of, but the great intangible machine of commercial tyranny, which oppresses the lives of all of us.'*

*'Art and Its Producers', Collected Works of William Morris, vol.XXII, London, 1914, p.352.

The practice of blaming machinery for bad design conveniently diverted criticism away from capitalism and focused attention on the technical problems of production rather than on the much more difficult and contentious social ones. It was, after all, much easier to see how machines might be redirected to make better design than to conceive how the social relations of capital and labour might be reconstituted to the same end. But what is so remarkable about the myth of the machine as the agent of bad design is its survival into the present despite far greater understanding of the nature of society. Whatever the reasons for its unnaturally long life, the myth has had the effect of obscuring the central place that design holds in production. To treat design in terms only of technical or artistic factors invariably makes it seem trivial and insignificant, detracting from its unique characteristic of embodying, in the most vivid and concrete way, not some but all of the conditions surrounding the production of commodities. In a nineteenth-century calico design, we are looking not only at the product of a steam-powered roller press, nor only at the results of the artistic skill of an individual pattern designer, but also at the product of a system in which it was possible for one man to profit by purchasing the labour of many others at a price which paid for little more than their subsistence.

4. Differentiation in Design

In its 1895 catalogue, the American mail order company Montgomery Ward & Co. offered 131 sorts of pocket knife. The knives were grouped into four categories, 'ladies'', 'men's', 'boys'', and 'men's heavy pocket and hunting'. Although there were differences between the categories, the variations within each category were relatively slight. The catalogues of other nineteenth-century mail order companies, department stores and manufacturers reveal that it was normal for such dazzling ranges of choice to be offered in everything from pens to sewing machines or dining-room chairs.

The profusion has continued, though to a much lesser extent, to this day and has often angered design moralists, who have seen it as an abuse of design and a waste of effort, since it does nothing to improve human existence.* However, while a dozen designs of pocket knife might have served the needs of Montgomery Ward's customers just as well as the 131 offered, the company could hardly be blamed for over-production of designs, when such wide choices were universal. The diversification of designs, not just to suit many different categories of use and user, but also in the great variety available within each category, was so much a feature of nineteenth-century industry that it cannot be written off as the result of mere wilfulness and irresponsibility.

Although the handicraft methods that were still used in most nineteenth-century industries lent themselves to the production of many different designs, standardisation would have been as

*For example, V. Papanek, *Design for the Real World*, London, 1972, chapter 4.

Pocket knives for ladies and pocket knives for men. Some of the range of folding pocket knives sold by the American mail order firm Montgomery Ward. The ladies' knives are universally distinguished from the men's by their smaller size and slimmer handles, usually of white bone (instead of horn as was common for the men's). From Montgomery Ward & Co. catalogue, no.57, 1895, pp.440-441.

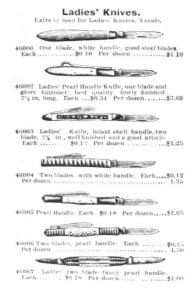

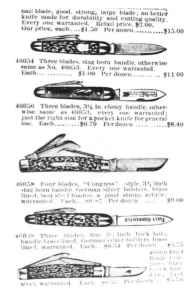

easy, and there was nothing in the system of production that compelled manufacturers to pursue variety. They evidently did so because they and their customers wanted the choice, and there was system in the diversity, for the designs fell into distinct categories which generally corresponded to their notions about the shape of society and the distinctions within it. The differences between the designs of manufactured goods thus became the incarnation of contemporary ideas of social difference. Unlike the muddled and contradictory form that these ideas usually took in the minds of ordinary men and women, design represented them in a form that was at once clear, tangible and irrefutable.

Montgomery Ward's designs of pocket knife were divided into four classes according to their function and the sex and age of the user. Each category had certain shared features. Ladies' knives were thus distinguishable from men's, while boys knives were superficially similar to men's but almost invariably had only a single hinge for the blades, making them simpler and cheaper. Such distinctions, which could be identified in many other products, rested on the assumption that people in each category of age, sex, class or rank, saw themselves as different from those in other categories and wanted this to be reflected in the goods they bought and used. Although the differentiation of designs expressed the divisions that the manufacturers saw in society, their view must have corresponded closely enough to what others saw for them to have been able to sell their goods. Taken as a whole, therefore, the entire range of manufactured goods constituted a representation of society.

The study of design not only confirms the existence of certain social distinctions, but also shows what the differences between the categories were thought to be. In the nineteenth century, great importance came to be attached to the distinctions between men and women, and between adults and children. The division between classes, although historically of overwhelming importance, can be seen less clearly in design, mainly because the poverty of the working class prevented them from buying much, and the middle classes were able to express their status sufficiently well merely by their power to buy goods unavailable to the working class. It was only when classes met in the relationship of master and servant and servants wore clothes and used articles bought by their masters that a differentiation of social class in design became easy to perceive.

Masculine and Feminine

*See L. Tickner, 'Women and Trousers' in *Leisure in the Twentieth Century*, Papers at the Second Conference on Twentieth Century Design History, London, 1977, pp.56-68.

*J.C. Flügel, *The Psychology of Clothes*, London, 1930, pp.200-202. See also Y. Deslandres, *Le costume, l'image de l'homme*, Paris, 1976, pp.241-249.

Throughout history, men and women have dressed differently, and even when, for example, women started wearing trousers or when 'unisex' fashions appeared in the 1960s, the convention, though temporarily interfered with, was never in serious danger of being abandoned.* Of the possible ways of classifying dress, such as by the class, age or race of the wearer, sex is the primary one, and the most common in histories of costume, for even though the design of clothes worn by men and women has changed, the dress of men at any one time and in any one place has almost always been instantly recognisable from that of women. J.C. Flügel in *The Psychology of Clothes* suggested that the reason why the sexes dress distinctively is to provide a warning against homosexual attraction in social encounters.* No such explanation, however, can be applied to sexual differentiation of articles purely for personal use, such as combs, watches and electric razors, which are hardly likely to function as signals of gender; their design is best explained through their conformity to accepted ideas of what is proper to men or to women – in other words, through notions of masculinity and femininity, which refer not to biological differences but to social convention.

Of the 131 pocket knives that were offered for sale by Montgomery Ward & Co. in 1895, 17 were described as ladies' knives. Although it is unlikely that there was any significant difference in the mode of cutting practised by American men and women, the ladies' knives were all smaller and had pearl or white handles; the men's knives were larger, and many of them had horn handles. The catalogues of nineteenth-century department stores and mail order houses reveal many other examples of designs which distinguished the sex of the user. The toilet cases illustrated in the Army and Navy Stores catalogue for 1907 were classified as ladies'

Below:
Ladies' hairbrushes and men's hairbrushes, Army and Navy Stores catalogue, 1908. The ladies' hairbrushes are distinguished by having handles, and, for the most part, a greater amount of decoration on the backs.

64

No. 51 W. 18-carat Gold Swiss Keyless Watch, in 15-carat gold London made Bracelet, complete with Safety Chain and Case £13 10

Fig. 116 W. 18-carat Gold Swiss Keyless Lever Watch, compensated balance, jewelled in 10 holes, in 15 carat gold London made Bracelet. Watch is detachable.
A quality £18 16
B   „ 18 10

Ladies' watches and man's watch, Army and Navy Stores catalogue, 1908. As well as being larger and having a leather instead of metal strap, the man's watch has Roman numerals on the face, unlike most of the ladies' watches, which have Arabic numerals.

*Mrs Ellis, *The Daughters of England*, London, 1845, p.3.

and gentlemen's, with differences in the contents of each, and the cases themselves were consistently different in design, the gentlemen's covered in pigskin and the ladies' in morocco leather. This was a distinction consistent with other leather goods, where pigskin, rawhide and alligator were the customary finishes for men's luggage, and the more delicate morocco or crocodile usual for women's.

Inside the dressing cases, articles common to the use of both sexes also differed. In the several pages of hairbrushes advertised in the Army and Navy Stores catalogue, gentlemen's hairbrushes were characteristically ovals, with little or no ornament; ladies' hairbrushes, even at an equivalent price, had handles and were generally carved or engraved. In wristwatches, the disparity in size between those for gentlemen and for ladies exceeded that between male and female wrists, and a lady's watch usually had more delicate features and face. Being smaller, ladies' watches have generally been more expensive, but when they can be compared to men's watches of a similar price, the ladies' models are still more ornamented. In the 1907 Army and Navy Stores catalogue, the men's watches were all calibrated with Roman numerals, while the ladies' watches all had Arabic numerals, whose form – curvilinear rather than angular – may be judged more delicate.

Articles where design is determined by the sex of the user can be found from all periods of history. The appearance of, say, sixteenth-century purses or modern electric razors will indicate whether they are for men or for women. But sexual differentiation in design has never been more widely applied than it was in the late nineteenth century.

The notion of great difference between the sexes was associated with the fact that nineteenth-century men and women of the middle and upper classes found themselves leading very separate existences. The gradual exclusion of middle and upper-class women from active political and commercial life from the sixteenth century onwards had reached the point by the mid-nineteenth century when the public life of women was restricted to the 'social' functions of entertaining and paying calls. This state of affairs was justified by the assumption that women were unsuited to any other kind of existence because of their supposedly fragile and delicate constitutions and their sensitive and emotional temperaments. Some of the feminine characteristics attributed to women were described by a popular author, Mrs Ellis, in her book *The Daughters of England*, published in 1845:

'As women, then, the first thing of importance is to be content to be inferior to men – inferior in mental power, in the same proportion that you are inferior in bodily strength. Facility of movement, aptitude, and grace, the bodily frame of woman may possess in a higher degree than that of man; just as in the softer touches of mental and spiritual beauty, her character may present a lovelier page than his.'*

The qualities of men, by contrast, were thought to lie in their strength, their vigour, their love of adventure and their ability to suppress emotion. These supposed differences, which betray a confusion of actual physical differences with attributed psychological ones, were to be found in nineteenth-century novels and scientific works alike. Even such a careful observer of the human race as Francis Galton wrote, without qualification, in his *Inquiry*

*Francis Galton, *Inquiry into Human Faculty and its Development*, London, 1883, p.56.

*C.W. Marsh, *Recollections 1837-1910*, Chicago, 1910, p.298, quoted in C.K. Dewhurst, B. MacDowell, M. MacDowell, *Artists in Aprons*, New York, 1979, p.39.

Philips man's electric razor, c.1980, and Philips 'Ladyshave' woman's electric razor, 1980. The lady's razor is coloured, and decorated with a floral device, so appearing more 'feminine' than the plain black model for men.

into Human Faculty and Its Development (1883): 'One notable peculiarity in the character of the woman is that she is capricious and coy, and has less straightforwardness than the man,' a statement which echoes exactly the differences between the men and women in Elizabeth Gaskell's novel *Wives and Daughters*, written nineteen years earlier.* There, the feminine qualities represented in Molly Gibson are moral virtue, sensitivity and susceptibiity to illness; in her stepsister, Cynthia Kirkpatrick, they are beauty and inconstancy. The leading men in the novel, Dr Gibson and Roger Hamley, are distinguished by their directness, by their dedication to a greater purpose (one to medicine, the other to science), by their energy and vigour, and by their capacity to surmount emotion. Roger Hamley's brother, Osborne, however, lacked all of these qualities – and accordingly did not survive to the end of the book.

Few statements can express the great distance that lay between the Victorian masculine and feminine ideals more succinctly than the following, from the recollections of a septuagenarian American, writing in 1910:

'Nature made woman weaker, physically and mentally, than man, and also better and more refined. Man, compared with her is coarse and strong and aggressive.'*

Because there is little evidence for such firm opinions as this having been expressed before the nineteenth century, it seems that masculinity and femininity took on these distinctive characteristics in the course of the century. The characteristics did not exist as realities, but as ideas; to live comfortably with them, people needed evidence of their truth. Fiction, education and religion all contributed and so, too, did design. The differences between the Army and Navy Stores toilet cases corresponded exactly to the differences that were said to exist between men and women: tough and rugged as against delicate and refined. However, unlike the other bearers of this ideology, which relied heavily upon words, design was more potent, for it provided enduring, visible and tangible signs of the differences between men and women as they were held to exist.

Childhood

Just as design could embody distinctions between masculine and feminine, so it could also express assumptions about the nature of childhood. The crockery and furniture intended for middle-class children that manufacturers first began to produce in quantity at the very end of the nineteenth century were characteristically painted in pastel shades or decorated with pictures of animals or scenes from nursery rhymes. These items would rarely, if ever, have been bought by children themselves, and their appearance must have had less to do with children's own desires than with adults' wishes to perceive children's needs as unlike their own.

How childhood came to be seen as a condition, not simply of weakness, but also of innocence, naivety and virtue has been discussed by the French historian Philippe Ariès in his book *Centuries of Childhood*. Even if Ariès is correct in placing the major changes in the sixteenth and seventeenth centuries, it is clear that the ideas did not stop evolving then. The growing belief in the absolute goodness of childhood culminated in the appallingly sentimental descriptions of childhood innocence that are to be found in turn-of-the-century literature; only with the discoveries of psychoanalysis did ideas about the nature of childhood start to change.

Signs of the changes in perception can be seen in the way children have been depicted. In a mid-eighteenth century portrait, *The James Family* by Arthur Devis, the daughters are given equal prominence with the adults in the composition and are dressed as miniature adults. C.R. Leslie's portrait of the Grosvenor family painted in 1831, makes the children the centre of the family's attention, but distinguishes the younger ones by their dress: the small boy near the left of the picture wears not adult clothes but a frock, a distinctive mark of childhood. These paintings present

Arthur Devis: *The James Family*, oil painting, 1751. An eighteenth-century perception of childhood: the children are dressed and depicted like the adults.

a reflection of the general tendency of the nineteenth century to be on the whole more inclined than earlier centuries both to treat childhood as a privileged state and to stress its differences from adulthood.

These changes, which can be documented in the child-rearing manuals of the eighteenth and nineteenth centuries, were visible particularly in dress. There is also evidence that toys, games and books for children began to be produced commercially in the late eighteenth century, but there are few signs of specially-designed furniture or crockery, apart from cribs and cradles.* The pattern books of eighteenth and early nineteenth century cabinetmakers and upholsterers do not contain nursery furniture, which they were only rarely called upon to supply.* However, nursery furniture had been recognised as a special category by the time that J.C. Loudon's *Encyclopaedia of Cottage, Farm and Villa Architecture* was first published in 1833. Among its very thorough descriptions of furniture designs and uses, there was a short section on nursery furniture. Most of the items were miniature versions of standard cane and Windsor chairs, the same as appeared from the middle of the century in the catalogues of large furniture manufacturers. A few, however, were not simply smaller versions of adult furniture, but were specifically for children. One of these, illustrated by Loudon, was the Astley Cooper chair, named after the surgeon who had designed it to make children sit up straight at table. Only at the very end of the century were there entire ranges of nursery furniture that were different from those for adults, not only in scale but also in form and appearance. Some of these new articles, such as the purpose-designed toy cupboards, specifically filled children's needs, some offered the advantage of being hygienic and easy to clean, while others were decorated with pictures of

*C. Gilbert, *The Life and Work of Thomas Chippendale*, London, 1978, pp.53-54.

*J.H. Plumb, 'The New World of Children in Eighteenth Century England', *Past and Present* no. 67, May 1975, p.90.

C.R. Leslie: *The Grosvenor Family*, oil painting, 1831. An illustration of the change in attitude to chidhood over a century: children are sharply distinguished from adults, by performing essentially childish activities in front of the family and being dressed in some cases, like the boy in the centre, in children's clothes.

Nursery furniture. Purpose-designed chairs of various types for the nursery. The Astley Cooper chair (bottom left) was intended to make children sit up straight at table. From J.C. Loudon, *Encyclopaedia of Cottage, Farm and Villa Architecture*, 1857, p.1086.

after the bassinet ; that is, when the child is about a year old, and has been weaned. We may here mention a description of crib, which has hooks or other fastenings ; by which, when one side of it is taken out, the crib can be made fast to the side of the mother's bed, so that she may have access to the child during the night, by merely stretching out her arms, and taking it to her.

2145. *Chairs* are the next articles made use of by children ; and those about London are of four kinds. Fig. 1999 is a child's chair of the first kind, having a night pan, and a matted seat. A small stuffed flannel of the size of the seat, and having a round hole in the centre, is generally placed over it when it is to be used, in order to prevent the pan from hurting the child. (In some districts of Italy, and other parts of the Continent, rings of stuffed cloth, or stuffed leather, or of rush matting, are used for the same purpose by grown-up persons.) In England, infants of ordinary health and strength are put into chairs of this kind, when between three and four months old.

Fig. 1998 is a child's high chair, to be used when it first begins to sit at table. There is a bar or stick put across between the arms, to keep the child from falling out, and sometimes there is a foot-board. A child in average health is put into such a chair when about twelve or fourteen months old.

Fig. 2000 is an Astley Cooper's chair ; being a form recommended by that eminent surgeon, with the view of preventing children from acquiring a habit of leaning forward, or stooping ; the upright position of the back affording support when the child is placed at table, and eating, which a sloping-backed chair does not. It is proper to observe that some medical men do not approve of these chairs.

Fig. 2001 is a child's elbow-chair, or bergère, as it is commonly called in England. This chair stands on a stool, to which it is attached by a thumb-screw ; and, when the

Nursery cups, mugs and beaker, decorated with animals. From Army and Navy Stores catalogue, 1908.

NURSERY CHINA.

English China, Coloured "Toys" Decoration, Gilt Edges.

Mug .... 0/6   Tea Cup and Saucer........... 0/8   Milk Tumbler...... 0/8   Small Cup and Saucer ... 0/8   Small Mug ... 0/5

Tea Plate to match, 0/6 each.

NURSERY FURNITURE

Furniture for Children's Use.

No. 950. Oak Arm Chair 8/6
No. 572. Oak Play Table, 2 ft. 9 in. by
1 ft. 9 in. by 1 ft. 6 in. high 17/6
No. 951. Oak Chair without arms 6/9

No. 625. Oak Work Table,
with flaps and sliding work bag,
size when open 4 ft. by 2 ft.
£3 12 0

No. 434. Clothes Cupboard in oak,
4 ft. wide by 4 ft. high £8 5 0

No. 267. Cottagers' Chest, painted
dark green picked out with bright red,
3 ft. 6 in. wide by 5 ft. high £8 15 0

Nursery furniture, Heal's,
c.1914. Heal's made a full range
of nursery furniture, including
not only chairs but tables,
cupboards and chests of
drawers. From Heal & Co., *The
Nursery Book*, n.d. [c.1914].

animals or with colours that were thought particularly appropriate
for children.

Among other things, these developments were an extension of
the distinctions between childhood and adulthood that had already
become accepted. The more convinced people became of the
innocence and virtue of childhood, qualities that are by no means
naturally evident in children, the more reliant they became on
external physical signs for corroboration of their beliefs; hence,
for example, the choice of animals such as rabbits and hedgehogs

Nursery china: Mister Rabbit
saucer, Shelley Potteries, 1926;
baby's plate, decorated with
teddy bears, Cetem ware,
c.1925.

to distinguish children's utensils. Where birds and mammals had appeared on china for adults, the association had tended to be with hunting, but the motifs on children's china were different, for the animals were anthropomorphised and the children were evidently meant to empathise with them. It is possible that the choice of these symbols to indicate childishness was associated with the stress that was placed in the late nineteenth century on play as an essential activity for children. That this was a middle class concern is illustrated by the observations about working-class childhood made by visitors to the new Board schools set up in Britain under the Education Act of 1870. These visitors reported being 'pained by the utter unchildlikeness of the street children,' and in one area of London, Bermondsey, a Children's Guild of Play was organised 'to make them little children again, and fill their minds with real child's play'.* Games where children imitated animals were thought particularly appropriate, and it may be because animals (especially rabbits) provided such good models for playful and hence childish behaviour that they appeared so often in children's stories and on articles for children's use, like the nursery wares that the Shelley Pottery began to produce in Britain in 1902.*

A few nursery articles, like the Astley Cooper chair, were designed to influence the physical development of children, but most of the special furniture and utensils had no bearing at all upon children's health or physique. For middle-class families to spend unprecedented sums on specially designed and decorated nursery articles that served no hygienic or physical purpose can only be explained by changes in ideas about the needs of childhood. The introduction to the Heal's 1914 catalogue of nursery furniture, hinted at just this:

Child Life, new series, vol.III, no.11, 15th July 1901, pp.181-182.

*See C. Watkins, W. Harvey, R. Senft, *Shelley Potteries*, London, 1980, pp.79-85.

Nursery china, Heal's, c.1925. Like most nursery ware, the decoration depicted animals, in this case ducks, hens and geese, from the farmyard.

Teapot as Mushroom House from a nursery teaset, Shelley Potteries, 1926, designed by Mabel Lucie Attwell. Nursery china taken to its most whimsical extremes.

'Formerly the children, even in the families of the well-to-do, were relegated to an attic or some room not thought sufficiently good for any other purpose, furnished with things discarded from other rooms. Nothing was placed there because it was specially suitable, but rather that it had become unsuitable or too dilapidated elsewhere.

'Now the nursery is carefully chosen, well lighted and well planned. The aspect, size, ventilation and general cheerfulness considered, in short everything is done to make the nursery a pleasant and convenient place, suitable to the needs of the occupants, and in every way a fit training ground, both physical and moral, for the young.

'Children are admittedly very susceptible to their environment, therefore, how important it is to surround them with things at once beautiful and useful. Place a child in the midst of bright and cheerful things and you go a long way towards making him happy and good-tempered; it is difficult to cultivate these virtues in a gloomy setting.'*

*Heal & Co., *The Nursery Book*, n.d. [1914], p.3.

If, as Heal's argued, the newly discovered needs of childhood demanded a special environment, the practical effect of applying this principle to design was to endow what were otherwise no more than speculations about child psychology with the character of objective truth, and to remove childhood further from adulthood than it had ever been before.

Social Class

Important though the development of social class has been historically, class distinctions in design are far from easy to trace. This has been partly because, at least until recently, distinctions between classes have been marked so clearly by different patterns of consumption that distinctions in design would have been irrelevant. However, the one commodity universal to all classes is dress, which therefore offers a promising subject in which to discuss class differentiation. Costume has long been regarded as an important social indicator, but never more than it was by the Victorians. Mrs Merrifield, in her book *Dress as a Fine Art* (1854), listed its

72

*Mrs Merrifield, *Dress as a Fine Art*, London, 1854, p.5.

function of marking the wearer's station in society third after the needs of decency and warmth.* Part of the reason for the nineteenth-century preoccupation with this function was the fact that the customary social distinctions in dress were increasingly being ignored or flouted. The development of cheap ready-to-wear tailoring made it possible for men of all ranks to wear virtually identical clothing. As the French *Journal des Tailleurs* commented on the dress of visitors to the Paris Exhibition of 1855:

'Between the black coat of M. Rothschild and the black coat of his lowest clerk, there are only imperceptible nuances which could be appreciated only by a tailor's apprentice – M. Rothschild's coat probably comes from the Renard workrooms and cost him 180 francs. The clerk's coat without doubt was bought at La Belle Jardinière and cost about 35 francs. For the present, that is the only difference, only M. Rothschild's coat will stay black, and the clerk's will turn from blue to dirty grey. M. Rothschild is also a little more free in his movements.'*

*Quoted by, and translated from, H. Vanier, *La Mode et Ses Métiers*, Paris, 1960, pp.155-156.

Because costume expressed conflicting desires to obscure social distinctions and to make them apparent, it is by no means a straightforward example of the expression of class structures in design and is complicated by the fact that the working classes frequently wore second-hand clothes. The only kind of clothing specific to the working class were the slop-made jackets and trousers sold by the clothing warehouses as working clothes.* These cheap, loose-fitting clothes were cut from jean, fustian or moleskin; in practice, those who wore them would have been identified as working class, but they were neither designed nor chosen with this intention in mind.

*Catalogues of E. Moses & Son, Aldgate, London, 1846-55.

A more rewarding subject for comparison is textiles, as printed cottons were among the first industrially made products to be sold to all classes. In the eighteenth century, printed cottons had been relatively expensive and fashionable wear for middle and upper-class women. Although printed cottons might have been bought by the middle classes for their servants to wear, as they were by Parson Woodforde, who recorded in 1801 buying '2 Cotton Gowns for my two maids, of Pink and White, 17 Yards at 2/6d, £2.2.6d'*, they would not have been bought by working-class women themselves. The cotton print dresses worn by working-class women would generally have been secondhand or cast-offs. It was more usual, though, for working-class people to wear woollen rather than cotton clothing.*

*J. Woodforde, *The Diary of a Country Parson*, edited by J. Beresford, vol.V, London, 1931, p.304.

*A. Buck, 'The Dress of Domestic Servants in the Eighteenth Century', in *Strata of Society*, Proceedings of the Seventh Annual Conference of the Costume Society, London, 1974, pp.10-16.

With the great expansion of the Lancashire cotton industry early in the nineteenth century, the market changed. For the first time, working-class women could buy new cotton dress material for themselves, and they did so on such a scale that by 1818 they were said to constitute almost the entire home market for the printed cotton trade. A London draper reported in 1818 that printed fabrics '. . . are worn principally by servants and the lower class of people.'* Sales of printed cottons to middle-class customers had declined in the 1800s and 1810s because of the fashion for wearing plain white dresses which was inspired, it was said, by the wish to imitate the form of classical figures. Although printed cottons came back into fashion in the 1820s, the working classes still dominated the home market.

*Minutes of Evidence taken before the Select Committee on the Duties on Printed Cotton Goods, *Parliamentary Papers*, 1818, vol.III, pp.305, 316 and 341.

*Select Committee on the Copyright of Designs, Minutes of Evidence, *Parliamentary Papers*, 1840, vol.VI, para.3749.

*Select Committee on the Copyright of Designs, 1840, paras 1697-1704.

*Select Committee on Printed Cotton Goods, 1818, p.320.

*Select Committee on the Copyright of Designs, 1840, paras 1708, 5035-37.

Henry and Augustus Mayhew, *The Greatest Plague in Life*, London, 1847, p.86.

Interior of a cotton mill, c.1830. The women are dressed in gingham and printed striped cotton, characteristic working-class wear of the date. From E. Baines, *History of the Cotton Manufacture in Great Britain*, London, 1835.

As the manufacturers themselves recognised, the market was now divided between working-class custom for prints mainly on calico, and fashionable buyers of prints on superior cottons.* In theory, the same designs could have been printed on any quality of fabric, but, in practice, the printers used different designs for the two markets. Certain patterns known to be popular with the working class were produced largely for that market.* According to evidence given to a Select Committee in 1818, the wearing of ginghams, both woven and printed, was normally restricted to the working class.* An engraving of the interior of a cotton mill in the 1830s shows a millhand dressed in gingham and another in striped cotton, suggesting that these patterns were characteristic working-class wear. According to evidence given in 1840, a large class of simple prints, particularly Bengal stripes and green or navy blue with white spots, were steadily in demand with the working class.* That such patterns typified working class wear in the 1840s is confirmed by the description of a maid in Henry and Augustus Mayhew's satirical novel *The Greatest Plague in Life*, published in 1847:

'When the conceited bit of goods came after the station, she looked so clean, tidy and respectable, and had on *such* a nice plain cotton gown, of only one colour – being a nice white spot on a dark green ground . . . that I felt quite charmed at seeing her dressed *so* thoroughly like what a respectable servant ought to be.'*

Apart from the familiar stripe and spot patterns, it is not possible to identify from the surviving pattern books which designs were aimed at a working-class market. Certain firms did specialise in cheap prints, but their pattern books are not on the whole the ones to have survived, and it is only occasionally possible to identify designs known to have been sold to the working class.

For the middle-class market, the cotton printers produced patterns, mostly on more expensive types of fabric, that were calculated to attract well-to-do customers by the refinement and quality of the designs, as well as by their novelty. A constant

Above:
Printed cotton dress, English, c.1784. In the eighteenth century, printed cottons, like this dress, were restricted to middle and upper-class wear.

Right:
White cotton dress, English, c.1810. The growth of a working-class market for printed cottons caused them to be abandoned by the middle and upper classes, who started to buy only fine white cottons.

*Select Committee on the Copyright of Designs, 1840, paras 948-950.

succession of new designs was produced in small quantities for middle-class women who wished to be dressed in patterns that they could be sure had not yet been reproduced on the cheaper fabrics worn by working-class women. It is hard to pin down exactly how the patterns for the middle class differed from those for the working class and whether they indicated anything about the differences that were supposed to exist between the two classes. In any case, many fashionable designs were subsequently reproduced by the manufacturers on cheap cotton, a practice which both attracted working-class customers wanting to follow the fashion, and caused the owners of dresses in the first, expensive printing of a pattern to discard them, because they had become 'common', and to buy new ones.* What evidence there is about the patterns intended exclusively for the working class suggests that these were thought to be distinguished by their vulgarity and crudity. However, this does not seem to have been a permanent characteristic, for, as one critic wrote in 1856:

'. . . good authorities in the Midland Counties, at least, say that the great mass of the people who usually buy these things prefer

Cotton print designs, English, 1850. These designs are rare instances of patterns which are known to have been produced specifically for the working-class market. From *Journal of Design*, vol.IV, no.31, September 1851, pp.9-10.

the smaller, neater and more simply coloured designs, to the blotchy abominations which used formerly to be sought after, and which in too many instances, are still presumed by the less observant manufacturer and retailer, to constitute the taste of the working class.'*

*G. Wallis, 'Recent Progress in Design as Applied to Manufactures', *Journal of the Society of Arts*, no.173, vol.IV, 14th March 1856, p.292.

Nor was the attempt to distinguish between the refinement of designs for the middle class and the coarseness of deigns for the working class always successful. How a pattern was judged could depend to a large extent on who was wearing it; as another critic observed,

'. . . it sometimes occurs that a staring pattern, which we should be disposed to call extremely vulgar on a commonplace person, is worn with impunity by one of ultra fashionable rank. A distinguished air, and a fine person, may carry off the extravagance of a design . . .'*

*'Counsel to Designers for Woven Fabrics', *Journal of Design*, vol.II, no.18, August 1850, p.179.

Thus, while the evidence leaves no doubt there was differentiation in cotton print patterns on the basis of class, identifying the class for which particular designs were intended is made difficult, if not impossible, by the nature of the market for cottons, where the manufacturers, their customers and the passage of time all conspired to obscure the distinctions as they might have existed at any one moment.

The history of another commodity, soap, shows design being used commercially to create demand in a particular class market. Unlike printed cottons, where class differentiation in design had long been accepted, soap products were not manufactured for specific classes of consumer until W.H. Lever began to market his new soap, Sunlight, by giving it a brand image with specific working class appeal. Soap for laundering clothes and for household cleaning was manufactured in Britain on a scale that grew steadily throughout the nineteenth century.* By 1885, there were a number of well-established firms in the business, but none of them had yet produced soap in a form that could be said to have been designed. There were about half a dozen basic varieties of household soap made by these firms according to accepted recipes.* The soap was supplied in long bars to the grocers who cut pieces

*On the history of soap, see Charles Wilson, *The History of Unilever*, London, 1954, vol.I, part I; and H.R. Edwards, *Competition and Monopoly in the British Soap Industry*, Oxford, 1962.

off and sold them by weight to the customers, much as if it were cheese. Until the 1880s, each soap manufacturer operated in a regional market in which he had a monopoly. There was thus little or no competition between the makers. Any stamp or brand on the soap was of no interest to the customer, who chose a kind of soap, such as 'mottled', 'curd', 'primrose', or 'Windsor', and not a make.* As one of the main soap manufacturers explained at the time:

*R.L. Wilson, *Soap Through the Ages*, Port Sunlight, 1952, p.13.

'. . . there is little or no difference in quality between different makes of Bar Soaps – there is a Thomas's Primrose, a Knight's Primrose, a Cook's Primrose – all the same soap. It is impossible therefore by the nature of the case to . . . [attempt] through advertising to create a demand in favour of any one particular make.'*

*Quoted in C. Wilson, p.41.

This state of affairs changed rapidly with the arrival of W.H. Lever in the soap industry in 1885. Lever had been a partner in a wholesale grocery business with branches in Bolton and Wigan, a business that depended for its prosperity on the rising standard of living of working-class customers. In 1884, he began to tire of grocery and turned his attention to soap, on which working-class households were tending to spend more and more money. Lever aimed to capture this market, which existing manufacturers of household soaps had not yet tried to reach, with a special product. He was to become so successful in selling his own new 'washer' soap that other soap manufacturers went out of their way to claim that their bar soaps were not for working-class customers. One established manufacturer was to explain:

*Quoted in C. Wilson, p.67.

'Bar soaps do not come into competition with "washers". That is a special soap sold in the lower-class neighbourhoods, and we find . . . that it does not sell in the best-class neighbourhoods. They still stick to the bar soap trade in some form or another.'*

Bar of soap and tablet of Sunlight soap. Bars, cut off by weight for the customer, were the normal form in which soap was sold until W.H. Lever started producing one pound tablets stamped with his brand name.

In his grocery business, Lever had sold bar soap made by other manufacturers but branded with his own name. In 1884, he realised that to increase his sales to working class customers, he had to advertise. For this, he needed a distinctive product with a distinctive name. In 1884 or 1885, he introduced the name 'Sunlight'

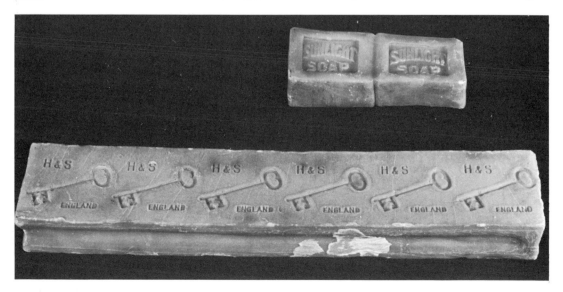

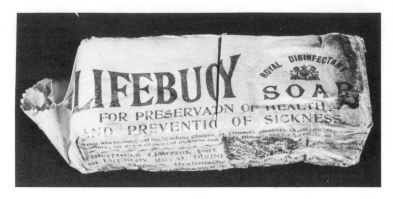

Printed paper wrapping for Lifebuoy soap. As well as selling soap in tablets, Lever wrapped it in paper wrappers printed with the brand name and publicity for the product. This ensured that his brand was distinguished from all others.

for all the bar soaps he sold; among them was a soap made with a high proportion of palm oil instead of tallow, so that it had an easy-lathering quality, which allowed Lever to publicise it as 'the soap which washes itself', or 'self-washer' soap. He anticipated a future for it as a household soap for the working-class market. To distinguish it from existing types of bar soap and to draw attention to the brand, he sold it in one pound tablets, ready-wrapped in imitation parchment with his name and 'Sunlight' printed on. Although there were precedents in America, forming household soap into tablets was a new development in Britain and one which made Lever's product instantly distinguishable by both appearance and brand name from all other soaps in grocers' shops.

Because of difficulties with the makers of the 'washer' soap, Lever leased a soap works in Warrington in 1885 and began making it himself. From then on, it was the only sort of soap to be called Sunlight, a name which identified it both as a type and as a make. Lever's business quickly became a phenomenal success: annual production increased from 3,000 tons in 1886 to 18,000 tons in 1890, the year after the move to his new factory at Port Sunlight, and to around 52,000 tons in 1900.

Much of Lever's success rested on having identified a distinct working-class market and having designed and packaged a product which he then could advertise effectively, an option not open to other manufacturers because of the lack of differentiation between their products. Lever took great pains with his advertising, using clever slogans, displaying advertisements on railway stations and roadside hoardings, and taking space in newspapers. Throughout, the advertising was directed specifically at working-class custom, as Lever himself later made clear:

'In the very first handbook we issued with Sunlight Soap, which was got up by myself, entitled *Sunlight Soap and How to Use It*, everything was brought down to the level of the working man's needs. The only point where I went beyond this was with instructions for cleaning pampas grass, feathers and so on, but I view these as to be found in many working men's houses, the pampas grass in a jar on the Bible in the sitting room and the feathers in the hats of the daughters.'*

*Quoted in C. Wilson, pp.38-39.

Lever's other advertising strategies, of which the most famous was the slogan, 'Why does a woman look older sooner than a man?' were also aimed at working-class customers. Such aggressive advertising techniques, which were deplored by other manufacturers, succeeded in making Sunlight popular with the

SUNLIGHT
FIRST!

SUNLIGHT
SOAP

CHEAP
FARES
TO
CANNES
NICE
BIARRITZ

"WHY GO SOUTH FOR SUNLIGHT
WHEN YOU CAN HAVE IT AT HOME?"

Advertisements for Sunlight soap. Advertising was only possible once Lever's product had a brand image. Advertisements like these were directed at working-class custom.

working class. With the sale of non-washer soaps confined to the better-class neighbourhoods, soap, which had never before been differentiated in any other way but by its composition, came to be distinguished by its class of user.

The history of Sunlight soap demonstrates an extremely simple use of design. Unlike printed cottons, where the design itself determined who would buy the fabric, there was nothing about the actual appearance of the tablets of Sunlight soap to identify it in consumers' eyes as a working-class soap. The role design played here was merely to create a commodity which was sufficiently distinctive to be advertised effectively.

Master and Servant

It was when the classes met as masters and servants or in organisations where there were hierarchies of employees that differences in design became sufficiently consistent to give a clear idea of the distinctions that were thought to exist. Whether the people were railwaymen, bank clerks or shop assistants, the design of the clothes they wore and of the articles they used helped define their status and the nature of their relationships with one another and with their employers.

The relationship between domestic servants and their employers, though by no means the only kind of master-servant relationship that existed in the nineteenth century, was one of the most complex and awkward. By the middle of the century, it was beginning to

Railway uniforms, North Eastern Railway, 1905. The railways were very hierarchical organisations. The occupations and ranks of employees were expressed in the cut and cloth of the uniforms. From North Eastern Railway, *Specifications of Uniforms*, Leeds, 1905, facing pp.63, 68, 101, 108.

*See L. Davidoff, 'Mastered for Life; Servant and Wife in Victorian and Edwardian England', *Journal of Social History*, vol.7, no.4, 1974, pp.406-428.

*For instance H. & A. Mayhew, pp.89-90, 94.

*P. Cunnington, *Costume of Household Servants*, London, 1974, chapters 4 and 5.

be referred to as a 'problem', which suggests that the relationship was undergoing some kind of change. Hindsight suggests that the problem lay not in domestic service itself, but resulted from changes elsewhere that were making it into an archaic form of employment.* Jobs where the employee lived in the master's house, ate his food, and was regarded as his responsibility had once been normal, but in most occupations this form of employment died out during the eighteenth century. Such customs survived in the nineteenth century only for farmworkers in some districts, and for domestic servants. On the whole, working-class men and women looked for jobs where they did not have to live in and were paid solely in money. The survival of domestic service's anachronistic form at a time when other occupations gave more freedom and independence provoked considerable discontent among servants, who saw their friends and relatives leading a more independent, though less secure, life and envied them for it.

This discontent led in the later nineteenth century to the increasingly common complaints from employers about 'headstrong' and disobedient servants. Any aspirations towards independence in servants were combated by the increasing concern of masters and mistresses to make sure their servants were identified as different from themselves. Symptomatic of this was the anxiety of mistresses at being mistaken for their maids or at their maids being mistaken for themselves, both popular subjects for cartoons and humorous stories in the middle of the century.*

Although male servants had normally worn livery since the eighteenth century, female servants, who greatly outnumbered them, did not wear distinguishing costumes until the 1860s.* Parson Woodforde's maids wore dresses made from printed cottons he bought for them, and eighteenth-century paintings show maids

Left to right:
Station Master's single breasted suit, summer style, in blue twill, with four mohair buttons. 'NER' in gold on both sides of collar.

Passenger Guard's double-breasted suit, winter style, in fine pilot cloth, piped with scarlet cloth, sleeves with red piping 4½in. from bottom, gilt pressed buttons, 'NER' in gold both sides of collar.

Goods Guard's single-breasted suit, in medium pilot cloth, no piping. Horn buttons. 'Guard' in red worsted on left side of collar, 'NER' on other.

Porter's single breasted suit in blued olive corduroy. Six small white metal buttons.

wearing clothes similar to the day-to-day clothes their mistresses would have worn at home. Since the employers provided their servants' clothes, there was no danger of maids appearing dressed in a way that might overshadow their mistresses; in any case, the relationship was sufficiently well-defined as not to be so easily threatened. However, by the mid-nineteenth century, the lowering of the price of printed cottons and the fact that printers would reprint fashionable designs upon cheap fabric made it possible for

Joseph van Aken: *An English Family at Tea*, oil painting, c.1720. Apart from her apron, the costume of the servant pouring the tea is not markedly different, except perhaps in the quality of the material, from that of the ladies seated.

because he is the chief of the floorists.
GEOGRAPHY FOR GIRLS. — Iceland is situated in Belgravia.

CRINOLINE FOR DOMESTIC USE.
Domestic. "BOTHER MISSUS! SHE WEARS IT HERSELF, AND I DON'T SEE WHY I SHOULDN'T."

QUESTION FOR SOLICITORS. — What nasty thing has more limbs than a centipede! The Law.

CRINOLINE FOR DOMESTIC USE.

Missus. "MARY! GO AND TAKE OFF THAT THING, DIRECTLY! PRAY, ARE YOU AWARE WHAT A RIDICULOUS OBJECT YOU ARE!"

Cartoon of a mistress and maid in crinolines, 1853. Servants imitating the costume of their mistress was a recurrent theme of cartoons and humorous stories in the 1850s, and indicates the anxiety that existed over this before servants' uniforms became normal. From *Punch*, vol.24, 1853, p.170.

*Margaret Powell, *Below Stairs*, London, 1968, p.63.

*M. Girouard, *The Victorian Country House*, Oxford, 1971, pp.20-22.

servants to dress themselves in garments that could be mistaken for the smart dresses in their mistresses' wardrobes. Faced with this prospect and with servants who were seeking greater independence, mistresses began to insist upon uniforms for their maids, particularly parlour maids, who would be seen by visitors. From the 1860s, it became normal for maids to wear black dresses, with white caps and white aprons, the distinctive garb of the domestic servant well into the twentieth century.

The inferior status of servants was emphasised by other strategies. Rules for servants' behaviour became increasingly elaborate and ritualised: for example, servants were expected never to hand an article directly to their employers or their guests except on a silver tray.* Restrictions on when servants might go out of the house and who might visit them reinforced the sense that they were their employers' property. As if the rules in themselves were not sufficient, the distinction between master and servant was made physically apparent, when large houses began to be designed in the mid-nineteenth century with entirely separate servants' quarters and independent circulation systems so that servants could carry out their work largely out of sight of their employers. Typical of the arrangements for segregating servants from their masters were those at Walton House in Surrey, remodelled by Sir Charles Barry in 1837. The servants occupied the top half of the building above the axis of the carriage porch and entrance hall, and their quarters connected with the master's end of the house only through a small door in the entrance gallery and through the passageway at the extreme left of the plan. Though Walton was a large house, much the same principle of strongly defined spatial segregation of masters and servants was to be found in smaller houses designed for the middle and upper classes in the nineteenth century.*

POOR VENUS OF MILO!

Cartoon of a mistress and maid, 1893. The servant wears the uniform of black dress and white apron and bonnet, making any confusion with the mistress impossible. From *Punch*, 18th March 1893, p.123.

Such complicated architectural solutions to the problem of the relationship between master and servant were available only to the wealthy. A more economical and, in many ways, more incisive method of indicating to servants the inferiority of their status was through the development of plain and humble designs for the beds they slept in, the chairs they sat upon, and the plates they ate off. The catalogues of nineteenth century furniture manufacturers usually contained a selection of kitchen and servants' furniture which was distinguished by its plain finish, lack of ornament and cheapness. The furniture was invariably made of deal, either plain or painted, and so was quite unmistakably different from that intended for the use of the master and mistress in the other rooms of the house. Heal's catalogue for 1896 illustrated a servant's

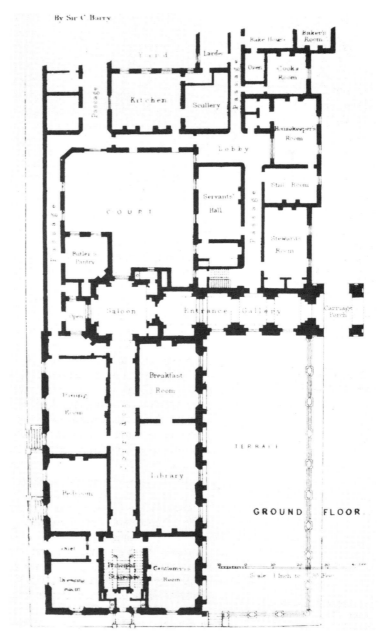

Plan of Walton House (now Mount Felix), Surrey, as remodelled by Sir Charles Barry, 1837-40. The segregation of servants and masters is a major principle of the design. From R. Kerr, *The Gentleman's House*, London, 1864, plate 28.

83

Folding bedsteads for servants, Heal's catalogue, 1896.

bedroom, furnished for £4.14.9d, with a simple iron bedstead and a chest of drawers, chair and washstand in plain deal. Though a servant with a room furnished as well as this might have considered herself lucky, the plainness of the designs left no doubt as to whom they were for. Even in this room, there was no sign of luxury, no accommodation for self-indulgent comfort or relaxation. The general standard of the furnishing of most servants' rooms was far more comfortless. They were often furnished with cast-offs and calculated to give the servant no chance to feel that there could be grounds for comparison between herself and her mistress.

The lesson that lay in the austerity of the servants' furniture was not lost upon servants themselves. The autobiographies of domestics frequently refer to the discomfort of the furnishings they were provided with. One former housemaid, who entered service in 1922, wrote:

'My second venture was a definite improvement, as under-housemaid of two in a private house . . . I had a room to myself here. The type of room I discovered through trial that one always expected in 'gentlemen's service' has an iron bedstead with lumpy mattress, specially manufactured for the use of maids, I suspect, a painted chest of drawers, with spotty mirror, lino-covered floor and a strip of matting at the bedside.'*

*L. Swainbank in *Useful Toil*, edited by J. Burnett, London, 1974, p.222.

Another former servant, Margaret Powell, who entered service a year earlier, has described the rationale for the choice of such furnishings:

'It was the opinion of "Them" upstairs that servants couldn't appreciate good living or comfort, and therefore must have plain fare, they must have dungeons to work in and to eat in, and they must retire to cold spartan bedrooms to sleep.'*

*Powell, p.80.

The one space in the Victorian house which was used by both master and servant was the hall. Masters and their visitors passed through the hall, when entering and leaving the house, while servants were required to be there to receive guests and take their hats and coats. Because of their combined use by servants and masters, halls needed a special type of furniture, particularly of chair. Although people of the master's class might pass through the hall, they were unlikely to linger or sit down; the only people

*C. Cook, *The House Beautiful, Essays on Beds and Tables, Stools and Candlesticks*, New York, 1878, p.33.

likely to spend long enough in it to need to sit down were inferiors, whether servants, prospective servants waiting for interview, or, as the American author of one nineteenth-century book on the decoration of the home put it, 'messenger boys, book agents, the census man, and the bereaved lady who offers us soap.'* Hall chairs would be seen by the master and his guests and thus had to conform to the standards of beauty found elsewhere in the house, but there was no reason for them to be any more comfortable than the rest of the furniture provided for servants. The same American authority on decoration explained:

*Cook, p.33.

'As visitors of this class are the only ones who will sit in the hall, considerations of comfort may be allowed to yield to picturesqueness, and any chair or bench that gives us that will serve . . .'*

The conventional hall chair was usually made of oak or mahogany, with an elaborately carved back and turned legs, but was distinguished from drawing-room or dining-room chairs by its plank seat and lack of upholstery; it was consistent with other

Servant's bedroom, furnished by Heal's, 1896. The plain furniture signified that it was for a servant. From Heal's catalogue, 1896.

Bedroom, furnished by Heal's, 1896. The contrast between this room, for the mistress, and the servant's room reinforced the social distance between the mistress and maid. From Heal's catalogue, 1896.

Hall chairs, c.1850. To be seen by all, but sat upon only by social inferiors, the hall chair characteristically had ornate back and legs, but a plank seat. From William Smee & Sons, *Designs of Furniture, a stock of which is always kept ready for sale at their cabinet and upholstery manufactory and workrooms, no.6 Finsbury pavement, London,* c.1850, p.357.

*See K.L. Ames, 'Meaning in Artefacts: Hall Furnishings in Victorian America', *Journal of Interdisciplinary History*, vol.IX, no.1, 1978, pp.19-46.

furniture for servants in its austerity, but its ornament made it quite unlike anything found below stairs. It was a hybrid, designed to be seen by one class and used by another.*

The distinctions in furniture were also expressed in tableware. In catalogues like those of the Army and Navy Stores in the 1890s and 1900s, the servants' ware was plain and unornamented, or decorated only with the most ubiquitous design of all, the willow pattern, and it contrasted sharply with the elegant and highly decorated china which was featured on other pages and would be seen standing on the shelves of the kitchen dresser while the servants ate off the plainest of crockery.

If such distinctions in design were intended to convince domestic servants of their own lowly status, it also helped employers believe that servants were as inferior as their occupation and accoutrements seemed to make them. Servants often complained that employers were oblivious of the conditions under which they worked and of the tasks they were expected to do: when they dared to point out the unreasonableness or impossibility of what was required of them, mistresses often appeared genuinely surprised and shocked by what was being expected of them. Had servants worn clothes like other people and lived in accomodation more like that of other members of the household and less like that of a penal establishment, the temptation to assume that they were not only poorer but mentally inferior and less civilised than their employers would not have been so strong. At a time when liberal thought was beginning to doubt the 'natural' inferiority of servants, the stigmatising of servants by the clothes they wore and the articles they used was convincing proof of the wrongheadedness of the new ideas for those who were unsympathetic to them.

Kitchen china for use by servants, 1908. Either the ubiquitous willow pattern, or plain and distinctly marked, such ware contrasted with the ornate china used by the masters, and reminded servants of their place. From the Army and Navy Stores catalogue, 1908.

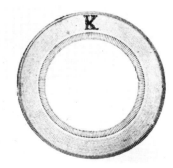

Variety

While the desire to embody social distinctions may have accounted for, say, the classification of pocket knives into ladies' and men's patterns, it does not explain why ladies should have required a choice of seventeen different designs, nor men a choice of 39 designs. How are we to explain the compulsion which gripped so many manufacturers to be so prolific with designs for their products?

One possible answer is that variety gave customers a degree of choice and enabled them to feel more sure of their own individuality. A masculine-looking pocket knife might underline the purchaser's view of himself as manly, but as long as it was the only men's knife available, it would do nothing to make him feel different from other men. What would do this would be the opportunity to choose from a range of knives or to have a particular design which he alone among his acquaintances might possess. Variety for such reasons occurred to the greatest degree in goods which were conspicuous to others, such as furniture and clothes, or in printed cottons, an industry where manufacturers were very conscious of trading on desires for individuality.

The belief that unusual or unique possessions bestow individuality upon their owners is an illusion that has been indulged in for a long time. This aspect of commodity fetishism was presumably derived from the aristocratic practice of collecting relics, curiosities and unique works of art, but how manufactured goods, by their nature never unique, ever came to be regarded in the same light is mysterious. Whatever the cause, capitalist manufacture was quick to take advantage of it, and produce ten, twenty or a hundred designs where one would have sufficed.

A second reason for the variety of designs was the manufacturers' anticipation of increasing their sales. Subtle variations in what was essentially the same product might persuade people to buy a second or third article where one would have been enough for their needs. Cake stands, shaving mugs and nursery ware fulfilled functions that could have been served equally well by standard china products, but they provided customers with a rationale for buying additional articles. Similar reasons explain why W.H. Lever, having established the success of Sunlight soap, began to market what was essentially the same soap in a number of slightly different forms. In 1894, Lever introduced Lifebuoy soap, which was Sunlight soap with the addition of phenol (carbolic acid) to give it hygienic properties, and in 1899, he introduced two more varieties, Monkey Brand which contained a scouring agent, and Sunlight in flake form, subsequently known as Lux.* Lever had recognised that there was a physical limit to any household's demand for soap, and that the only way to increase sales was to offer new variants for specialised uses, which consumers could be persuaded to buy in addition to the original brand. The principle of diversifying the product in order to increase sales, which has been followed ever since in soap manufacture, was at work in a great many nineteenth-century industries.

A third possible reason for variety was that manufacturers and their designers may initially have been uncertain of the appropriate imagery to represent the qualities attributed to each social group. Manufacturers stood a greater chance of finding, say, a hairbrush that exactly fitted assumptions about masculinity if they started by offering a large number of designs rather than a few or only one. It was the decision as to which designs would represent people's

*C. Wilson, pp.55-57.

notions of the elusive qualities of social class that proved the most difficult, and it was therefore not surprising that the greatest proliferation and fastest change was to be found in this category of consumer goods.

To most manufacturers of consumer goods in the nineteenth century, the commercial advantages of producing a great many different designs far outweighed the disadvantages in cost. However, the relative profitability of producing one or many designs depended somewhat upon the method of production employed. Handicraft industries lent themselves more easily than mechanised industries to the production of many different designs. Where the forming of each component and the final assembly was the work of a craftsman, it made little difference whether he worked to one design or another, but in more highly mechanised industries, the preparation of new dies, templates, jigs and moulds entailed great expense and was a disincentive to variety.

The effects of the change from entirely handicraft to more mechanised methods of manufacture upon the range of designs can be seen in the output of the Windsor chair manufacturers of High Wycombe. From early in the nineteenth century, each component of the chair, its seat, legs and balusters, was made by an independent craftsman, who sold his work to a chair master. The masters employed framers to assemble the chairs, and undertook the distribution and sale of the chairs. All the processes of production, from sawing up the logs to the framing, were carried out by hand labour; one of the processes, the turning of the legs and stretchers, was the work of craftsmen known as 'bodgers', who worked in huts in the woods around High Wycombe, turning the legs on primitive treadle lathes from timber that they themselves had felled. The number of designs of Windsor chair available was very great, as the surviving catalogues show. Many of the masters would buy a standard, locally printed catalogue with three to four hundred designs in it and would have their own name overprinted on it, with an indication of which designs they manufactured. The larger firms generally offered well over a hundred designs, and one master, Edwin Skull, who had a specially printed broadsheet, advertised 141. As long as the masters relied on hand labour, there was almost no economic limit to the variety of designs they could offer, for they had only to instruct the craftsmen to produce a different design to obtain it.

In the last quarter of the nineteenth century, the masters gradually began to introduce machines into their workshops, principally as a means of employing labour that was less skilled and therefore cheaper. Machines were developed that shaped the seats to a preset pattern, work formerly done by a man using a curved adze. Other machines were introduced to bore holes at preset angles in the seat for the legs and uprights, a task previously done with a brace and bit by the framer, whose skill had lain in his ability to judge by eye the different angle needed for each hole. Increasingly, during the twentieth century, the masters began to employ machinery for every process: balusters were cut to jigs, and finally even the low-paid work of the bodgers was replaced by electric lathes in the factories, though several bodgers survived until 1939. With the use of so many machines, a major cost of production became the preparation of jigs to sufficiently high standards of accuracy to ensure that all the components of

Chair bodgers shaping legs by hand, near High Wycombe, c.1920. Until the arrival of machinery, the components of the chairs were made by men working in the open, using the simplest of tools.

the chair would fit together. Because of the expense of making the jigs and setting up the machine tools, it ceased to be economic to vary the designs to any great extent, and as a result the number produced by each manufacturer fell in the inter-war years. By 1980, the largest firm making Windsor chairs, Furniture Industries Ltd (whose products are known by the brand name Ercol), produced only seventeen designs, compared with the 141 offered by Edwin Skull a century earlier.*

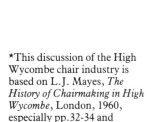

*This discussion of the High Wycombe chair industry is based on L.J. Mayes, *The History of Chairmaking in High Wycombe*, London, 1960, especially pp.32-34 and pp.61-68.

Edwin Skull & Co. broadsheet, c.1860. Such a large range of designs was usual among High Wycombe chair manufacturers in the nineteenth century.

Chair framer boring holes in the seat, High Wycombe. The skill in this job was in judging the angles correctly.

*Select Committee on the Copyright of Designs, 1840, para.2851.

*Select Committee on the Copyright of Designs, 1840, para.2883.

*Select Committee on the Copyright of Designs, 1840, para.3755.

*Select Committee on the Copyright of Designs, 1840, para.2885.

During the nineteenth century it was not only handicraft production that manufactured variety; so, too, did many mechanised industries. Many cotton print masters who gave evidence to the 1840 Select Committee on design stressed the great number of patterns they produced every year. One printer, who annually introduced between four and five hundred new designs, said 'we endeavour to make a trade by variety rather than by excellence'.* They were most explicit about their reasons for this policy – as the same printer explained:

'I should expect that the more I sowed, the more I should reap; that the more pains I took in producing new and good things, the more likely I should be to be rewarded by the public for my labour and expense.'*

Another manufacturer, who said he printed around four hundred new designs each year, commented, 'I think I should get more money by continually reproducing styles, as frequently as possible.'*

To these manufacturers, variety of design was a principle of business and the key to profit, for it was the means by which they persuaded their middle-class customers to purchase textiles in excess of their needs. By constantly producing new designs, manufacturers were able to promote fashion; a lady who saw that the material of which her dress was made had become widespread and popular would purchase a new and original design to keep ahead in fashion, even though the first dress might be barely worn. As the same manufacturer who thought that the more he sowed the more he would reap replied when he was asked if he thought more patterns would lead to more dresses being worn:

'I think it is exceedingly probable, because what is a dress after all? It is mere fancy and taste, it is not a mere covering, otherwise we should not have had any printed dresses at all. It is like paintings, there is no reason why a gentleman should possess a painting, but when he sees a good one, he wishes to have it.'*

Seat boring machine, High Wycombe. This machine, introduced in the late nineteenth century, made the chair framer's skill redundant, and, like other machines, discouraged manufacturers from proliferating designs.

The principle of 'the more I sow, the more I shall reap' belonged in some measure to all manufacturers of consumer goods, whether chairs, cutlery or clocks. Profit was determined by the volume of sale, and, since more designs stimulated fashion, they promised more sales and played an important part in the accumulation of capital.

The activity of design was therefore of great assistance to the development of capitalism in industries making consumer goods, supplying the variety that enabled manufacturers constantly to be increasing their sales and their profits. If design was of such great service to capitalism, capitalism has been no less good for design. Not only did it bring design into existence as a necessary activity within the division of labour in manufacturing, but its appetite for novelty and variety guaranteed the prosperity of designers. Capitalism may have been very bad for many crafts and trades, eroding their skills, their status and their rewards, but design is one activity that capitalism has caused to flourish.

Theories of Diversity

The tendency for manufacturers to multiply the designs of their products has not gone unnoticed by writers on design. The majority of books on the history of design and the decorative arts are filled with lists of designs produced by one manufacturer or a set of manufacturers. Few historians, however, have made the attempt to explain the reasons for the differences between these many designs. The presence of diversity has usually been taken for granted as normal and therefore, to the mind trained to find interest only in irregularities and curiosities, unworthy of comment.

When historians have tried to explain the diversification of designs, they have invariably fallen back on one of two theories. Some have seen the development of new and different designs as the result of the evolution of new needs; for example, the development of new and different designs of spanners – ring spanners, cranked spanners, and socket wrenches – would be explained by the need for tools to assemble and dismantle machinery whose designs had become increasingly complicated and compact. Other historians have attributed the development of new and different designs to the desire of designers to express their ingenuity and artistic talent. Both theories may indeed explain the diversity of designs in particular instances, but they fail to cover all cases.

A good example of the all-too-common failure to make sense of the diversification of designs occurs in Siegfried Giedion's *Mechanization Takes Command*, the only previous attempt to relate design to the history of society in a comprehensive way. Giedion observed the development in mid-nineteenth century America of many designs for the adjustable chair, a novel type of furniture. He tried to explain the introduction of the new type, and the great variety of designs for it, by means of both the standard theories for diversity. He began by arguing that the nineteenth century adopted a new, more relaxed, semi-reclining posture of sitting, in which people sought comfort by constantly shifting their bodies:

'The posture of the nineteenth century . . . is based on relaxation. This relaxation is found in a free, unposed attitude that can be called neither sitting nor lying. Once again the painters are the first to voice the unconscious inclinations of their time by surprising and capturing their model in this indefinite posture. In a

Folding chair frame, design by G. Wilson. One of many designs for adjustable chairs developed in the United States in the nineteenth century. (U.S. Patent no. 116784, 4th July 1871.)

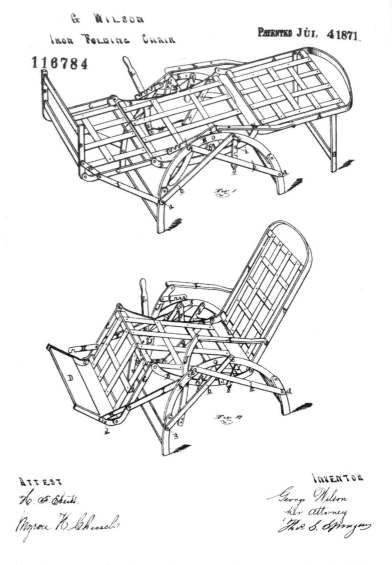

rippling water-color of 1826, Richard Bonnington paints his 'Reclining Woman' relaxedly using an upholstered sofa as if it were a reclining chair.'*

*Giedion, p.396.

Giedion saw the development of patent furniture as a response to this new posture of sitting; he wrote of new furniture, its 'aim is to serve needs previously without claim or without solution.'* This explanation was quite consistent with Giedion's position as a supporter and publicist of the early twentieth-century Modern Movement in architecture and design, one of the precepts of which was that 'form follows function'. However, Giedion's attachment to functionalism and his determination to believe that all designs, or at least all the designs that he admired, must be derived from the discovery of new uses led him into some distinctly rickety arguments. Applied to adjustable chairs, the 'functionalist' theory of design development seems doubtful, for it is most unlikely that after several millenia mankind should suddenly have discovered a new way of sitting in the nineteenth century. The inadequacies

*Giedion, p.394.

of the 'functionalist' theory become even more apparent when applied to other products. Could Montgomery Ward's 131 different designs of pocket knife be said to be the result of the discovery of new ways of cutting?

Giedion's second reason for the proliferation of the designs of adjustable chairs was a supposed surge of creative ingenuity amongst designers: 'when creative power comes to life, objects that centuries of use have left unchanged – plows, hammers, saws or furniture – take on a new aspect.'* This explanation seems even more suspect. The many different designs may reveal great ingenuity on the part of designers, but this is hardly a cause of the proliferation of adjustable chair designs. Why should the rapid multiplication of designs not have occurred at some other time in history? There seems no reason to believe that nineteenth-century designers were more inventive and ingenious than people at other times.

*Giedion, p.419.

However, the greatest weakness of the 'ingenious designer' theory is that it betrays a misunderstanding of the process of design and manufacture, for it attributes to designers a power and autonomy that they do not in practice possess. Designers, unless they also held managerial positions in manufacturing industry would have had no influence on how many or what type of articles should be made, other than to determine their form. The decision to increase the number of designs must, like any other decision about production, rest with the manufacturer. The reason for producing many different designs was that it was profitable for the manufacturer to do so.

The arguments which have been advanced in this chapter, unlike the 'functionalist' or 'ingenious designer' theories of diversity, place the products of design in a direct relationship to the ideas of the society in which they are made. The evidence is that manufacturers themselves made distinctions between designs on the basis of different markets: in some cases, as with printed textiles, the manufacturers explicitly acknowledged that they made distinctions of this kind in their production of patterns; in other cases, the classifications in manufacturers' catalogues provide silent testimony of the fact that their various designs were intended for different groups of people.

To look at the ranges of goods illustrated in the catalogues of nineteenth century manufacturers, department stores and mail order houses is to look at a representation of society. Through the designs of knives, watches, clothes and furniture to suit every rank and station in life, one can read the shape of society as manufacturers saw it, and as their customers learned to see it. For, like any representation, be it in the form of painting, literature or film, this strange and cumbersome masterpiece created by manufacturing industry not only corresponded to what was seen to exist, but, without recourse to language, metaphor or symbolism, also showed people social boundaries and distinctions that might otherwise have been invisible to them, or to which they might have been indifferent. Yet, unlike the audience for works of art, which is generally only a minority, that for manufactured artefacts in the nineteenth century was enormous: even though people might have possessed only a few of them, or even none, the range of designs would have been familiar to them. And to know the range of different designs was to know an image of society.

5. The Home

'We went down three steps to the main part of the living-room. The carpet almost tickled my ankles. There was a concert grand piano, closed down. On one corner of it stood a tall silver vase on a strip of peach-coloured velvet, and a single yellow rose in the vase. There was plenty of nice soft furniture, a great many cushions, some with golden tassels and some just naked. It was a nice room, if you didn't get rough. There was a wide damask covered divan in a shadowy corner, like a casting couch. It was the kind of room where people sit with their feet in their laps and sip absinthe through lumps of sugar and talk with high affected voices and sometimes just squeak. It was a room where anything could happen except work.'*

*Raymond Chandler, *Farewell My Lovely*, Harmondsworth, 1949, p.46.

As Chandler's Philip Marlowe observed, the home, as well as providing shelter, is also an icon. The appearance of its contents makes evident what it is and what people are meant to do, or not do, in it. Ideas about the home vary between cultures and between periods, but at any one time and in any one place, there is likely to be a consensus about what a home should be like, what is right and proper there, and what is out of place.

Notions of what is proper, and therefore beautiful, in the home have shaped the design of articles for domestic use. However, the relationship also works in the other direction: as well as conforming to the consensus of taste, designs tell people what they ought to think about the home and how they ought to behave there. A good example of the kind of influence that ideas of domestic propriety can have upon the appearance of objects is the sewing machine, which, in its early history, presented manufacturers with great problems through the need to distinguish domestic machines from those for industrial use.

The first sewing machines were manufactured in the United States in the early 1850s. All the main mechanical inventions used in sewing machines until the 1890s were patented between 1846 and 1850, and so, by the late 1850s, there was no difficulty in making a reliable and efficient machine employing any combination of about half a dozen basic principles of machine sewing.* However, since the early machines were individually made by handicraft methods, they were costly and were thus sold almost exclusively for industrial use, where the expense could be justified. Yet, as the sewing-machine manufacturers found to their cost, the market for industrial machines was limited and rapidly satisfied. Singer & Co. did very badly in the mid-1850s, when they were selling only industrial machines: in spite of extremely grand premises in New York and agents across the country, they sold only 810

*Grace R. Cooper, *The Sewing Machine, Its Invention and Development*, 2nd edition, Washington D.C., 1976, is the source for most of the following account.

Wheeler and Wilson sewing machine, 1854. The first small sewing machine with a potential domestic market.

*R. Brandon, *Singer and the Sewing Machine, A Capitalist Romance*, London, 1977, p.114.

Steam-powered sewing machines in the factory of G. Holloway & Co. of Stroud, 1854. At this date, the normal place to find a sewing machine was in a workshop. From *Illustrated London News*, 16th December 1854, p.624.

machines in 1853, 879 in 1854 and 883 in 1855.* Wheeler & Wilson, the largest manufacturers in the business until they were overtaken by Singer in 1867, managed rather better because their machine, being smaller, lighter and simpler than Singer's, was potentially attractive to the domestic market. Right from their start in business, Wheeler & Wilson had aimed at making a machine that could be used domestically as well as industrially; they had seen that, although the market for industrial machines might be small, domestic sales need be limited only by the number of households in the country. They were the first manufacturers to present the sewing machine as a domestic appliance, an example that was very quickly followed by other firms when they realised that it was their only chance of staying in business.

Singer 'Family' sewing machine, 1858. Singer's first domestic machine, introduced to compete with Wheeler and Wilson's.

The problem for all the manufacturers was then to persuade Americans that they needed a sewing machine at home. Any household that could afford the price could just as well afford to pay a seamstress or servant to do its sewing. And because sewing by machine had been an industrial technique used only in work-shops, a sewing machine seemed not only unnecessary but also undesirable in the home: it was like having a machine tool in the living room. Singer's first 'Family' machine, introduced in 1858, was not a success: at $125, it was too expensive, but it was also a

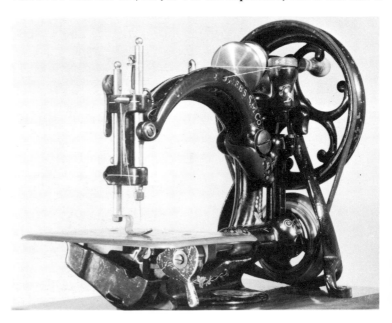

Willcox and Gibbs sewing machine, 1857. The first low-priced sewing machine for the domestic market.

victim of the prejudices against the domestic use of the sewing machine.

To make the sewing machine a desirable piece of equipment for the home, the manufacturers tried various approaches. The first was reducing the price of the machines, in which the pioneers were Willcox & Gibbs, who invented a very simple mechanism that sewed with a single-thread chainstitch and sold for only fifty dollars, half the price of the Wheeler & Wilson model. As prices came down, manufacturers also began to sell the machines on hire purchase, to put them within reach even of households that could not afford to pay someone else to do the sewing. Singer was the first to introduce a hire purchase scheme, offering machines for a five dollars down payment, with monthly instalments of between three and five dollars. Their sales quadrupled within a year.*

There were still the machine's unwanted industrial associations to be overcome: how were people to be convinced that it was suitable for the home when they thought of it as belonging in workshops and being operated only by working-class girls? One response was intensive advertising. Manufacturers took every opportunity to convince the public of the machine's appropriateness for the home: for instance, they had sewing machines illustrated in domestic settings, as in the fashion plate of 1867 that featured a Wheeler & Wilson machine. Singer's own publicity made much of the machine's advantages to domestic life. One of their early publicity booklets announced:

*Brandon, p.117.

Fashion plate, September 1867, illustrating the Wheeler and Wilson machine, suggesting it as appropriate to the home.

Singer 'New Family' sewing machine, 1858. After the unsuccessful 'Family' machine, Singer quickly introduced a new model for the domestic market.

'The great importance of the sewing machine is in its influence upon the home; in the countless hours it has added to women's leisure for rest and refinement; in the increase of opportunity for that early training of children, for lack of which so many pitiful wrecks are strewn across the shores of life; in the numberless opportunities it has opened for women's employment; and in the comforts it has brought within the reach of all, which could formerly be attained only by the wealthy few.'*

*Quoted in Brandon, p.126.

Yet manufacturers were very aware that advertising alone was not enough and that they had to make their domestic models look appropriate to the home, as is quite clear from the brochure introducing Singer's first 'Family' machine in 1858:

'A few months since, we came to the conclusion that the public taste demanded a sewing machine for family purposes more exclusively; a machine of smaller size, and of a lighter and more

Squirrel sewing machine, 1858. Another, more fanciful attempt to domesticate the sewing machine. The squirrel was chosen because of the creature's frugality and providence.

*Quoted in G.R. Cooper, p.34

elegant form; a machine decorated in the best style of art, so as to make a beautiful ornament in the parlor or boudoir . . . To supply this public want, we have just produced, and are now preparing to receive orders for, "Singer's New Family Sewing Machine".'*

Singer had identified the problem of the design of the domestic sewing machine and seen that the solution was to make it 'exclusively' domestic and distinct from all industrial models; this was done, as the brochure states, by the application of beauty and art. However, while Singer and other manufacturers knew they had to make their domestic models unlike industrial machines, they seem to have been unsure of what appearance would be suitable to ornament the parlour or boudoir. In the late 1850s and early 1860s, a plethora of new designs for sewing machines were launched in the United States, as every manufacturer tried to produce something that would conform to the market's idea of what was appropriate to the home. Some of the designs were obvious novelties: incorporating animals or cherubs, they were intended to appeal through their idiosyncrasy. Almost all were distinguished by some degree of ornament and by lightness of construction.*

*G.R. Cooper, pp.46-53.

In practice, though, the sewing machine so rapidly proved its domestic value that, after a few years, it was no longer necessary to devote much effort to making it look different from its industrial counterparts. The designs began to be broadly similar, although the domestic models were usually distinguished by a larger amount of gilded ornament. Nevertheless, for a short time, manufacturers had deemed it extremely important to design a domestic machine that would be regarded as an entirely separate species from the industrial version.

A Place for Anything but Work

It is obvious enough that factories are the result of the industrial revolution, but we rarely think of homes, as we know them today, as a creation of the same revolution. Previously, most production and commerce had been carried on in the homes of the craftsmen, merchants or tradesmen concerned, and a house was understood to be a place that incorporated both work and the habitual activities of living, eating, sleeping and so on. However, once productive

Right:
Handloom weaver, making Donegal in a cottage in Bunerana, c.1915. A late survival in rural Ireland of the once normal condition of the home, where production took place alongside domestic life.

Left:
Cherub sewing machine, 1858. In the rush to develop domestic sewing machines a large variety of ornamental machines, such as this, were marketed in the late 1850s.

work was removed to factories, offices or shops, the home became exclusively a place for eating, sleeping, raising children and enjoying leisure. It acquired a new and distinctive character, which was vividly represented in its decoration and the design of its contents.

Those who went to work in factories subordinated themselves to the rules and directions of managers and overseers for the duration of the working day; unlike domestic craftworkers, they had, for example, no freedom to decide when they worked, or for how long. Part of the intention in building factories had been to provide an instrument for the management of the workers, which led to their reputation for oppression.* Similar changes in the lives of workpeople took place in trade and commerce, where expansion obliged merchants and brokers to employ men in the subordinate jobs of book-keeping and recording and invoicing transactions. From the beginning of the nineteenth century, these activities increasingly happened outside the merchants' own houses, in places exclusively devoted to work – counting-houses or offices. The rise of both factory and office turned work for a large number of people into an activity that was characterised by being done for a wage, in a place specially devoted to it, under the supervision of the employer.

*E.P. Thompson, *The Making of the English Working Class*, Harmondsworth, 1968, pp.393-398.

Not only did the factory and the office cause work to become physically separate from home, but the oppressive conditions also encouraged people to keep the two separate in their minds. Giving the home positive virtues made it into a haven where some of the self-respect that was lost in the workplace could be recovered. Keeping home and work apart has remained important, and a great deal of feeling has been invested in the separation.* There are plenty of ways in which people signify the distinction, for example by wearing different clothes at home and at work. A particularly vivid illustration of the strength of feeling in keeping the two apart in the nineteenth century was given by the fictional character of Mark Rutherford, a clerk in a particularly unpleasant office:

*For recent evidence see J.H. Goldthorpe, D. Lockwood, F. Bechhofer & J. Platt, *The Affluent Worker in the Class Structure*, Cambridge, 1969, pp.101-103.

'Another stratagem of defence which I adopted at the office was never to betray to a soul anything about myself. Nobody knew anything about me, whether I was married or single, where I lived, or what I thought upon a single subject of any importance. I cut off my office life in this way from my home life so completely that I was two selves, and my true self was not stained by contact with my other self. It was a comfort to me to think the moment the clock struck seven that my second self died, and that my first self suffered nothing by having anything to do with it. I was not the person who sat downstairs and endured the abominable talk of his colleagues and the ignominy of serving such a chief. I knew nothing about him. I was a citizen walking London streets; I had my opinions upon human beings and books; I was on equal terms with my friends; I was Ellen's husband; I was, in short, a man.'*

Mark Rutherford's Deliverance, London, 1888, pp.250-251. (First edition, 1885.)

For employees like Mark Rutherford, the detachment of home from work made it possible to retain some self-esteem. But for employers, managers and entrepreneurs, whose work was not oppressive or alienating, the distinction that was established between home and work arose from rather different motives. In the late eighteenth and early nineteenth centuries, entrepreneurs

Interior, 7, Chesterfield
Gardens, London,
photographed in 1893. The
nineteenth-century bourgeoisie
turned the home into a palace of
illusions, which encouraged
total dissociation from the
world immediately outside.

*Discussed more fully by W.E.
Houghton, *The Victorian Frame
of Mind*, New Haven, 1957,
pp.341-348, and R. Sennett,
The Fall of Public Man,
Cambridge, 1977, p.20, and
chapter 8.

*W.Benjamin, 'Louis-Philippe
or the Interior' in *Charles
Baudelaire, a Lyric Poet in the
Era of High Capitalism*,
London, 1973, pp.167-169.

had generally chosen to live near their factories: Sir Richard
Arkwright's house at Cromford in Derbyshire was close to his
mill, and the Crossleys at Halifax lived within sight of their
factory. However, by the later nineteenth century, employers
increasingly built their villas and mansions in different neighbourhoods from their factories and offices.

Their wish to separate home from work has generally been
explained by the argument that many entrepreneurs and professional men found the world in thich they worked increasingly
brutal and deceitful.* While participating in it, they felt it necessary to find some way of experiencing and expressing the moral
virtues and honest emotions that they saw being submerged in the
commercial world. The home, therefore came to be regarded as a
repository of the virtues that were lost or denied in the world
outside. To the middle classes in the nineteenth century, the
home stood for feeling, for sincerity, honesty, truth and love.
This representation of the home involved a complete dissociation
of all things good from the public world, and of all things bad
from the domestic world. It was to turn the home into a place of unreality, a place where illusions flourished.* These conditions of the
artificial exclusion of all 'bad' feelings from the home combined
with enforced intellectual idleness provided, as Sigmund Freud
and Josef Breuer were to observe in the 1890s, the climate for

Domestic hysteria. In an environment where illusions flourished and where women had nothing to do, hysteria became a familiar complaint. From Mrs Ellis, *The Mother's Mistake*, London, 1860, p.57.

hysteria, one of the most common malaises of nineteenth-century bourgeois women.*

To make the home so totally virtuous required much hard work, and the Victorians adopted various strategies to satisfy their illusions. They set up special codes for behaviour at home, and special roles were given to certain actors, principally women. Some of these aspects of nineteenth-century domestic life have been discussed in Richard Sennett's book *The Fall of Public Man*, and the process of evolving special roles for women has been written about by various historians, among them Leonore Davidoff and Patricia Branca.* One of the most important of the strategies to be evolved was the development of special standards of taste and design for the home.

Underlying all these standards, whether in the choice of furnishing style or in the artistic harmonies of the colour scheme, came the basic requirement that the environment should kill all associations with work. Writing in 1879 about the furnishing of drawing rooms, Rhoda and Agnes Garrett explained: '. . . out of the laudable desire to exclude all work-a-day thoughts and objects, the modern drawing room too often displays a tawdry and theatrical style of decoration and furniture . . .'* Their underlying assumption, that the home should be the antithesis of the environment of work, has been a recurrent theme in advice to home decorators (not that people have needed reminding, so generally has it been taken for granted). For example, a book on home decorating published in the 1950s began with the following words: 'A tastefully planned home provides a wife with a gracious background and a haven for a husband where business worries can be temporarily banished.'*

One method of making home as unlike work as possible has been to construct in it the antithesis of environments in which work has habitually taken place. Out of the desire to make the home everything that the office was not has come a regular inter-action between the designs of furnishings for each. Until well into the twentieth century, offices were austerely furnished in utilitarian colours with hard surfaces, and people sought to make their homes colourful, soft and plushy. Recent attempts to introduce some of the comforts of the home into offices have made the

*See especially the remarks on the case study of Anna O. in S. Freud & J. Breuer, *Studies in Hysteria*, Standard Edition of the Complete Works of Sigmund Freud, vol. II, London, 1955, pp.22, 41.

*L. Davidoff, *The Best Circles*, London, 1973 and P. Branca, *Silent Sisterhood*, London, 1975.

*R.& A. Garrett, *Suggestions for House Decoration*, London, 1879, p.56.

*News of the World *Better Homes Book*, London, n.d. [c.1953], p.4.

*On the High Tech Style, see J. Kron & S. Slesin, *High Tech*, London, 1979.

distinction less clear cut. It is in this context that some designers have taken the perverse step of imitating the hard, metallic finishes of industrial environments for domestic interiors in a style that has become known as 'high-tech'.* It seems unlikely, however, that this style of domestic furnishing will ever appeal to more than the tiny professional and commercial élite whose choice of imagery related to the factory seems mainly determined by their wish to distinguish their homes from those of the working class, which remain furnished as the antithesis of the workplace.

However, the pursuit of an antithesis does not, on its own, provide a model to be followed in the design of domestic interiors: 'not an office' or 'not a factory' are not themselves descriptions that provide any useful source of imagery for the home. What is the appropriate scenery for a place of non-work? One source of examples and imagery can be traced in the metaphors and similes that have been used for the home. The Victorians frequently described their homes as like heaven, and so, for example, we find a mid-nineteenth century sermon inspiring women 'to strive to make a home something like a bright, serene, restful, joyful nook of heaven in an unheavenly world.'* While the analogy of home with heaven made sense in that both were expected to be free from production and strong in virtue, it was of little practical use

*Baldwin Brown, *Young Men and Maidens, A Pastoral for the Times*, London, 1871, pp.38-39, quoted in Houghton, p.345.

Interior of a house in Hampstead, London, designed by Michael Hopkins, completed 1977. Details, finishes and furnishings derived from industrial enviroments are the basis of 'high-tech' but the interference with the home's customary image as a 'no-work' place has limited the popularity of the style.

to the home decorator – how was heaven furnished? In Victorian art and literature, heaven bore a tautological resemblance to the ideal of domestic life.

In the nineteenth century, the most available source of imagery for a place free from work was the homes of the aristocracy, who were perceived by the bourgeoisie to live a life of idleness. Many middle-class homes in Britain, Europe and America until the 1860s strove to imitate aristocratic taste, though generally that of the past rather than the present; contemporary aristocratic taste allowed little scope for illusion, whereas that of the past was less inhibiting.

Home as a Sign of Character

In her book, *The House in Good Taste*, published in 1913, Elsie de Wolfe wrote:

'We take it for granted that every woman is interested in houses – that she either has a house in course of construction, or dreams of having one, or has had a house long enough to wish it right. And we take it for granted that this American home is always the woman's home: a man may build and decorate a beautiful house, but it remains for a woman to make a home of it for him. It is the personality of the mistress that the house expresses. Men are forever guests in our homes, no matter how much happiness they may find there.'*

*Elsie De Wolfe, *The House in Good Taste*, New York, 1913, p.5.

These were truths that had already been commonplace in Anglo-Saxon culture for at least half a century: women were identified with the house, and were expected to deal with domestic furnishing, which would become an expression of their personalities. Just why these should have become such usual assumptions is worth considering.

As a metaphor for a woman's body, the house is an image long established in poetry, mythology and the unconscious: it was, for instance, one of the more potent symbols for female sexuality picked on by Freud in *The Interpretation of Dreams*. It is hard not to ignore this metaphorical meaning of the house in the quote from Elsie de Wolfe, particularly in its last sentence. The correspondence of house and body affects each, and establishes an identity between them; among its effects is the supposition that a woman is under an obligation to care for her house as she cares for her body.

This psychological explanation for the identification of women with houses is not specific to modern society and could be expected to apply in all cultures. However, the material conditions of modern society have made women's association with the home especially strong. Middle-class women in the nineteenth century were effectively excluded from all forms of work, domestic or otherwise, with exceptions made only for single women, who could work in a very few occupations, for instance as governesses or nurses. The enforced idleness of married women was a reflection of the wealth and success of their husbands: rather than consuming leisure themselves, the men consumed it through their wives and daughters.

That women should consume leisure vicariously for men was not the reason put forward at the time for their exclusion from work, but is one that has been supplied since by Thorstein Veblen in his *Theory of the Leisure Class*. The usual nineteenth-century justification was unsuitedness: women were thought to have

*J. Ruskin, *Sesame and Lilies* (first published 1865) in *Collected Works of John Ruskin*, edited by E.T. Cook & A. Wedderburn, vol. XVIII, London, 1905, pp.121-122.

*Rozsika Parker, *The Subversive Stitch*, London, 1984.

*Mrs Ellis, *The Mother's Mistake*, serialised in *Family Friend*, new series, vol III, 1854, p.2.

*J. Ruskin, letter to *The Times*, 25th May 1854.

qualities that made them unfitted for work. Thus, John Ruskin wrote in his lecture 'Of Queens' Gardens', 'The woman's power is not for rule, not for battle – and her intellect is not for invention or creation, but for sweet ordering, management and decision.'*

However, the very same characteristics were thought to make women suited to the management of the home. The innocence attributed to women might have been out of place in the deceitful world of business, but their supposed virtue and purity fitted them perfectly for the ordering of cookery, servants and children. Their alleged sensitivity to beauty was also of special value in the home, even though, until the late nineteenth century, its only outlet was in needlework and the embroidery of upholstery, hangings, covers and pictures, through which women were expected to express their feminine and individual qualities.* Before the 1860s, the choice of domestic furnishings seems to have been primarily a male activity, as was suggested by the opening of a novel published in 1854, *The Mother's Mistake*. A recently married couple go round the house which the husband has furnished, and he asks his wife, 'Is this not sufficient?' to which she replies, 'You have done all, and more than all, I could have imagined, to make me happy.'* However, from the 1860s, the choice of domestic decoration and furnishing became an accepted and even expected activity for middle-class women, a good subject for their sensitivity which had hitherto found an outlet only in needlework. The domestic manuals of the last quarter of the century usually assumed that women would be responsible for the choice of decor and furnishings. In many cases, the activity must have been a welcome escape from enforced idleness; it was no doubt out of a desire to find occupations for women that some manuals encouraged them to undertake the decorating themselves, even to the extent of papering and painting rooms.

The many late nineteenth-century handbooks gave a wealth of detailed advice on domestic decoration from which certain principles can be deduced. After making the home as unlike the husband's place of work as possible, the second general principle, as mentioned by Elsie de Wolfe, was that the interior should express the personality of its occupants, especially that of the lady of the house.

The idea that domestic decor expressed personal character comes out of a general nineteenth-century fascination with appearances. The more reserved people were in public, the more they were driven to study the minutest clues of each other's appearance and possessions for signs of their true character. For example, John Ruskin's judgement of the shallowness and unworthiness of the man and woman in Holman Hunt's painting 'The Awakening Conscience' was based upon his observation of the furnishings, of which he wrote:

'. . . there is not a single object in all that room – common, modern, vulgar . . . but it becomes tragical, if rightly read. That furniture so carefully painted, even to the last vein of the rosewood – is there nothing to be learnt from that terrible lustre of it, from its fatal newness; nothing there that has the old thoughts of home upon it, or that is ever to become part of a home?'*

By the late nineteeenth century, it was principally women whose characters were revealed by the choice of furnishings. The pressures on women to take part in this bourgeois charade were considerable. So close had the identification between woman and the house become that a woman who failed to express her personality in this way was in danger of being thought lacking in femininity. In an essay published in 1869, Frances Power Cobbe wrote:

'The unhomeliness of the homes . . . of women in whom the feminine element is lacking is pitiable . . . The more womanly a woman is, the more she is sure to throw her personality over the home, and transform it, from a mere eating and sleeping place, or an upholsterer's showroom, into a sort of outermost garment of her soul; harmonised with all her nature as her robe and the flower in her hair are harmonised with her bodily beauty. The arrangement of her rooms, the light and shade, warmth and coolness, sweet odours, and soft or rich colours, are not like the devices of a well-trained servant or tradesman. They are the expression of the character of the woman . . . A woman whose home does not bear to her this relation of nest to bird, calyx to flower, shell to mollusk, is in one or another imperfect condition. She is either not really mistress of her home; or being so, she is herself deficient in the womanly power of thoroughly imposing her personality upon her belongings.'*

*F. Power Cobbe, 'The Final Cause of Woman', *Woman's Work and Woman's Culture*, edited by Josephine Butler, London, 1869, pp.10-11.

In the light of such attitudes, it is easy to see why women felt compelled to pursue the ideal of individual personal expression in home furnishing. So commonplace did the principle become that it has been repeated endlessly in books on home furnishing ever since. Thus, Emily Post wrote in her book, *The Personality of a House*, published in 1930:

'Its personality should express your personality, just as every gesture you make – or fail to make – expresses your gay animation or your restraint, your old-fashioned conventions, your perplexing mystery, or your emancipated modernism – whichever characteristics are typically yours.

'The house that does not express the individuality of its owner is like a dress shown on a wax figure. It may be a beautiful dress – may be a beautiful house – but neither is animated by a living personality.'*

*Emily Post, *The Personality of a House*, New York, 1930, p.3.

As domestic environments have come to be regarded as signs of the occupants' characters, people have gone to great lengths to present a satisfactory account of themselves. The advice supplied in handbooks and magazines on home decorating has been based heavily on the assumption that furnishings indicate personality, while the furniture trade has taken great advantage of the fact that its customers are buying what is regarded as an image of themselves. Bereft of other ways of expressing their personalities publicly, people have been driven to catalogues of domestic furnishing to find a persona. Homes that lack signs of individuality are usually regarded as dead, which is often a criticism of schemes designed by professional interior decorators; it is to avoid such deadness that some designers lay great emphasis on the need for personal collections of ornaments and often leave spaces in their schemes for displaying them.

There is a paradox in the pursuit of individuality in home furnishing, for while most of the authorities on domestic decoration have insisted that every home must distinctively express the

William Holman Hunt: *The Awakening Conscience*, oil painting, 1853. Ruskin's commentary on the painting interpreted its meaning largely through the appearance of the furnishings.

character of its occupants, the same authorities have also laid down rules to be followed in the design of the decor. The pursuit of individualism cannot be compatible with the observance of preordained principles of design. In practice, many of the qualities of domestic environments come from attempts both to be individual and simultaneously to conform to standards of taste and domesticity imposed from outside.

The Ideal Home: from Beauty to Efficiency

Over the last two centuries, homes have changed considerably, most obviously in their appearance. It is important to recognise that the changes have not only been physical, for homes, as well as being made of bricks and mortar, melamine and foam rubber, are also made of ideas. Perhaps the most important change within the last century in the ideas constituting the home has been the shift from its role as a source of moral welfare to one of physical welfare, represented in visible terms by its turning from a place of beauty into one of efficiency.

The metaphorical connection of home with heaven made it easy for the Victorians to look upon home as a moral haven: innocent, uncorrupted and raised above the deceits of the world. This elevation to celestial status gave support to a very widespread middle-class desire to make the home superior to all other institutions. The earnestness and evangelical zeal with which this opinion was promoted suggests that it was relatively new and, at the time, far from universally held. This would account for the fervour with which *The Family Friend*, a magazine devoted to the virtues of domestic life, wrote as follows in 1853:

'In how small a compass lie all the elements of man's truest happiness . . . A marriage contracted with thoughtfulness and cemented by a pure and faithful love, when a fixed position is gained in the world and a small fund has been accumulated . . . a dwelling comfortably furnished, clean, bright, salubrious and sweet . . . a small collection of good books on the shelves – a few blossoming plants in the window – some well selected engravings on the walls . . . these are conditions of existence within the reach of everyone who will seek them – resources of the purest happiness, lost to thousands, because a wrong direction is given to their tastes and energies, and they roam abroad in pursuit of interest and enjoyment which they might create in abundance at home.'

*'Happy Homes' in *Family Friend*, new series, vol. II, 1853, p.66.

With such propaganda, the nineteenth-century bourgeoisie sought to elevate family life to an unprecedented importance. One explanation for so much being made of the family can be found in the retreat from the public modes of life of the eighteenth-century coffee houses, theatre, and pleasure gardens, where strangers had engaged freely in conversation on all subjects; home became the only place in which authentic behaviour and feelings could still be displayed.

Further explanation for the emphasis on the family lay in the belief that a good home might be a beneficent moral influence upon its inhabitants, as was more or less universally accepted by the Victorians. The sanitary reformer Dr Southwood Smith, quoted in *Recreations of a Country Parson*, published in 1861, made the principle clear:

'A clean, fresh, and well-ordered house exercises over its inmates a moral, no less than a physical influence, and has a direct tendency to make the members of the family sober, peaceable, and considerate of the feelings and happiness of each other; nor is it difficult to trace a connexion between habitual feelings of this sort and the formation of habits of respect for property, for the laws in general, and even for those higher duties and obligations the observance of which no laws can enforce. Whereas, a filthy, squalid, unwholesome dwelling, in which none of the decencies common to society . . .

Recreations of a Country Parson, London, 1861, p.299.

are or can be observed, tends to make every dweller in such a house regardless of the feelings and happiness of each other, selfish and sensual.'*

There was a strong body of opinion that wanted to go much further than this and make the home not just a place where respect for law and property was learnt, but also the source of religious sentiments. In an age greatly concerned by the decline of religious practices, the family seemed to offer a context in which faith could be preserved. The analogy of home with heaven was therefore attractive, for it implied a sanctity lacking in other institutions and provided assurance of the survival of religion despite the neglect of regular churchgoing.* But how were faith and sanctity to be represented in the home? Cleanliness and orderliness were not enough on their own; it was argued that only the cultivation of beauty would arouse the higher feelings. Preaching the power of beauty, the journalist W.J. Loftie wrote in 1879 about the homes of the poor:

*The 1851 Religious Census had drawn attention to the low church attendance in towns. See General Register Office, *Religious Worship in England and Wales*, London, 1854.

'A few bare walls hung with pictures, a few flowers in the window, a pretty tile on the hob, would, in my opinion, do more to keep men and women at home, and to promote family love, than libraries of tracts and platforms full of temperance lecturers.'*

*W.J. Loftie, *A Plea for Art in the Home*, London, 1879, p.96.

Everything that the Victorian middle class said about beauty in the dwellings of the poor applied with just as much force to their own homes. Beauty was consistently attributed a moral value in addition to its purely aesthetic significance. An article in *The Family Friend* in 1867 emphasised the moral value of beauty not only in the home, but in the wife as well:

'One of the grandest points to be attended to, in making a home happy, is to make it attractive. The husband should do his best to render it comfortable and attractive to the wife, as she should to the husband and children . . . Beauty, as one of the most powerful characters with which the Supreme Being has impressed the most prominent objects of his creation, is one of the most essential elements of the attractiveness of human life in every condition. Therefore, it is not to be so lightly esteemed as some parents would seem to consider it in giving moral instruction to their children . . . It is not, however, merely in his wife that a husband should look for and expect beauty within the walls of his own dwelling. It should, as far as possible, be made to appear in everything with which he is surrounded . . . The influence of such a disposition of things in soothing the appetites with which the outward life of man is assailed, would hardly be believed, if not witnessed.'*

*J. Sherer, 'The Management of the Home', *Family Friend*, 5th series, vol.III, no.3, March 1867, pp.201-203.

For all the emphasis on the moral significance of beauty, there is no suggestion here of what form beauty might take; it was assumed that the readers knew for themselves. Nevertheless, what the Victorians thought of as beautiful did not remain constant. For the early part of the century, the homes of the aristocracy, with their connotations of freedom from work, had provided the main standard of beauty, but in the 1860s and 1870s ideas began to change and new, specifically middle-class models were developed. The rather heavy, sub-Renaissance look of early Victorian furnishing was replaced by a somewhat plainer style under the impact

Art furnishing. An example of the new 'moral' furnishing of the 1880s. The construction of the furniture is plainly visible, and upholstery is kept to the minimum. From Mrs Orrinsmith, *The Drawing Room*, 1878, p.57.

of the religious revival in the mid century and of the design reformers associated with the Arts and Crafts Movement. In the new taste of the 1870s, the early Victorian style was characterised as particularly ugly. In her book *The Drawing Room*, published in 1878, Mrs Orrinsmith described such an interior:

'Who does not call to mind the ordinary lower middle class drawing room of the Victorian era? The very headquarters of commonplace, with its strict symmetry of ornament and its pretentious uselessness. All things seem as if chosen on the principle of unfitness for any function; everything is in pairs that can possibly be paired. The cold, hard, unfeeling white mantelpiece, surmounted by the inevitable mirror, varying in size only with the means of the householder, totally irrespective of any relation to the shape or proportions of the apartment; the fireplace a marvellous exhibition of the power of iron and black lead to give discomfort to the eye. At the window hang curtains in the harshest folds, trimmed with rattling fringes. On the carpet vegetables are driven to frenzy in their desire to be ornamental. On a circular table (of course with pillars and claws) are placed books – too often selected for the bindings alone – arranged like the spokes of a wheel, the nave being a vase of, probably, objectionable shape and material. Add a narrow ill-curved sofa, and spider-legged chairs made to be knocked over, dangerous as seats even for a slight acquaintance, doubly so for a stout friend – and all is consistently complete.'*

*Mrs Orrinsmith, *The Drawing Room*, London, 1878, pp.1-2.

The reaction against such taste was, at least initially, restricted to the fashionable minorities of the art furnishing movement and devotees of the Queen Anne style, and involved a well-developed philosophy of design in relation to morality. The intention was to establish a form of beauty that corresponded approximately to the moral virtues that the aesthetic reformers believed should be represented in the home.

From the 1860s onwards, the design and furnishing of domestic interiors received a greater degree of attention than before, which was reflected partly in the increasing number of books on interior furnishing published in both Britain and America. Among the best known were Charles Eastlake's *Hints on Household Taste* (1868), Colonel Edis's *Decoration and Furnishing of Town Houses* (1881), the 'Art at Home' series of books edited by W.J. Loftie in the late 1870s, Mrs Haweis's *The Art of Decoration* (1881), Mrs Panton's *Suburban Residences and How to Circumvent Them* (1896), and R.M. Watson's *The Art of the House* (1897). In the United States, there were C. Cook's *The House Beautiful* (1878), Edith Wharton and Ogden Codman's *The Decoration of Houses* (1897) and Elsie de Wolfe's *The House in Good Taste* (1913). Not only were many of the authors women, which was significant given the general belief that women were especially suited to home furnishing, but many also practised as professional interior decorators. For example, Rhoda and Agnes Garrett, authors of *Suggestions for House Decoration* (1879), one of the titles in the 'Art at Home' series, worked professionally as interior decorators and ran a school of interior decoration. Mrs Panton wrote a weekly advice column on home furnishing in *The Lady's Pictorial* in the 1880s and 1890s as well consulting privately, while Edith Wharton and Elsie de Wolfe both acquired considerable reputations as practising interior designers in New York.* The arrival of professional interior decorators indicated a new attitude towards home furnishing. Since the eighteenth century, interior design and decoration had generally been carried out by firms of upholsterers, whose business was both in making furniture, or having it made, and in supplying the whole ensemble of domestic furnishing. In the late nineteenth century, there was a reaction, particularly from the middle-class intelligentsia, who deplored the failure of the trade to provide furniture and decorative schemes which met the moral and aesthetic standards of beauty they expected in their homes. Although there were hardly enough independent interior decorators to influence the decor of most homes directly, these individuals did have a considerable effect on the fashion in furniture: it was partly because of them that 'art furniture' came to be widely manufactured in the 1880s.

The general principles of art furnishing were to reduce the amount of furniture and to create more space in rooms. Heavily upholstered furniture was eschewed in favour of wooden-framed chairs and settees with loose cushions. Sombre furnishings, gilding and such colours as crimson were banished in favour of paler tones and white-painted joinery work. Rugs on wooden or parquet floors were preferred to fitted carpets. Throughout, an air of casualness and informality was aimed at, with symmetry in furnishing schemes being discouraged. Finally, and most important of all, shams and deceits were forbidden: furniture which disguised the way it was made, or the materials of which it was made, was

*N.Cooper, *The Opulent Eye*, London, 1979, pp.171-177; and A. Callen, *The Angel in the Studio*, London, 1979, pp.171-177.

Sitting Room, 'Glen Roy',
Wake Green Road, Moseley,
Birmingham, photographed in
1890. A partial application of
the principles of art furnishing.

regarded as dishonest and therefore to be avoided. Often, the application of these principles led to results that were not as different from earlier Victorian interiors as one might have expected. The first of the two illustrations of art furnishing shows a sitting room photographed in 1890. While it reveals signs of art furnishing principles in the design of the mantelpiece and the painted wood-work of the fireplace and surrounding panelling, as well as in the two William Morris wallpapers and the William Morris carpet, the room still contains much that belongs to an earlier era of Victorian taste. The profusion of furnishings and ornaments, and the upholstered chairs with tasselled fringes are alien to the declared principles of art furnishing, although they were often found in interiors that were said to be beautiful. The second illustration, of a London drawing room designed a few years later, shows a very much purer application of the principles of art furnishing. There seems to be altogether more space in the room, an effect achieved by having less furniture, fewer ornaments and the white-painted ceiling and wall-panelling. The only patterns are those of the furniture covers and of the wallpaper on the frieze, and although these are bold, they both have white grounds and are sufficiently similar to give the room an air of harmony.

The attraction of a scheme like this, which would have made it seem beautiful at the end of the nineteenth century, was that it conformed to the Christian virtues that it was believed that domestic life should demonstrate. No material imitates something that

Drawing room, Rosslyn Tower, Putney, photographed in 1907. Furnished in the best turn-of-the-century taste, conforming to the principles of art furnishing.

*R.W. Edis, 'Internal Decoration', in *Our Homes and How to Make Them Healthy*, edited by S.F. Murphy, London, 1883, p.356.

it is not, and, it would have been said, each part makes sense in relation to the whole. Furnishings which obeyed such criteria of beauty were, it was argued, bound to have a good moral influence upon the members of the household. As Colonel Eddis had warned of the dangers of 'dishonest' design:

'If you are content to teach a lie in your belongings, you can hardly wonder at petty deceits being practised in other ways . . . All this carrying into everyday life of "the shadow of unreality" must exercise a bad and prejudicial influence on the younger members of the house, who are thus brought up to see no wrong in the shams and deceits which are continually before them.'*

Throughout the late nineteenth century, beauty was the principal means by which the home was to fulfil its purpose as a place of sanctity. Among its characteristics, beauty included comfort and the satisfaction of the aesthetic senses, but above all it meant the representation of the moral virtues of truth and honesty. In the responsibilities attributed to women in the home, it was the pursuit of beauty that was emphasised most strongly for the sake of its moral effects upon the members of the household.

The home of the twentieth century followed that of the nineteenth in certain respects, such as the physical and emotional separation from the place of work, but differences in appearance and organisation revealed some major changes in underlying values. The relative importance attached to the various rooms was

Dining room of a house in Hampstead Garden Suburb, designed by Robert Atkinson, early 1920s. In a much smaller house, this interior shows some of the changes in taste characteristic of the 1920s. With plain painted walls, the most minimal joinery, and little upholstery, the room is not 'decorated' in the sense apparent in the earlier interiors, apart from the grate and mantelpiece. From C.H. James & F.R. Yerbury, *Modern English Houses & Interiors*, London, 1925, plate V.

no longer the same – for instance, kitchens came to receive far more attention than they had before, and drawing rooms rather less. These changes were symptoms both of new social realities in the twentieth century, such as the growth of a middle class without servants, but they were also an indication of the new ideas about what constituted a home. Most importantly, the nineteenth century view of the home as a stronghold of beauty and spiritual virtue was replaced by the idea that the home's main function was as the source of physical welfare and health. Although it would be wrong to suggest that cleanliness and child-care had not mattered in the nineteenth-century home, they had never been more than subsidiary to the moral functions of the dwelling in the responsibilities of wives and mothers. In twentieth-century literature about the home, preoccupations with motherhood, children and hygiene replaced instructions about needlework and the Christian virtues; in practice, this was signified by the reversal of roles between drawing room and kitchen as the core of the house. The change took place on both sides of the Atlantic in the first two decades of the twentieth century.

Just how different the home had become by the 1920s and 1930s can be seen in the following quotation, taken from a book on household management published in the 1930s. It describes the house in terms that would have been utterly unfamiliar fifty years before:

'The home is by far the most important institution in the lives of the British people. It is a centre of interest, not only in the immediate family life, but equally in the wider hustling world of trade and commerce, for its influence is far-reaching and all-embracing.

'For the average British man and woman, each day begins and

ends in the family centre. The influence of a happy, harmonious home is therefore a national asset.

'The early-morning family contact will have its reaction on business life throughout the day; the return to the home at night will bring rest and peace and a laying aside of worries and cares.

'Psychologically as well as physically, the home is the centre of recreation and relaxation. The powerful influence of a well-run home is therefore a matter of national importance and must be recognised and encouraged as such. Never before has there been such a demand for well-built, scientifically planned houses. A new consciousness of home-making has been born. Men and women are equally enthusiastic. Together they study houses, plans and schemes of decoration; together they devise ways and means of owning homes of their own; and their interest is fostered and encouraged by manufacturers and designers of home equipment and household utilities. For indeed a modern, well-equipped home is a worthwhile possession, whether it consists of three rooms or thirty. It gives a sense of security and comfort and intimacy essential to real family life.

'Contributions to home service come from world-wide sources. Each year – almost each month – science brings some new discovery to the home. Ether waves are utilised for the preservation of food; wireless waves are made to boil water for the household; invisible rays protect the home from unwelcome intruders; and many other such wonders are rapidly being included in everyday household services.'*

*The Home of Today, published by Daily Express Publications, London, n.d. [c. 1935], p.7.

This passage contains a number of important assertions, the most notable being that an efficient, well-run, harmonious home is a national asset. It is also stated that attitudes towards the home are influenced by the manufacturers of domestic equipment, a significant view in the light of the rapid growth of such industries in the inter-war years. In addition, the ownership of a home is seen as a necessity for real family life (which is important in the context of the steady increase of owner-occupation as a form of tenure throughout this century). Finally, it is suggested that all the problems of domestic life can be solved by the application of science, an attitude that was to have important effects upon the character and appearance of the domestic environment.

All this creates a picture of the home that is not too far from that widely held today. The idea with the most far-reaching effects was the proposition that the quality of the domestic environment had a major influence upon the physique and health of the nation. In European countries and in America, this idea took root around the beginning of the twentieth century. In Britain, the immediate cause was widespread concern about the apparent physical deterioration of the race and about the threat of a declining population. The dangers had been highlighted by the discovery that one in four army recruits during the Boer War was physically unfit for military service, and by the evidence of a high rate of infant mortality. Revealed at the height of colonial activity and imperial expansion, these facts presented an issue of major national importance, for they suggested that the British would be able neither to defend nor to populate their empire in the future.

The causes of poor physique and of the high rate of infant mortality were thought to lie principally in the domestic sphere.

As Major General Frederick Maurice wrote in an influential article,

'Whatever the primary cause . . . we are always brought back to the fact that . . . the young man of 16 to 18 years of age is what he is because of the training through which he has passed during his infancy and childhood. "Just as the twig is bent the tree's inclined." Therefore it is to the condition, mental, moral and physical, of the women and children that we must look if we have regard to the future of our land . . . Mr Barnett in Whitechapel . . . found that the health and long life of the Jews, whose women did not go out to work, compared most favourably with that of the Christian population, the women of which worked without adequate regard to their function as mothers. It does not follow that a stereotyped copying of the habits of the Jews would be desirable, but it may explain and justify the view of the Emperor of Germany that for the raising of a virile race, either of soldiers or of citizens, it is essential that the attention of the mothers of a land should be mainly devoted to the three Ks – *Kinder, Küche, Kirche*.'*

*F. Maurice, 'National Health: A Soldier's Study', in *Contemporary Review*, January 1903, quoted in A. Davin, 'Imperialism and Motherhood', in *History Workshop*, no. 5, Spring 1978, p.16.

Although the General's explanation overlooked the much more relevant factors of malnutrition and poverty, the view that defective mothering was the root of the problem was widely shared. A variety of measures were introduced to improve the physique of the race, among them free school meals, school medical inspections and attempts to improve housing conditions, but the greatest emphasis of all was placed on improvement in standards of motherhood and domesticity. Schools of motherhood were set up to teach young mothers how to carry out their responsibilities better, and basic lessons in hygiene and domestic work were given to girls in schools.* Parents were encouraged to see their responsibilities in a new light; a book on household administration, published in 1910, stated:

*Described by Davin.

'The burden of responsibility or the privilege of promoting progress . . . rests with those people who propose to be or already are parents . . . Parental care and intelligent home management are thus intimately concerned with the physical evolution of the race, as well as with its moral development. They must, therefore, assume an increasing rather than a diminishing importance if the full development of potentialities is to be insured in the rising generation, and racial progress promoted. Any proclivity to depreciate the dignity or to undermine the influence of these institutions must be carefully examined and, if necessary, sternly repressed.'*

*A. Ravenhill, 'Some Relations of Sanitary Science to Family Life and Individual Efficiency', in *Household Administration*, edited by A. Ravenhill & C.Schiff, London, 1910, p.252.

Underlying statements like this were the beliefs that the family was the basis of the nation, and that the duty of improving its condition rested on parents, particularly mothers. Whether or not the training in motherhood had any practical effect upon welfare, the widespread political concern with standards of domesticity laid a heavy responsibility upon individual families. The people likely to have been most affected by the propaganda about health and welfare and to have been made the most sensitive to the need for efficiency and hygiene, were those at school during the first two decades of the century, the adults of the inter-war years. It is not surprising, then, that the pursuit of hygiene in the home reached its most vivid expression in the 1920s and 1930s. Take, for example, the illustration of a bathroom from a sanitary ware manufacturer's

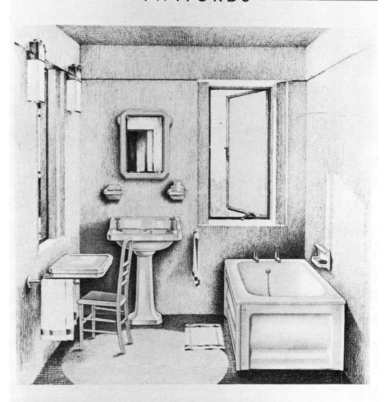

FEATURES—The most popular suite. Panelled corner bath in enamelled iron much easier to keep clean than the ordinary exposed type with feet. Pedestal lavatory adds to the attractiveness of the outfit and the pottery dressing table is a most useful addition. Toilet is not included but can be added if space permit.

No. 44 Twyfords Bathroom Suite

Minimum size of bathroom 7'0" × 7'0" (215 × 215 c/m)

Comprising—

No.							
321/1	Corner Bath ..	..	..	..	page	107
„ 619P/1	Pedestal Lavatory	..	..	..	„	31
„ 1550/1	Dressing Table	..	..	..	„	58
„ 1031	Towel Rails (2)	..	..	..	„	125
„ 1020	Soap and Brush Tray	..	..	..	„	121
„ 1056	Soap Tray ..	..	..	..	„	118
„ 1057	Tumbler Holder	..	..	..	„	118
„ 986	Tumbler ..	..	..	..	„	118
„ 1059	Mirror ..	..	..	..	„	117
„ 1050	Bathroom Chair	..	..	..	„	58
„ 962	Towel Rail ..	..	..	..	„	125

Twyfords bathroom suite no. 44, 1935. In the twentieth century, the importance of kitchens and bathrooms increased in relation to drawing and dining rooms. The bathroom suite design reflects this change, and the value attached to hygienic appearances.

catalogue of the 1930s where the design's stress on hygienic considerations was calculated to appeal to the consumer. No bathroom has to look like this; indeed, bathrooms before and since have not. But here, the white enamel bathtub and basin, the tiled walls and the chromium fittings, all with hard, bright finishes, made a virtue of cleanliness. This imagery of hygiene corresponded to, and indeed reinforced, the consumers' belief that physical cleanliness and efficiency were among the worthiest of aspirations.

If the pursuit of domestic hygiene was one arm of the campaign for greater national efficiency, another was the more effective use of domestic labour. By making domestic work less laborious, it was argued that it would be carried out better and with less waste of physical effort. One side of this policy was to make housework a systematic job, an approach encouraged by schools of housecraft and by groups like the Good Housekeeping Institute and Better Homes in America, and signified by the title of 'domestic science' for what was otherwise known as housework. Alongside this went the introduction of mechanical appliances to lighten the load of domestic chores. In Britain, the development of these products was closely related to the structural change in the economy away from exporting industries and towards those making consumer goods for the home market. That such industries were able to build up a demand for domestic appliances owed something to the pressure that was being placed upon people to achieve greater efficiency in their homes. It is clear from the advertising for domestic appliances that manufacturers took advantage of the heightened sense of domestic responsibility. Increased efficiency was also expressed in the design of furnishings and of houses themselves: the 'labour-saving house', a cliché of the 1920s, was not only a response to the perceived shortage of servants, the so-called 'servant problem', but also to the demands of national efficiency. The recurrent features of the labour-saving house – hot and cold running water on all floors, dumb waiters and no dust-catching mouldings – were all means of reducing domestic work and so of enabling more human resources to be devoted to the major problem of physical welfare. By the 1950s, many of these features, as well as the values they represented had become normal and part of the accepted standards of domestic design.

Freedom and Constraint at Home

The 'fifties interior illustrated was not entirely the creation of its occupants or their architects, in spite of all that has been said about the importance of individualism in domestic furnishing. In the pursuit of efficiency, in the lightweight furnishings, the easily movable rugs, the flush doors and recessed cupboards, the interior conforms to a set of outside standards that were intended to make the home the basis of the nation's welfare. In this sense, flush doors, for example, introduce a set of political values into the home: what is considered to look best in the home is what enables the housewife to fulfil her role of caring for children and workers most efficiently. However reasonable and acceptable this might seem, it must be stressed that this idea did not originate within the home and so conflicts with the principle that the appearance of the home should express individual personality.

The extent to which individualism in the home is an illusion is brought out by the similarity of the interior to other fashionable interiors of its date. Its appearance was determined by the contemporary standards of taste, and by what was available in the shops to buy. However much people may wish to pursue an entirely original treatment in their interiors, they invariably find themselves constrained by the market. For all the illusion of freedom at home, the things people spend their money on are fixed by what the economy provides for them to spend it on; the standards and mores that they maintain at home are to some degree determined by the obligations and beliefs that are thrust upon them – there is a sense in which they are actors playing out roles into which they have been cast by the economy. This is not a new phenomenon: an article in the *Cornhill Magazine* in 1864 described the experience of an imaginary couple in furnishing their home:

'But the interior of the house is a field in which his taste, or his wife's taste, may find full scope. That they have a taste probably neither of them doubts for an instant. Let us grant the fact for argument's sake, and then watch how they exercise it. At the furniture warehouse, they are in the upholsterer's hands; at the china-shop, they are as easily talked over by the obsequious vendor of wine glasses and dinner plates. The carpet merchant leads them by the nose . . .'*

*The Fashion of Furniture', *Cornhill Magazine*, vol. IX, March 1864, p.339.

Yet, even if it is actually impossible for people to be free agents in furnishing their homes, the wish to be so is extremely strong. The special value attributed to homes is summed up in the statement, 'Home is where I can do what I want when I want.' To anyone doing a routine job under the supervision of a manager or an overseer, home takes on great importance as the place where it is possible to make choices and to have some self-esteem. Hence the value of individualism in home furnishing: it becomes a sign of being capable of independent thought and emotion, of having a life apart from the millwheels of the economy.

The conflict of the desire for individuality with the constraints of the economy and of dominant ideas thrives in the furnishing of domestic interiors. Every choice, every decision about the decoration of the home is a new episode in the same drama: the conflict is always there and never resolved. It is the fact that the home is both a factory of private illusions and a catalogue of ready-made tastes, values and ideas that makes all design for the home so extraordinarily revealing about the conditions of modern life.

Sitting-dining room, house at Oulton Broad, Suffolk, designed by Tayler and Green Architects, 1954. An excellent example of the best taste of the 1950s. Plain brick, quarry tile, plaster and plywood veneer are the main finishes; mouldings and skirtings are minimal; the amount of furniture is small, and as much of it as possible is fitted. But was this simplicity a product of the taste of individuals, or of received notions about the proprieties of domestic life?

6. Design in the Office

In modern industrial societies, the majority of people work in factories and offices, places that have acquired quite unmistakeable design characteristics, above all because of their nature as instruments of management. Not only has the design of the buildings and of their internal organisation been arrived at to suit the purposes of the managers, but so too has the design of the interiors and of all the furnishings and equipment.* Whether in the factory or the office, design has been used to represent ideas about the nature of work and about the behaviour expected of people doing it. It is the presence of such ideas in the design of working environments and equipment that makes it easy to see why similar forms for objects, furnishings and decor would not have been welcome in the home.

*On the relationship between office buildings and management theory see F. Duffy, 'Office Buildings and Organisational Change', *Buildings and Society*, edited by A.D. King, London, 1980.

This chapter concentrates exclusively on design in offices during the last century. Over that time, the changes in office environments have been more pronounced than those in factories, and the ideas that management has tried to represent to office workers through design have been more various and more complex. Design in offices has been used to resolve, or at least calm, anxieties and conflicts that have been set up by the introduction of new theories of management and by uncertainties about the status of office work in relation to other occupations; in both cases, the results have been much more successful than the open exercise of authority.

The Sociology of Office Work

Over the last century, clerical workers, who make up the majority of those employed in offices, have formed an increasing proportion of the total occupied population. Nevertheless, their status and rewards have deteriorated. In Britain, until the last quarter of the nineteenth century, clerks were almost all men, many of whom enjoyed quite a high status through regular contact with their employers, by the trust that was often placed in them, and because their wages were generally not less than those of the most skilled of the working class and could be very much more. But though clerks had a degree of respectability, they rarely earned enough to live up to the standards considered appropriate to the middle class. This was one of their most common grievances, to which the employers' customary reply was that middle-class respectability was an additional benefit of being a clerk and, far from requiring a higher salary, was in itself a form of reward (though one that cost the employer nothing). Underlying this dispute was the ambiguity of the clerk's status: was he or was he not middle class? Notwithstanding his modest wages, the clerk was not seen by the working classes as one of their number. But equally, the

*The sources of this account of clerical work in the nineteenth century are F.D. Klingender, *The Conditions of Clerical Labour in Britain*, London, 1935, chapters 1 and 2; D. Lockwood, *The Black Coated Worker*, London, 1958, chapter 1; and G. Anderson, *Victorian Clerks*, Manchester, 1976.

'Elbowing Him Out.' The arrival of women in offices, shown in this cartoon of 1900, did much to depress the status of male clerks. From *The Shorthand Writer*, 1900.

*Klingender, pp.58-98; and Lockwood, pp.72-94.

secure and established middle class of employers and professional men did not see him as belonging with them.* The uncertain standing of the clerk accounted for much of the social discomfort experienced by the fictional Mr Pooter in George and Weedon Grossmith's *The Diary of a Nobody* and has survived to some extent to the present.

In insurance offices and banks, the clerks were better paid and had higher status than their counterparts in business counting houses, railway companies and solicitors' offices. Clerks in the superior category were generally involved in the whole sequence of office work and have thus been compared to industrial craftsmen before the division of labour, as they were responsible for all the stages of a transaction and were able to control the rate at which they worked. The lower category of clerk was usually responsible for fewer stages and had less control over the way he worked. The disparity between the two categories was acknowledged by contemporaries and meant far more in social terms than the differences in the grades of clerical workers today. By the turn of the century, office work and its status had changed in various ways. As the quantity of trade increased rapidly, offices had to expand and employ a higher proportion of clerks to senior staff, thus reducing the clerks' chances of contact with their employers. With the introduction of education for all from 1870, the number of potential clerks increased, as middle-class children no longer had a monopoly of reading, writing and arithmetic, the basic skills of the clerk, and working-class children could compete for office jobs. The introduction of the typewriter in the 1880s brought women into offices to operate it, and, from the 1890s, their number grew so rapidly that by 1911 women constituted a quarter of all clerical workers. Their presence further increased the labour supply and, because women had lower status than men in any occupation and worked for lower wages, further depressed the status of clerical work. In the early twentieth century, the amalgamation of many banks, insurance companies and merchant houses again increased the size of offices and consequently the proportion of clerks in them; the chances of personal contact with employers became even less.

The combined effect of these changes was to make the clerk's job seem more lowly, and even the distinction between superior and inferior clerks was eroded, leaving them all merged into the same general class. As their social position declined, so, too, did their earnings compared to those of other workers, notably manual workers whose relative incomes increased over the first half of the twentieth century, a development that accelerated during and immediately after World War II. By the 1950s, many factory workers were earning more than office staff.*

Roughly simultaneous changes took place in the United States in the late nineteenth and early twentieth centuries, although the decline in the relative wages of clerical workers was much more pronounced, since the wage differential between clerks and manual workers had originally been much greater. The erosion of the status of clerks was more noticeable in the United States than in Britain because the changes that were made in the organisation of offices happened on a more comprehensive scale, and rather earlier, in America. As the scale of office business increased, it became subject to the principle of division of labour that had already been

The Time Clock, 1911. This American advertisement implied that office and shop floor staff alike should be subject to the same timekeeping routine. From *The Factory*, January 1911.

*On the history of clerical work in the United States, and the introduction of scientific management into offices, see H. Braverman, *Labor and Monopoly Capital*, New York & London, 1974, chapter 15.

*For the history and development of scientific management, see Judith A. Merkle, *Management and Ideology*, Berkeley, 1980.

applied in factories. From the beginning of the twentieth century exactly similar processes of management and rationalisation began to be applied in offices: clerks were divided into departments, each of which carried out one stage of the work process, and every clerk in a department did the same work. With departments con-nected only by the flow of work, the American office of the early twentieth century came to resemble a factory, at least in its organ-isation. The clerical worker, instead of being the equivalent of a craftsman, with responsibility for the whole of a transaction, lost this control over his work, and became no more than a process worker. Perhaps the most potent sign of the clerk's reduction to the level of a factory worker was the appearance of the time clock in offices in the first decade of the century.* The department-alisation of large offices seems to have become general both in America and in Britain in the early years of the century and it opened the way for the application of the techniques of scientific management, that had been developed in America and were later adopted in Europe.* The history of scientific management goes back to the 1880s, when Frederick Taylor began his studies of factory work. He realised that wasted movements, misdirected effort and badly designed tools and equipment prevented most workers from operating with maximum efficiency. If these things could be overcome and the worker could be taught to operate in the most efficent way, his output (and the firm's profits) would increase. Taylor assumed that there was an optimum method for each job and that the task of managers was to discover 'the one best way', record the time it took and set it as the standard rate. For the Taylor system to work, the labour process needed already to have been divided into stages, for it depended on perfecting each worker's handling of a single task; Taylor believed that a worker who had to perform too many tasks would never reach the optimum rate at any of them.

Taylor's work had become known in the 1900s, although his first popular work, *The Principles of Scientific Management*, did not appear until 1911. By then, manuals on the scientific management of offices were already being published in the United States.★ Scientific management set out to reduce each clerk's work to a single task, such as opening the mail, unpinning the remittance or invoicing the order, so that each could be studied with the aim of reducing it to its essentials, which could be carried out using the minimum of time and movement. Truly amazing results were promised: correspondents who had previously managed with difficulty to handle 20 letters per hour through the day found themselves able without strain to deal with 60 per hour, while the rate of opening letters was increased from 100 to 300 per hour when the process had been analysed and the correct method taught to the clerk.★ Scientific management was said to make workers happier through the discovery that they could work more efficiently, although the primary motive was to get more work out of office staff for the same or very little more pay. Managers were advised to cultivate friendly relations with their staff, to drop casual hints about how much more work one was managing to do than another, to chart the production of each worker and offer gold stars to those who exceeded the weekly norms, and to set up, in a spirit of healthy fun, office competitions to see who could achieve most in a week. A similarly indirect approach went towards the interest that scientific managers took in workers' health and welfare: fatigue was widely acknowledged to be a cause of poor work and was accounted for by such doubtful physiological theories as the build-up of toxins in the body. Its elimination would maximise efficiency

★One of the first manuals recommending scientific management in the office was Walter D. Scott, *Increasing Human Efficiency in Business*, New York, 1911.

★W.H. Leffingwell, *Scientific Office Management*, Chicago, 1917, p.5.

Adjustable Desk for Typists, c.1918. The caption to this illustration explained 'To work standing for short periods of time is found to relieve fatigue. With the chair and desk raised, the change from a sitting posture can be made almost instantly.' From L. Galloway, *Office Management. Its Principles and Practice*, New York, 1919, pp.192-193.

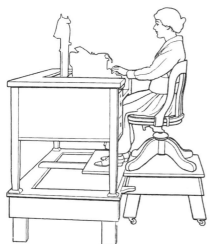

Figure 29. (a) Adjustable Desk—Stenographer Sitting
The desk and chair are placed on platforms so that the operator can work either in a sitting or standing posture, as she prefers.

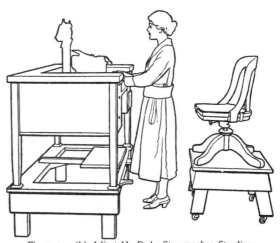

Figure 29. (b) Adjustable Desk—Stenographer Standing
To work standing for short periods of time is found to relieve fatigue. With the chair and desk raised, as shown above, the change from a sitting posture can be made almost instantly.

and therefore profits. At the same time, though, the reduction of fatigue could be calculated to appeal to the worker; new designs of furniture and equipment were introduced to office workers as improving comfort rather than profit. Because, for example, it was recognised that changing position at work helped to reduce fatigue, a special desk and chair were designed, the main virtue of which was that the typist would waste a minimum amount of time changing from one position to another. Scientific management continued the erosion of the office worker's status, which had already been undermined by the division of labour. Even management theorists acknowledged what had happened. One of them wrote in 1919: 'Much of the routine of the office employee resembles in one respect that of the factory.'* By 1920, the organisation of work in large, scientifically managed American offices had become indistinguishable from that in many factories, though with a different product in the shape of words and numbers written on pieces of paper.

*L. Galloway, *Office Management*, New York, 1919, p.75.

The development of the office desk and of other office furniture and equipment needs to be seen against this background of the deteriorating status of the clerk and the pressure from management to increase efficiency. The standard nineteenth-century clerk's desk had a high back with pigeon-holes and drawers in it, and sometimes a roll top. The supporting pedestals contained drawers down to floor level. The other common pattern of desk had a sloping top to support ledgers, at which the clerk could work standing or sitting. A clerk seated at a high-backed desk could see his work in front of him and a little to either side, but he could not see ahead beyond his desk, nor could anyone else see what he was doing without coming to look over his shoulder. Such a desk assumed that the clerk was responsible for its contents, and for his work; it represented a small private domain, perhaps with a roll top that could be closed down at any time to secure its privacy. From his desk, the clerk could collect and deliver office papers as his own pace of work required them to be moved around, and he could file papers as he chose in the drawers and pigeon-holes. Such a desk encapsulates the responsibility, trust and status given to some clerks. To the supporters of scientific management, the desk had great significance as the main piece of equipment

Below:
High-backed roll-top desk in use in an American office, c.1900. The desk in the centre allowed the clerk privacy and some freedom in how he organised his work.
Right:
Roll top pedestal desk. The standard late nineteenth-century desk, with a large amount of filing space. From Montgomery Ward & Co. catalogue, 1895, p.609.

Clerks in a London Insurance
Office, c.1900. The flat-topped
desks with racks for ledgers
gave the clerks some privacy
and autonomy at their work.

*J.W. Schulze, *The American
Office*, New York, 1913, p.62.

used by the clerical worker, and it was the first item in the office
to be redesigned in the interests of greater efficiency:

'The desk is the most used piece of furniture in the office. The
office employee is at it constantly. The highest type of working
efficiency in a desk is obtained when the desk itself is so constructed and so arranged that it doesn't in the slightest degree
interfere with the progress of a person's work, but on the other
hand aids it in every possible way.*

First the pedestal bases of the desk were replaced by legs, so that
there was a clear space of eight to ten inches between the bottom
drawer and the ground. This was to make cleaning easier and
prevent the harbouring of dust and germs, an improvement equally
in the interests of employer (because it might reduce the working
time lost through sickness) and employee, to whom it offered
better health. The other change in design was the elimination of
the high back with pigeon holes and the roll top.

'The chief objection to the roll top is that it becomes a receptacle
for important papers which are forgotten . . . Most papers that are
filed in the pigeonholes should be placed in the files where they
are accessible to everyone who needs them . . . Moreover the unnecessary height of a roll-top desk cuts off valuable light and air.'*

*Schulze, p.63.

The loss of filing space in the desk mattered little in the organisation of the office, because the division of labour had made filing a
separate activity, with its own department; individual clerks were
no longer responsible for filing and storing the papers they worked
on. Scientific management had a general, at times pathological,
hatred of desk storage space and saw any cavity in the desk as
providing an opportunity to hoard vital documents and obstruct
the flow of paper through the office. Thus the typical clerk was
left with a flat-top desk, with at most six drawers in it. The transformation is illustrated by the new design adopted by the Equitable
Assurance Co. during the 1910s. It was described as follows:

'The desk finally selected for the use of employees engaged in routine duties is little more than a table with three shallow drawers . . .

125

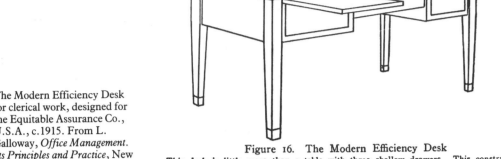

The Modern Efficiency Desk
for clerical work, designed for
the Equitable Assurance Co.,
U.S.A., c.1915. From L.
Galloway, *Office Management.
Its Principles and Practice*, New
York, 1919, p.89.

Figure 16. The Modern Efficiency Desk

This desk is little more than a table with three shallow drawers. This construction
makes it impossible for clerks to stow away and so overlook papers.

The center drawer holds the employee's tools and the side drawers his stationery. The advantages of a desk of this simple type are that clerks cannot stow within it papers which will be later overlooked. As there is no room for placing current work in the drawers, any tendency to defer until tomorrow what can be done today is nipped in the bud. The simplicity of this equipment reflects the celerity with which business is conducted today. The desk is no longer a storage place – nor even ornamental – but a tool for making the quickest possible turnover of business papers.*

*Galloway, pp.89-90.

The new design signified the change in the nature of clerical work. Taking away the high back meant that the clerk no longer worked in a private space: the chief clerk or supervisor was able to see whether he or she was working at maximum efficiency. Equally, though, the clerk could more easily see what was going on in the rest of the office (which might or might not be an inspiration to harder work) and talk to those at neighbouring desks. However, conversation in the office was a subversion of the principles of scientific management, interrupting concentration, and most employers made silence the rule in their offices – a rule that managers were advised to explain to employees on the grounds that silence in the office would reduce fatigue.* In some offices, partitions were built between the desks to make conversation impossible, but they defeated the object of better supervision unless the overseer constantly patrolled the office.

*Leffingwell, 1917, p.11.

With the disappearance of the roll top, the clerk lost the ability to make his or her desk private: work was constantly exposed to view, and the top of the desk was expected to be in such good order that anything could be found at a moment's notice. In the interest of efficiency, clerks were to be taught to arrange the contents of their desks according to a prescribed system:

'Desk system should be taught to all the clerks, and close watch kept until they have thoroughly learned it. To ascertain just how well they are proceeding, suddenly ask for an eraser or a ruler, or some other item that is not in constant use, and see how long it takes to locate it. If it cannot be located at once, without the slightest loss of time, the lesson has not been learned.'*

*Leffingwell, 1917, p.208.

Even the drawers were to conform to the system: they should be used in the way that had been established as the most efficient

*Schulze, p.64.

and, since each clerk in a department would be doing the same work, the best arrangement would be equally applicable to all. Once a standard system had been fixed, with, say, the top left drawer for unfinished work and the top right for stationery, the office manager was periodically to inspect the desk drawers to see that it was being followed. In one office, the clerks were awarded points for, among other things, the condition of their desks.* One reason why desk systems were considered necessary was that the clerk no longer brought work to and from his desk. The movement of papers was handled instead by a messenger, whose efficiency depended on his being able to locate unerringly the papers to be collected on each desk. With messengers or even (in some cases as early as 1915) mechanical conveyor systems for files, the clerk worked only at his desk and no longer had any control over the pace of work. The responsibility and trust given to the nineteenth-century clerk had entirely disappeared: the clerk now worked to a tempo imposed by management at a desk which had been designed and organised to prevent its being in any way a private space. The change in desk design in America during the 1910s both reflected, and was to some extent responsible for, the change in the status of the clerk from craftsman to proletarian – the employer was buying not only his or her time, but also the right to supervise every movement. Even if not all desks were actually used so rigorously, they were marketed as if they could be. The rationally designed desk, 'trained down to fighting trim', provided an image of efficiency to office managers, and the mere presence of 'scientific' desks in an office was a sign of aspirations towards efficient management.* In British offices, where scientific management never achieved quite the same ruthlessness, the reformed desks adopted in the 1920s, might have created an impression of efficiency, but the extent of the reorganisation of work was probably less drastic.

*Galloway, p.90.

The impression of efficiency was, of course, greatest if all the desks in an office were the same, or at least designed according to the same system. American office managers were encouraged by the scientific management experts to believe that the standardisation of furniture would have good general psychological effects, as well as improving overall efficiency; it suggested well-ordered methods and demanded of the employee the same care and regard for order:

Partitions in an American typing office, c.1915. The partitions ensured that the typists would not be distracted by gossip and chatter. From W.H. Leffingwell, *Scientific Office Management*, Chicago, 1917, p.140.

Mechanical Conveyor for Files, c.1925. The conveyor removed the need for clerks to leave their desks. From W.H. Leffingwell, *The Office Appliance Manual*, 1926, p.381.

'Various kinds of shapes, and irregular arrangements of desks, suggest on the other hand that there is no general scheme of supervision that is in harmony with a well-founded principle. There are

*Schulze, p.72.

*Leffingwell, 1917, p.20.

*Leffingwell, 1917, p.72.

*Schulze, p.63.

*Galloway, p.91.

so many different ways of doing the same thing that each employee feels he is more or less called upon to "improve" upon the methods used by everyone else.'*

Standardisation extended down even to the pens with which the clerk wrote. It was argued that there was no need to have a large supply of different pens to suit the handwriting idiosyncrasies of individual clerks, but that one style of nib would be more economical, and anyone could learn how to use the standard nib within a few days.* Thus, even in handwriting, the most individual and personal characteristic left to the clerk, non-conformity was to be eliminated on the grounds that it was inefficient.

In theory, scientific management should have been applied with equal force to all grades of office workers. In practice, though, exceptional reasons were found to justify executives having different tools and materials from clerks, although their basic activity in time and motion study terms – sitting reading or writing at a desk – was exactly the same. While clerks had dip pens, the executive was justified in having the much more prestigious fountain pen, 'because he is often called upon to write in all parts of the office, where an inkwell might not be handy,' and so was excused the uniformity imposed on the clerk.* Similarly, the reasons for the redesign of the clerk's desk should have applied with equal force to the executive's desk: filing had eliminated the need for storage, and efficiency demanded that the desk be no larger than was needed for writing on. This was where the principles of scientific management came into conflict with the need to maintain and demonstrate status, a conflict in which 'scientific' principles seem to have been defeated every time.

Executives' desks continued to be distinguished from clerical desks in size, capacity and appearance. In their recommendations for executive desks, the management experts emerged with contradictory statements on all three factors. On the size of desks, one writer notes:

'It will be found that for most purposes a 48″ desk without a center drawer, or with two drawers on either side will be found sufficient. Only in the case of employees charged with executive duties should it be necessary to use large desks.'*

It would seem that the only explanation for this necessity was one of status, as the executive's desk was not for storing documents, and indeed executives were severely warned against the dangers of allowing this to happen. In another office management manual, under an illustration of an extremely capacious desk for the executive, are the following remarks:

'Whatever the form of executive desk adopted, the test of its usefulness is based on its effectiveness as a working tool and not its use as a store house . . . At best, any type of storage system is a passive agent in business, and when the executive's desk takes on this function, it shows that his activities are not in harmony with the modern methods of business.'*

The efficiency experts acknowledged that the drawers of the executive's desk would normally be empty, but they did not dare suggest doing away with them altogether, as was done much later and under different conditions. The rolltop desk, which had been

Figure 17. Standard Double-Pedestal Flat-Top Desk
A type of desk widely used by executives, providing free working surface and ample drawer room for necessary storage purposes.

American executive's desk, c.1915. The type of desk recommended by scientific management for executive use. From L. Galloway, *Office Management. Its Principles and Practice*, New York, 1919, p.91.

Top right:
Roll-top desk used by an executive in precisely the way scientific management objected to. From *The Factory*, September 1912.

Below:
Flat-top desk with folding cover, c.1935. A compromise solution to preserve confidentiality without allowing the desk to accumulate papers unnecessarily. From V.E. Jackson, *Modern Office Appliances*, London, 1936.

B. CONSTRUCTORS "ROLLS" DESK

Right:
American tabulating machine office, c.1915. The woman is sitting on a wooden chair of the kind approved for clerical workers. From W.H. Leffingwell, *Scientific Office Management*, Chicago, 1917, p.108.

banished from the clerical office, continued to be preferred by many executives on the grounds that it was useful for protecting confidential papers from inquisitive eyes. In spite of the threat of disorder posed by such desks, the office manuals of the 1910s accepted their use by executives, albeit with disapproval; indeed one compromise solution was developed, a flat-top desk with a roll-top cover. Similar considerations applied to the use of finish, ornament and fittings to distinguish executive desks from clerical desks. Whatever a neo-Georgian desk might do for the prestige of the user, its greater expense, its unnecessary number of drawers and the additional mouldings that acted as traps for dust and disease would have been anathema to the theorists.

Scientific management was no less partial in the advice it offered on office chairs. Clerks clearly needed the best design of chair for desk work and this was said to be swivel-based, with a wooden

Manager's desk of ornate design, U.S.A. mid 1920s. From W.H. Leffingwell, *The Office Appliance Manual*, 1926, p.734.

saddle seat and a slatted wooden back. If this was actually the chair that best minimised fatigue, it should have been thought equally appropriate for executives' use as well. Executives, however, were recommended to have cane seated chairs, which were said to be superior to wooden-seated ones; status debarred clerical workers from enjoying the same benefits. It was through inconsistencies like this that scientific management revealed itself to be much less than the science it claimed to be, and not so much concerned with overall office efficiency as with changing the character of clerical work.*

*See Braverman for further discussion.

Specialised Furniture in the Office

Once office work had been rationalised to the extent of allocating particular activities to each department and giving its clerks an identical work routine, there became a case for designing specialised furniture for the various functions. If the desk was thought of as a tool, then each clerical job needed its own tool. From about 1910, specialised desks were designed in increasing variety. One of them was the tub desk, with a top that was not a flat surface, but consisted of a range of trays for filing cards. However, it was in the development of typists' desks and chairs that specialised furniture received most attention. Partly because typing was a new form of office work and partly because it was women who did it, typing was treated from the start as a specialised activity, and typists tended not to perform other functions in the office. In the United States, patents for typing desks appeared in considerable numbers in the 1880s and 1890s; there was lull in applications after the turn of the century, but an increasing number of patents were registered from 1910 until the mid 1920s, when the number again fell off. The second phase of interest in typing desks was closely connected to the introduction of scientific management into offices. Typing had a particular attraction for the scientific managers, because the rate of work could be measured so easily. The techniques for recording typists' output included stroke counters on the machine to record each character typed, and, as typists soon discovered the advantage of using the space bar instead of the tabulator, squared transparent overlays from which the number of square inches of typed material could be read off. Characteristically, even the time required for the supervisor to carry out this action was recorded, and a standard rate was established of six sheets a minute.*

*Leffingwell, 1917, pp.147-149.

130

Tub desks in an American office, c.1915. The original caption explained, 'Every desk is visible to the supervisor. One clerk with a modern "tub" desk can handle as many cards as with the card drawer cabinet, and thousands of waste motions made by pulling out and putting in the drawers . . . are eliminated.' From W.H. Leffingwell, *Scientific Office Management*, Chicago, 1917, p.187.

The sunken well desk, the first to be purpose-designed for typing, had been introduced in the 1880s; it provided surfaces at different heights for the typewriter and for writing. The innovations of the 1910s involved making the height of the typewriter adjustable, with the storage drawers redesigned to reduce the time the typist spent reaching for paper and carbons, and devices added for holding the copy or shorthand notes. The fully developed result looked more like a work bench than a desk. At the same time, the sunken well started to go out of favour for stenographers' desks, on the grounds that their work was entirely limited to typing and so there was no need to provide an alternative height for writing. The well desk was gradually superseded by a low level flat top desk.

Purpose-designed typists' chairs were apparently not developed until the early 1920s, when use began to be made of the studies of

Sunken-well typist's desk, c.1915. There were many different designs for the two-level typing desk. From L. Galloway, *Office Management. Its Principles and Practice*, New York, 1919, p.187.

Right:
The purpose-designed typist's chair was developed through the study of posture. Note the way such studies perceive the worker as a mechanism. From W.H. Leffingwell, *Office Management*, 1927, p.413.

Far right:
Purpose-designed typist's chairs in use. The original caption drew attention to the similarity to factory furniture. From W.H. Leffingwell, *The Office Appliance Manual*, 1926, p.740.

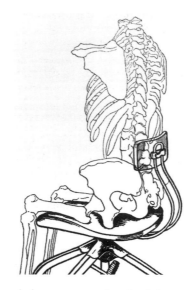

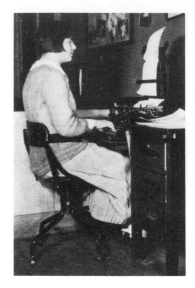

sitting posture that had been undertaken in factories. The new chairs were closely based on those designed for factory use: they were made of steel, with adjustable, upholstered seats and backs. Although they were efficient and comfortable, they looked unmistakably industrial. The widespread use of steel for office furniture on the grounds that it was more durable than wood (a questionable argument, since it was true of the material but not of the finish, which was easily scratched or chipped) had the effect of making the office more and more closely resemble a factory. To the theorists of scientific management, this association had great attractions, for it provided visible proof that their methods and analysis applied universally to all kinds of work, regardless of the social pretensions of the workers. The industrial appearance of office furniture and equipment in the inter-war years was not, as has been suggested, the result of an absence of design, or of the failure to conceive of any alternative image, but rather expressed a deliberate intention to associate office and factory.

Right:
Gestetner duplicating machine, c.1930. An overtly industrial piece of equipment. From *Design*, no.40, p.12.

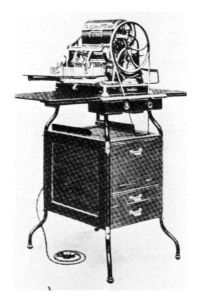

Far right:
Powers printing tabulator accounting machine, c.1935. This equipment could easily be mistaken for a machine tool.

Office Equipment

*An extensive selection of inter-war office equipment is illustrated in Vincent E. Jackson, *Modern Office Appliances*, London, 1936.

*Klingender, pp.86-98.

Powers-Samas accounting machine office, mid 1930s. But for the clothes of the clerks, there is nothing to distinguish this office from a factory.

With the exception of a few articles like dictating machines and telephones, most office equipment before 1940 was overtly mechanical and industrial in appearance. The appearance of the British Gestetner machine, as produced until the early 1930s, was typical: its general form was the result of primarily mechanical considerations, its mechanism was exposed, it was supported on a tubular frame structure and was painted black. This description would equally well fit most other items of office equipment made in Britain and America in the 1920s and 1930s; addressing machines, typewriters and mechanical accounting machines were equally mechanical in appearance.* There would be little reason to comment on them were it not for the fact that almost all items of office equipment underwent such a major change of image in the late 1940s and early 1950s as to leave little doubt that the original form of these machines was neither 'neutral' nor derived unthinkingly from factory tools and equipment. While the designs may have been determined partly by technical considerations, they nevertheless presented a strong set of associations that, by the 1950s, manuacturers were very anxious to discard.

While levels of employment were low, as they were in Britain and the United States in the 1920s and 1930s, offices had little difficulty in attracting staff. In the early 1930s, London employers were able to cut wages, sometimes by as much as half, and many clerks lost their jobs altogether.* In such conditions, no clerk was likely to make complaints about the work environment. Employers had little interest in making their offices appear other than highly utilitarian, which could be seen as the product either of indifference or of the desire to express efficiency. The early 1930s London accounting machine office illustrated below, with its heavy industrial-looking machines and plain decor, is distinguished from a factory only by the clothes worn by the clerks.

Management aims did not affect the design of all office machines in the same way. The appearance of some, including typewriters and adding machines, changed in a uniform way, but others, like dictating machines and telephones, acquired particular images, for reasons peculiar to their functions.

Underwood no.1 typewriter, 1897. An early typewriter, for use in offices.

After their arrival in offices in the 1880s, typewriters became increasingly plain and industrial in appearance. The only embellishments usually to be found distinguished machines from those of other manufacturers or assisted in faster and more efficient typing. The first changes in typewriter styling appeared not in office machines, but in portables.

Portable typewriters were originally intended for use by travelling salesmen and other itinerant businessmen who needed to type letters away from the office. From 1920s, however, typewriter manufacturers recognised, as sewing machine manufacturers had done earlier, that there was an enormous market among home users. At first, the association of typewritten letters with commerce resulted in a prejudice against them for personal correspondence,

Smith Corona portable typewriter, 1922. Early portables conformed to the industrial style of the office machines.

Business Equipment Topics, vol. LXXVIII, no.4, August 1931, pp.7-8.

Gestetner duplicating machine no.66, early 1930s. Restyled by Raymond Loewy from the model shown on p.132. From *Design*, no.40, 1952, p.13.

*R. Loewy, *Never Leave Well Enough Alone*, New York, 1951, pp.83-84.

Below:
Monarch portable typewriter, 1932. A low-priced portable designed for mass sales. From *Business Equipment Topics*, 1932.
Right:
Smith-Corona portable typewriter, 1932. A lightweight machine, clearly directed at the domestic market. From *Business Equipment Topics*, November 1932.

to which the marketing response was that even in the home their proper use was in business correspondence and that typewritten letters to bank managers and the like would achieve better results than handwritten ones.* The industrial appearance of the machines themselves, which made them seem unattractive in the home, was overcome by redesigning them in a more appropriate form.

In practice, there were two approaches to marketing portable typewriters. One was to produce the cheapest possible machine, however ugly it might be, and sell it on its low price. The more common alternative was to produce an attractive object, which cost very little more, especially as the manufacturers were aiming at a very large volume of sales. The machines made by Smith Corona in America from the early 1930s, and Olivetti in Italy from the mid 1930s are good examples: they were slim, cased in a single casting which ran around the keyboard, and finished in light colours instead of the customary black of office machines. The neat and elegant result succeeded in making the portable typewriter a popular object for home use. It was not until later that similar restyling was applied, for rather different reasons, to office typewriters.

A very few office equipment manufacturers in the 1930s re-designed their products in a way that anticipated the general changes of the 1950s. Such a firm in Britain was Gestetner, which had made a typically industrial-looking duplicating machine in the 1920s, but in the early 1930s employed Raymond Loewy to redesign it. His new design effectively demechanised it by enclosing the mechanism in a casing. Loewy described the design as a 'face-lift' job, in which he arrived at 'a form which enclosed everything that could be enclosed'.*

Interestingly, it was a face-lift that survived and continued to be used, with a few more wrinkles removed, for Gestetner duplicators until the 1950s. Although Loewy may not have been aware of it at the time, one reason for the continued success of his design lay in its recognition that the operator was not interested in seeing how the machine worked and would very much rather not have known that it was a machine at all.

When the typewriter was introduced in the 1880s, shorthand was the available and obvious method to use for taking down the spoken word to be turned into typescript. Shorthand and typing were at once acknowledged to be complementary skills, both of which were necessary for the typewriter to be of real use in the office.

Distributors wanted for the "MONARCH PIONEER"

A new practical and thorough-ly tested portable typewriter with standard keyboard of 42 keys. Net weight 9 pounds.

At the lowest price in history for a <u>Real</u> Typewriter
. . . . Unlimited Sales Possibilities

Edison phonograph, 1890s.
Despite the carved oak
cabinets, the first office
dictating machines were not
well received.

Dictating machines in an
American office, c.1915.
Interest in office dictating
machines revived through the
influence of scientific
management. From W.H.
Leffingwell, *Scientific Office
Management*, Chicago, 1917,
p.132.

From 1888, however, shorthand skill was threatened by Edison's development of the phonograph and its application as a business dictating machine. The promoters of the early phonograph believed that it would have a very limited appeal in the house, because it was expensive, its sound reproduction was mediocre, and there were problems in the quantity production of pre-recorded wax cylinders to play on it. It was seen as having a much more promising future as an office dictating machine. Edison's system was to rent phonographs to businesses through concessionary companies, which were set up in the United States in 1888, in Britain in 1892, and in Germany in 1894. The phonograph, though, did not turn out to be a success in the office; it was resented by stenographers, and it was too expensive and insufficiently advanced to offer any real savings in the office. Some office phonographs were supplied in elaborate ornamental cabinets, which were presumably part of an attempt to overcome the opposition of office staff and convince them that it was a prestigious piece of office equipment. Such attempts must have had little success, as all the Edison subsidiary companies had stopped promoting the phonograph as a dictating machine by the end of the 1890s and had turned to other markets for it.*

*V.K. Chew, *Talking Machines*, London, 1967, pp.14, 26.

Interest in the dictating machine was revived in the 1910s with the arrival of scientific management, which was attracted to shorthand-typing as an occupation in which it seemed that the separate tasks might advantageously be divided. All the time that a stenographer was taking down shorthand, her typewriter and her typing skills were idle, which the theorists saw as an offensive waste. The dictating machine made it possible effectively to separate the two tasks. Experiments in US government offices were quoted to show that the average cost of producing a letter could be reduced from 4.3 cents to 2.7 cents if dictating machines were used.* Such

*Schulze, p.36.

examples encouraged some businesses to install dictating machines, which were certainly common in large American offices by the 1920s. The American machines were marketed in Britain and Europe, where they seem to have been less common.

The dictaphone enabled the typist to devote all her time to typing, while the executive could dictate at any time that suited him. These inducements, with their cost savings, did not make the dictating machine a popular instrument with either shorthand-typists or executives. Special pleading by the office efficiency experts suggests that they realised how unpopular the dictating machine was, yet wanted to convince people of its value. The arguments put forward in its favour were not financial ones, but were to do with the quality of work. The dictating machine was alleged to encourage inspirational thought and closer concentration, and even improve letter-writing style:

'The dictator is guaranteed certain privacy of thought with the machine acting as a sort of silent, untiring stenographer, with no human failing or variableness with which to reckon. Moreover there is an absence of the human factor element which often intrudes itself between dictator and stenographer, and by reason of a peculiar sensitiveness on the part of the dictator prevents the best expression of his thought . . . Men who formerly dictated stilted letters . . . have been taught by the dictating machine to express themselves lucidly.'*

*W.H. Leffingwell, *The Office Appliance Manual*, 1926, p.344.

Such exaggerated praise was intended to overcome executives' worry that dictating machines would make relations in the office impersonal. Shorthand-typists had much stronger reasons for hostility, as one of their two skills was being eliminated and they were left working continuously at their typewriters, often in a typing pool where their rate of work was checked by a supervisor. Underlying all the special pleading in favour of dictating machines was the knowledge that it was not 'an entirely unknown occurrence for dictator and stenographer to engage in conversation entirely unconnected with the business in hand.'* The chance of cutting out time-wasting gossip made dictating machines highly attractive to office management experts. An additional attraction, and a further reason for hostility from both executive and typist, was that each wax cylinder was accompanied by a card on which the time of dictation and the time of typing had to be recorded; by looking at this, the office manager could find out the speed of production of each letter without having to watch his staff at work. The dictating and typing of a letter, which shorthand had kept as a personal affair controlled by two people, was made by the dictating machine into an impersonal process open to the scrutiny and control of the office manager.

Dictating machines in the 1920s and 1930s were very different in appearance from other office machines. They were boxed in cabinets with more obvious style to them than any other piece of office equipment, and the quality of the finish was high. The dictating machine was one of the few office machines used personally by executives, and it therefore needed a superior appearance to fit in with the other furnishings in his office and to avoid damaging his status by making him appear a machine minder. The machine needed to be at his service, rather than vice versa. In any case, the really efficient executive would need to have a dictating machine in his home. 'By placing a machine in his home, [he] may dictate

*W.H. Leffingwell, *Office Management*, Chicago and New York, 1927, p.465.

Dictaphone dictating machine, early 1930s. This was the machine used by the executive; the cabinet has the form and finish of a piece of furniture, and can be closed to conceal the machine. From V.E. Jackson, *Modern Office Appliances*, London, 1936, p.274.

Transcribing machine, in use by a typist, mid-1920s. Unlike the executive's machine, this showed no attempt to disguise its mechanical aspects. From W.H. Leffingwell, *The Office Appliance Manual*, 1926, p.336.

Edison Voicewriter, magnetic tape dictating machine, 1953. Scrupulous attention to the form of this machine made it suitable for use anywhere. From *Design*, no.83, 1955.

*Schulze, p.37.

*Manual of Modern Business Equipment: Dictating Machines, 2nd edition, 1962, p.22.

overflow work, or ideas that come to him.'* In order not to affront all the ideas of the separation of home from work, the machine's appearance had to reach the standards of home furnishing. On the other hand, the typist's transcribing machine was an obviously utilitarian piece of equipment. The conditions of clerical employment at the time made it unnecessary to appease shorthand-typists with stylish design to compensate them for the loss of one of their skills.

Apart from being unpopular, dictating machines were cumbersome, the quality of the voice reproduction was not good, and they needed the attention of an office boy to reshave the wax cylinders. These disadvantages discouraged much further extension of their use in the 1930s and 1940s. It was not until the 1950s that the introduction of the magnetic tape recorder provided a technically satisfactory machine that was small enough to be easily portable. Nevertheless, the machine still served the same function, and there was every reason for it to be just as unpopular as its predecessor.

Realising the large potential market for an efficient dictating machine, several manufacturers employed top designers to style their products, which were therefore closer to contemporary standards of high quality design than other office equipment. The Edison Voicewriter, designed by Carl Otto and marketed from 1953, was widely admired, but other makes were no less highly styled. The great advantage of the miniature tape machine was that it was portable and could be used not only in the office, but anywhere it could be plugged in. (Battery-powered models introduced a little later had no significant limitations on where they could be used.) Outside the office, dictating machines were most often used in cars or in executives' homes, where they raised the same problems as the original dictating machines and portable typewriters. If the meaning of home, as a place distinct from work, was to be preserved, dictating letters at home for later typing in the office was inadmissible. Yet advertisements for dictating machines in the 1950s did suggest that manufacturers expected them to be used in homes – hence the adoption of a domestic image, with smooth plastic casings, pastel colours and delicate controls, which gave dictating machines more affinity with portable radio sets than with other office equipment.

Dictating machine advertisement, England, 1955. As well as the 'a child can do it' copy line, the advertisement implied that dictating machines were likely to be found in homes. From *Office Magazine*, February 1955.

MY name's Johnny and I'm six. I haven't really got an Agaphone and this isn't my desk. But the Agaphone's so easy even I can use it. It doesn't matter if I press the wrong key—nothing goes wrong, and if I whisper into it—I can hear what I've said all over again as loud as anything. My Daddy says the Agaphone is easy to use and he likes it because it saves him lots of time. Sometimes he brings it home with him when he's busy and sometimes he uses it in his car.
Miss Brown that's Daddy's secretary likes the Agaphone too. She says she always gets away on time now and is never late for a date—whatever that is.
If you're as important as my Daddy, I think *you* should get an Agaphone.

Agaphone Small, Sound, Simple

M. & L. HAYCRAFT LTD.

ST. STEPHEN'S HOUSE (Adjoining Scotland Yard), WESTMINSTER, LONDON SW1

Telephone : WHItehall 9618/9

Up to an hour's dictation with the spools of wire held in a foolproof magazine. Can be used for conference recording. Time control enables dictation to be automatically located for playback. Signalling device warns the secretary of remarks, instructions, etc., which are not to be transcribed. Key controls are simple and positive. Small and compact. Handsome appearance. Operates on any voltage or can be used in a car.

Domesticating the Office: Post-war Office Design

During the 1950s and 1960s, not only did almost every item of office equipment undergo radical change in design, but so too did the entire environment of the office. In many cases, offices began to resemble the contemporarily-furnished homes of the wealthy. The decisive cause of this new image was the change in the market for clerical labour. On both sides of the Atlantic, the steady growth of the service sector of the economy created an increasing demand for clerical workers, while relatively full employment placed offices in direct competition with factories for the same labour. Factory employers tended to respond to these conditions by paying higher wages, but office employers chose in general not to compete on wages, and instead to rely on the greater respectability and 'pleasantness' of office work to attract people who might otherwise have gone into factories. The wage differential between industrial and clerical jobs was gradually eroded, so that by 1968 in Britain, the median earnings of women office machine operators were only 3% above those of semi-skilled factory machine operatives, while in the United States the median earnings of clerical workers had by

*Great Britain, Department of Employment, *British Labour Statistics Historical Abstract, 1886-1968*, London, 1971, Table 68; Braverman, p.297.

*L. Bruce Archer, 'Honest Styling', *Design*, no.108, 1957, p.38.

*Jon M. Shephard, *Automation and Alienation: a Study of Office and Factory Workers*, Cambridge, Mass., 1971, p.63; see also Braverman.

Data processing in a Manchester office, mid 1970s. Although this is called an office, the conditions of work differ little from those of a factory.

1971 actually fallen below those of all other urban occupations except service workers.* Although there had ceased to be any distinction between office and factory work in their material rewards, there was, however, a major distinction established in the images attached to the two kinds of work. To some extent, this had been achieved through devices such as the relabelling of all clerical jobs as 'secretarial work', but the major cause of the different perception of office work was the radical transformation of the physical environment of most offices. The overtly industrial references of pre-war offices were discarded as wholly unsuitable for the new labour conditions and replaced by a different set of references. Not only did the style of management change, but so too did the ambience, the style of the furnishings and of the equipment. As one industrial designer observed during the 1950s, the main object of office equipment styling became 'to identify the machine as an appliance for the office rather than the factory'.* Explicit though it was as an aim, finding a suitable image for the office presented considerable problems in practice, particularly since the actual changes taking place in the work of the office were tending in many cases to make it more rather than less like a factory.

Automation, and especially computerisation, are often said to have liberated office staff from dull and repetitive work but those advances have not affected all office workers in the same way. Management and executive staff have certainly benefited by the introduction of computers, which can provide them with more recent and more comprehensive data and necessitate their spending less time on interpreting it before making their decisions. But computers have also eliminated a wide middle range of clerks whose job was to prepare business data. In their place, computers have created a heavy demand for clerks to process the data into a form in which it can be used by a computer.* This group of workers, data processors and key-punch operators, are mostly women and work at a task more monotonous and repetitive than the preparation of ledgers ever was. Because punched cards are an easily visible and quantifiable product, the efficiency of each operator can be watched closely and standards of output set. The work is almost identical to that in many factories and is carried

IBM offices, Segrate, Italy, c.1980. The quality of furnishings, finishes and physical environment in the modern 'landscaped' office is inifinitely superior to that in most office workers' homes.

*Braverman, p.366.

out under a similar régime, often in buildings in the industrial zones of cities or their suburbs, or in provincial towns, since corporations have realised that there is no need for their data to be processed in high-rental central business districts. Thus two of the attractions of office work – the metropolitan environment and the chance to mix with other sorts and ranks of office workers – are lost: in location, as well in the conditions of work, much data preparation has become like factory work. The key punch operator has no knowledge of the process in which she is involved beyond what goes on in front of her, and her rate of work is set to a standard created initially by the scale of the investment in the capital equipment. The similarity between this and factory work has been acknowledged by employers as well as employees:

'The vice president of an insurance company, pointing to a room filled with key-punch operators, remarked: "All they lack is a chain," and explained himself by adding that the machines kept the "girls" at their desks, punching monotonously and without cease. And the workers themselves are under no illusions about their "white-collar" jobs: "This job is no different from a factory job except that I don't get paid as much," one operator in a large farm equipment office said.'*

Accompanying such jobs have been found all the signs of stress, proneness to sickness and dissatisfaction that are normally associated with assembly-line workers.

Computer operations represent office work at its most factory-like, while most clerical work is still concerned with the production of writing on pieces of paper. In the hands of an executive's personal shorthand secretary, who also makes appointments and receives visitors, office work can still be seen as a craft, made meaningful by the personal contacts between people. But the growing tendency in large corporations and government offices has been to eliminate the personal secretary, a position that is regarded as an inefficient use of labour, and to replace her by centralised typing services, so that the executive never dictates to anything but a tape recorder, and the typist never types from anything but a tape. The complete division of labour dreamed of by efficiency experts of the early part of the century has over the last twenty years increasingly become a reality.

The striking fact is that while office work itself has become more and more impersonal, the environment of offices has become infinitely more pleasant. Lighting levels and standards of heating and ventilation are now better than most office workers will have in their own homes, while the layout and furnishing of offices and the design of equipment have all been improved to a very high standard.* Even if the work made the place seem like a factory, the environment was designed to prove that it was an office. An indication of the significance attached to the office environment in attracting staff is the appearance from the late 1950s of the phrase 'modern office' in advertisements for clerical jobs in London evening papers.

Since the 1940s, two important developments in the layout and design of offices have affected working conditions. One was the 'landscaped' office, the other was the 'personalising' of office space. Office landscaping was developed in Germany in the late 1950s as an alternative to the regular rectilinear grids of desks favoured by scientific management theorists. 'Scientific' principles still applied in office landscaping, in that the layout was determined by work flows, though these no longer followed the straight lines that had been assumed to be correct before. Supposedly more efficient than the grid layout, the landscaped office also made distinctions between staff invisible. It gave the impression of obliterating hierarchies; only a trained eye could distinguish between the desk of a manager and that of a clerk.* Landscaped offices were generally furnished to a very high standard, carpeted throughout, and fitted with furniture which demonstrated taste and style, as well as being efficient. For a manager anxious to prevent his staff from feeling that they had become a clerical proletariat, the landscaped office was a valuable innovation.

The egalitarian appearance of the landscaped office brought with it an assumption that good personal relationships among staff mattered, as executives and clerks worked on the same floor in informal contact with each other. Instead of hierarchical layout and imposed silence, the landscaped office allowed the organisation of space to be determined not just by the dynamic of the worker's movements, but partly by his or her own choice, in which relationships with other people in the office might be a factor. In this way, the landscaped office proposed a different standard of behaviour, as the impersonality that had compelled people to wear a mask at work was replaced by a norm based on personal 'openness' and on the understanding of others as individuals. It looked like a place where people got on well together and enjoyed each other's company; since a large proportion of clerical staff in the post-war world consisted of married women looking for relief from the isolation of domestic life, this message carried a strong

*See *Interiors Second Book of Offices*, edited by J. Pile, New York, 1969; and S. Mullin, 'Some Notes on an Activity', *Planning Office Space*, edited by F. Duffy, C. Cave & J. Worthington, London, 1976, pp.16-21 (subsequently referred to as Duffy Cave & Worthington).

*F. Duffy & C. Cave, 'Bürolandschaft, an Appraisal', in Duffy, Cave & Worthington, pp.68-77; and F. Duffy, 'Bürolandschaft '58-'78', *Architectural Review*, vol.CLXV, no.983, January 1979, pp.54-58.

Director's office, Phoenix
Assurance Co., London,
c.1910. This interior is
indistinguishable from a room
in a private house of the same
date.

*R. Sennett, *The Fall of Public
Man*, Cambridge, 1977,
chapter 12.

attraction. To create an impression of personal friendliness and the
absence of oppressive management, landscaped offices used furnishings that suggested domestic interiors (albeit those of the
British and American commercial élite) and relied on the image of
home as the place in which people are authentically themselves
and as the source of all sincere personal relationships.*

Domesticity in the office was not a discovery of the 1950s. Half
a century earlier, the offices of some directors and managers had
been furnished as domestic interiors, usually in a traditional style,
Georgian or Louis XV; what was new was the provision of a high
quality environment for everyone below the managing director.
The tastefully furnished director's office in the early twentieth
century said, 'this is a place in which personal relationships and
gentlemanly behaviour matter more than purely commercial ones,'
with the implication, 'I am a man of culture and good taste with
whom you may be proud to do business.' In the landscaped office,
these messages were translated from individual into corporate
statements: 'in this office, it is our sensitive understanding of
personalities that makes things go,' and 'we are an enlightened

Company Secretary's office, Wincarnis Tonic Wine Factory, Norwich, in 1913. At a more modest level, this office, too, had some domestic touches in the pictures on the walls and the upholstered chairs.

Director's office, Metal Box Company, Reading, in 1978. The offices of top management use 'personal' features, that are usually, like the patterned upholstery cover, drawn from the domestic sphere, to distinguish the character of their occupants.

corporation, for whom you may be proud to work, or with whom you may be proud to do business.'

Scaling up the message from an individual to a corporate level lost part of the original meaning, as the environment no longer had anything to say about the worth of the individual. In compensation, it was acknowledged that senior management might still need private offices, and that they should have individual and personal furnishings for them; only thus could they impress other businessmen with their individuality. The senior executive's office would have a very high standard of luxury and comfort, but would also incorporate some notation of the occupant's individuality and

Centraal Beheer offices, Apeldoorn, Holland, in 1978. The interior of this building was a bare shell, and staff at all grades were encouraged to decorate their workspaces themselves, and even provide their own furnishings if they wished.

taste, often through the display of works of art on the walls or shelves. Some office designers have gone further and attempted to extend the licence to express individuality to less exalted staff by encouraging them to furnish their space with objects and pictures of their own. The most famous and extensive version of this principle is incorporated in the Centraal Beheer at Apeldoorn in Holland, designed by Herman Hertzberger. But even in more ordinary offices, the same principle can be seen in the posters, plants, photographs and mascots that staff bring in to decorate and personalise their work spaces. Even if any of these things would have been permissible in the scientifically managed offices of the inter-war years, the interiors were certainly never photographed showing them. Sticking up a poster or watering the plants would have deprived the firm of a few seconds of the clerk's time and, in any case, the expression of individuality was wholly against the 'scientific' principles. An office that could insist that all clerks should use the same style of pen nib and, if necessary, change their handwriting, would have been unlikely to approve of such overt displays of individuality as having pictures around the office.

The change from this state of affairs was deliberate and was the result of developments in the theory of management. Its origins were a series of experiments done between 1927 and 1932 by the Harvard Fatigue Laboratory at the Hawthorne Works of the Western Electric Co. to find ways of reducing fatigue and increasing output among a group of six women assembling telegraph relays. The researchers started by introducing breaks and rest periods into the day and changing the work schedules. They found that each new experiment produced better results than the last. In the twelfth experiment, they reintroduced the original working day, and output rose yet again, to a level that was higher than at any previous time during the experimental period. Puzzled by these results, the researchers were driven to conclude that the organisation of work, on which scientific managment had placed so much emphasis, was not important and that the key to the constant increase in output was connected to the relationship that had built up between the researchers and the workers, as well as in the strong personal attachments that built up amongst the six women, who came to see themselves as a special and privileged group. During the twelfth experiment, the researchers had started to interview the women in some depth about their attitudes to work, and their social life and opinions; this special attention was thought to be connected to the good results being obtained. The Hawthorne experiments and a later experiment on lighting levels for office workers showed that the study of the work of individuals in isolation, as practised in scientific management, was far less important than the study of the workers as part of a social group.

The 'Human Relations' school of management that developed out of the Hawthorne experiments emphasised the importance of the worker's relationships with other employees and with management, and was responsible for the changed attitudes towards office environments.* It had been found at Hawthorne that the women liked having a say in how the experiments were run. The lesson of this for management was that employees who had some influence on the organisation of their work would produce better results. Hence, workers who could influence the appearance of their surroundings could be expected to do better than those in offices of which the appearance and decoration were dictated by the management. On the other hand, an office in which the management had little control over the environment would fail to provide a corporate image, and would look inefficient. The Human Relations principle of management therefore set up some tension in the running of offices, between the need to promote the social relationships of office staff and the need to present a uniform image to indicate efficiency and constancy in the conduct of business. In resolving this and other conflicts in the organisation of offices, post-war furniture design played an important part.

With relatively full employment in the three decades after World War II putting clerical workers in a seller's market and encouraging them to change jobs frequently or move to factory work, employers chose a strategy of enhancing the respectability of office work and of making it seem unequivocally middle class rather than offering significantly higher wages. If the characteristics of factory work were routine, servility to the machine and rigorous efficiency, maintained by intensive supervision, the office was to be shown as fundamentally different in its apparently relaxed style of work, the absence of routine, the egalitarian relations and the subservience of machines. Nothing can describe the intended atmosphere better than the word 'friendly' which appeared so ubiquitously in advertisements for office jobs from the 1950s.

Even so, office hierarchies had to be preserved to avoid a descent into anarchy and chaos. The entire operation of bureaucracies and administrations depends upon knowing who is responsible to whom; without this certainty, the mainspring of the office would be lost. It was therefore important that the attractive appearance of office egalitarianism should remain no more than an appearance,

*The Hawthorne experiments are described in E. Mayo, *The Human Problems of an Industrial Civilization*, New York, 1933, chapter 3, and in more detail in F.J. Roethlisberger & W.J. Dickson, *Management and the Worker*, Cambridge, Mass., 1943, in which the principles of the 'Human Relations' school of management are also outlined.

although for it to have any useful effect, it had to be reasonably convincing. It was the capacity of office landscaping to contain this apparently insoluble contradiction in office work, between apparent egalitarianism and actual hierarchies, that made it so attractive as a system of design. The same ideas were represented in the design of office furniture in such a way as to make them seem not in the least contradictory, but entirely harmonious and compatible.

Post-war Desks and Equipment

In the context of the plain and utilitarian furniture manufactured in Britain during the post-war years, the desks that were custom-designed for senior staff in prestige offices were very much an exception. They followed high standards of contemporary domestic taste and were finished in light-coloured hardwoods, with rounded corners and legs, while the accompanying chairs were upholstered in brightly coloured materials. The intention was to break away from the drabness of pre-war prestige executive offices, which had usually been furnished in dark-coloured period furniture. This furniture was not produced in any quantity and was purely for managers and senior executives in a few image-conscious offices.

The quantity production of prestige furniture for offices began in the United States in the 1950s. The first and best known firm to do this was Herman Miller Inc., which in 1949 commissioned George Nelson to design a desk. The result, a minimal desk on a round-section chromed tube frame, has provided the form for a great many later designs. The original desk, however, was for executives and not for universal office use; it still preserved for the time being the distinction between executive and clerk. The extension of the smart, modern image to all ranks of staff can be explained partly by the demands of apparent egalitarianism and partly by the development of open-plan offices in which diverse

Office desk manufactured by Herman Miller, designed by George Nelson, 1949. This executive desk was the precursor of many office desk designs for the next thirty years.

There's a Status desk for non-stop directors,

. . . for dedicated young executives

and for pretty typists

Advertisement for Hille office desk range, 1961. The problem of office management in the 1960s was to create an illusion of equality while preserving hierarchies. This furniture range, designed by Robin Day, offered one solution. From *Design*, no. 202, 1965, p.72.

designs would have made it more difficult to sustain the vision of an orderly, and therefore efficient organisation. In Britain, Hille and Co. were the first office furniture manufacturers to make use of design to express the new ideas about management. Hille's innovation was to make furniture which had as much style as that of Herman Miller (whose designs they made under licence in Britain from 1958), and in which the style and quality were identical for all grades of staff, with desks for secretaries having exactly the same standards of elegance as desks for superior ranks. The Hille range of desks thus gave a semblance of common identity and even of equality to everyone in the office, while the differences between the desks made it clear that there were still hierarchies.

Offices of the *Liverpool Echo*, with the Herman Miller Action Office screen-mounted system, c.1975. Screen-mounted furniture, which enabled hierarchies to be visibly restored in open offices, became increasingly common after about 1970.

*I owe this explanation for the development of screen-mounted furniture to Francis Duffy.

It was the need to protect office hierarchies that was responsible for another major change in office furniture design in the 1960s: the introduction of screen-mounted furniture systems. Particularly as offices began to depend heavily on a new group of high-status but non-management professionals, the computer programmers and analysts, the openness of the original landscaped offices began to be broken up into partitioned cubicles formed by the screens.* While the uniformity of the design of a 'system' marketed by an individual firm maintained the apparent integrity of the organisation, the partitions allowed hierarchical divisions to be re-asserted.

The other changes in office desks have been less concerned with their image than with their use as a functional tool, involving their size and their relation to work routines. The enormous rise in rents, particularly in London, over the last twenty years has made office space a very costly commodity; unnecessarily large desks caused wasted space and were an expense to be avoided. The British Civil Service, which occupied much more office space in London than any other organisation, realised that very large savings could be made by economising on desk sizes. The range designed by the Ministry of Public Buildings and Works in the late 1960s aimed to make worktops the smallest convenient size for a single task; if a clerk needed more surface area, more units could be added, creating surfaces in sectors around him or her, a more economical use of the area than that given by a single large rectangular surface.* The addition of more standard units, rather

*J. Manser, 'New Thinking in Office Furniture', *Design*, no.236, 1968, pp.16-18.

Ministry of Public Buildings and Works prototype clerical desk, stage 1, 1968. The design economised on space and, to prevent personal filing, dispensed with drawers altogether, relegating storage to separate open units.

than the provision of different sorts of furniture, could also be used to indicate differences in hierarchy – always a problem in the status-conscious bureaucracy of the Civil Service. In the new clerical desks designed in the 1960s, such as the Ministry of Public Buildings and Works prototype, concealed storage space was reduced to the absolute minimum, usually one or at most two drawers, exclusively for stationery. (The MoPBW prototype design had no drawers at all.) All other storage was moved to exposed racks or shelves. This made private storage of papers and files by individuals virtually impossible, so that the desks ensured that the Civil Service practice of forbidding personal filing at all grades was observed. Nevertheless, office workers do need space for personal possessions, shopping, and so on. The first prototype of the MoPBW system provided a cage holding wire shelves, which, by being open, made it impossible to hide files in them. The wire racks, which also left the clerks' personal belongings on public display, were very unpopular, and later versions of the system gave them enclosed shelves, a compromise between office efficiency and the clerks' desire to retain some privacy in the office.

The MoPBW clerical desks were purpose-designed objects fitted to the functions of a clerk: although much more attention was given to their appearance, they had close affinities with the purpose-designed clerical desks of the early part of the century. However, as desks for specialised kinds of work, they conflicted with the idea that distinctions between office ranks should be minimised. Although there were still similarities between the appearance and finish of clerical and executive desks in the new

Ministry of Public Buildings and Works, prototype clerical desk, stage 2, 1968. Objections about the lack of personal storage space in the stage 1 design led to a compromise with an open shelf beneath the top.

Executive Desk, Gordon Russell Series 80, 1977. Storage has been entirely detached from the desk and placed in an optional independent unit, leaving a table with the finish of a domestic dining table.

*D. Rowntree, 'Desk and Chair: Basic Tools of Urban Life', *Design*, no.105, 1957, pp.16-21.

ranges of office furniture generated out of the study of work functions and marketed from the mid-1960s, there were some very big differences in form. In particular, the traditional executive's desk, which had served the combined purposes of storage, status symbol and defensive bulwark, was replaced in several ranges by a rectangular or round table with no storage facilities whatever. While this represents a victory for management science by finally wresting filing from even management and top executives, and also indicates the greater importance of small meetings in the modern executive's work, the designs did mark a change in image. The desk had become an object with wholly domestic associations and was in some cases quite indistinguishable from a contemporary domestic dining table. The same applied to chairs: back in 1957, Diana Rowntree wrote: 'There is difficulty in defining the difference between executive and dining chairs.'* Although table-like desks might seem to contradict the principles of generating furniture forms out of work studies, this was not entirely so. In all cases, the designers were as much concerned with image as with utility, and the image that mattered for the executive was personality, which has been consistently conveyed by reference to domestic environments, for, in contemporary Western society, home life is the only effective signifier of personal authenticity. We can see evidence of this in the way that politicians have to publicise details of their family lives, and in the ubiquitous framed photographs of wife and children, positioned on the executive's desk so that not only he but also his visitors can see them.

Office equipment also went through radical changes in appearance in the 1950s. Office typewriters, which had changed little in appearance since the last century, underwent a similar redesign to that which had already been given to some portable machines. From about 1950, almost all office typewriter manufacturers gave their machines light-coloured, all-enveloping steel cases which concealed the mechanism and attempted to give some elegance to the overall proportions. Some manufacturers had anticipated this general change, notably Olivetti, who had employed Marcello

Nizzoli to redesign their office machine, the Lexicon, as early as 1945. According to the advertising, the typewriter ceased to seem like a machine and became instead an instrument on which the typist, rather than being a mere operative, could reveal her talents in a virtuoso performance. If part of the point of being a secretary or a typist was not to be seen as a manual worker, then it was clearly important that typewriters should not look like machines, but should convey a more respectable and less oppressive image. The apparent demechanisation was made more complete in electric typewriters. Although they were in production from the 1930s, electric typewriters did not come into widespread use in America until the early 1950s and in Britain until the late 1950s. Although the electric typewriter is a more complex machine than the manual version, it is less mechanical for the operator, as it responds to the most sensitive touch: it has more of the qualities of an instrument than any manual typewriter. In their styling, electric typewriters have received more attention than manual ones. The most famous electric typewriter, the IBM Executive, with its fixed platen, had the least resemblance to a machine, while its two-tone finish and rounded form, the result of Eliot Noyes's design consultancy to IBM, make it closer to table-top art.

More recently, a new image for high technology, one which is unconnected with the industrial world, has been established. Technological design for space exploration has provided a new set

Advertisement for Adler Typewriters, 1960. Advertisers stressed the change that the new designs were intended to bring about in typists' self-image. From *Office Magazine*, September 1960.

Below:
Olivetti Lexicon 80 typewriter, designed by M. Nizzoli, 1945. Olivetti was the first manufacturer to make the standard office typewriter into an object of high style.

Bottom right:
Remington Standard typewriter,1950. Light colour and a faired casing gave the machine some elegance.

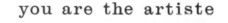

you are the artiste . . . .

Your touch on the keys, your virtuosity, produce the accomplished results which ensure your Chief's "applause" and a universal ovation!

ADLER IS THE INSTRUMENT OF YOUR CHOICE

Constructed with the superb technical skill and craftsmanship that ensures your complete confidence at the "overture" and "finale" of each working day. It is therefore not surprising that the Adler Universal receives the spontaneous acclamation of the World's Premier Typists!

ADLER *Universal*

BUSINESS EFFICIENCY EXHIBITION, OLYMPIA, OCT. 3-12. See us at STAND 157.
(De Luxe Balcony Level)

Above:
IBM Selectric Typewriter,
designed by Eliot Noyes, 1961.
Even greater attention was
given to electric typewriter
design than to that of manuals.

Right:
Olivetti 'Summa Prima' adding
machine, 1960. The blue plastic
case was a contrast to the black
metal covers of the pre-war
machines. From *Design*,
no.144, p.60.

*Ettore Sottsass Jr interviewed
by Stephen Bayley in BBC
'Horizon' programme *Little
Boxes*, 1980.

of references, so that, for example, a black finish on a machine no
longer signifies factory conditions, but high prestige and sophistication. Business machine manufacturers almost universally
stopped using black finishes in the 1950s, but the recent reappear-
ance of black for typewriters, such as Olivetti's Lexicon 83, and
other equipment suggests that the meaning of the colour is no
longer what it was.

Duplicating machines, adding machines, addressing machines
and even staplers have all received cosmetic treatment, normally
by being enclosed in pressed steel or moulded plastic covers and
given bright or light colours. Advertising has played less and less
on the cost-cutting, labour-saving aspects of the machines and has
emphasised instead what a pleasure it is to work in the company
of such attractive objects. All this has minimised the effect of
working in a factory and increased the sense of being engaged in
an enjoyable activity. That designers themselves were aware of
the changes in meaning that they were being called upon to create
was revealed by the remarks of the Italian designer Ettore Sottsass
Jr about his design for the Olivetti typist's chair, of which he said
in an interview:

'I thought that it can be a little bit humoristic, to get away from
this idea that the secretary has to sit on a mechanism. So that's a
little bit a Mickey Mouse object . . .'*

The falsity of the illusion about office work has nowhere been
greater than with the computer and its progeny, the microprocessor
and the word processor. Although the computer has been responsible for some of the dullest and most monotonous work in the
modern office, it has received more attention from stylists than
any other machine and has attracted the most glamour. So successful
has the packaging of the computer been that it has spawned a
whole aesthetic, which has been applied to many domestic products,
most of which, like the washing machine, have no connection
with the computer beyond the incorporation of a 'programme'.
The success of computer styling has not been confined to the
extent of its influence, but has also created great commercial benefits. For firms to continue to attract data processing staff, in
spite of the unpopularity of the work, they had to offer the incentive
of an atmosphere of non-industrial respectability in the computer
office. Attractive entrances, carpeted floors, tasteful colours and
finely designed equipment all contributed to make the work seem
'clean'.

As in all offices, the introduction of soft lighting, colour, varied
finishes and designs that suggested fun rather than brutal industrial

IBM 3667 Communication Terminal, 1974. The clean look of computer styling offered the illusion of a new, glamorous kind of work.

Below:
Olivetti Z9 typist's chair, designed by Ettore Sottsass Jr., late 1970s. Designs like this intentionally brought wit and humour into office furniture and equipment styling.

Right:
Olivetti Lexicon 830L, portable electric typewriter, 1978. In the late 1970s, the colour black returned to office equipment styling, signifying not factory efficiency, as it had in the 1920s, but sophisticated advanced technology.

efficiency all helped to persuade people of the importance placed upon personal relations. Nevertheless, the inescapable reality was that efficiency was the ultimate aim of the office. Though the means of attaining it may have changed, efficiency has been the main consideration behind the selection of every design for every article of office furniture or equipment during the twentieth century. However hard designers tried to blur the distinction between home and work, management aims remained at the root of all design for the office. It may be a compliment to say that an office looks like a home, but it is easy to see why there are few criticisms of a domestic interior worse than to say 'it looks like an office.'

7. Hygiene and Cleanliness

'Order and Cleanliness are the origins of Beauty.'*

*Th. Bondroit, 'Le bon goût à la Campagne', in *Congrès International de l'Enseignement Ménager*, 1908, vol.I, p.643, quoted in G. Heller, *Propre en Ordre*, Lausanne, 1979, p.190. Heller's book contains discussion, within the Swiss context, of many of the issues presented in the chapter.

In 1935, the industrial designer Raymond Loewy was invited by Sears Roebuck to design a new refrigerator. At this point, the market for refrigerators in America had been growing for a decade or so, and the emphasis in advertising was consistently on their life-enhancing, health-giving and hygienic properties. However, while a model like the 'Leonard' with its varnished wooden cabinet, may have been effective as a refrigerator, its appearance did nothing to support the manufacturer's claims that it 'offered hygiene'. Where such refrigerators had been angular and cumbersome, Loewy's design, the Coldspot, with its pressed steel casing and seamless finish, not only offered the operational efficiency of other refrigerators, but also conveyed an image of absolute cleanliness and hygiene. The seamless exterior and rounded corners, the brilliant white finish, and the absence of dust-catching crevices and mouldings (apart from the ribbing at the base of the bottom panel) all meant that when it was clean, it looked the physical embodiment of health and purity.

In the decades since the 1930s, the aesthetic of cleanliness has become the norm in the domestic landscape. The visible display of cleanliness seems to have been accepted unquestioningly as the proper appearance for household goods of all kinds. Likewise, the imagery of exaggerated hygiene appears in many other modern environments, such as trains, aeroplanes and public buildings.

Whatever the cause of the twentieth-century preoccupation with cleanliness, there is no doubt that notions about it have had as much effect upon design as have ideas of taste and beauty. As

Left:
The Leonard refrigerator, 1929. The varnished cabinet of this machine did not convey as well as that of the Coldspot the manufacturer's wish, that it be 'like a clean china dish'. From *Ladies' Home Journal*, May 1929, p.254.

Right:
Sears Roebuck Coldspot refrigerator, 1935. Styled by Raymond Loewy. The smooth finish, concealed hinges and door mechanism gave an impression of purity.

well as the visible evidence from the objects themselves, this judgement is borne out by the statements of designers. Among the most famous expressions of the beauty of cleanliness was Le Corbusier's 'Manual of the Dwelling' in *Vers Une Architecture*, published in 1923. The manual set out the requirements that clients should demand in their houses, and it began:

'Demand a bathroom looking south, one of the largest rooms in the house or flat, the old drawing-room for instance. One wall to be entirely glazed, opening if possible on to a balcony for sun baths; the most up-to-date fittings with a shower bath and gymnastic appliances.

'An adjoining room to be a dressing room in which you can dress and undress. Never undress in your bedroom. It is not a clean thing to do and makes the room horribly untidy . . .

'Demand bare walls in your bedroom, your living room and your dining room. Built-in fittings to take the place of much of the furniture, which is expensive to buy, takes up too much room and needs looking after.

'If you can, put the kitchen at the top of the house to avoid smells . . .

'Teach your children that a house is only habitable when it is full of light and air, and when the floors and walls are clear. To keep your floors in order eliminate heavy furniture and thick carpets.'*

*Le Corbusier, *Towards a New Architecture*, trans. F. Etchells, London, 1927, pp.114-115.

In Le Corbusier's own architecture of the 1920s, the imagery of hygiene was as important as that of machines, and it had an equally significant place in the work of countless other designers. However, unlike the rather exclusive aesthetic principles of design professionals that were based, for example, on abstract art or on machines, the principle of cleanliness has been not only shared by the uninitiated public, but has also been accepted enthusiastically as the basis of beauty in preference to other criteria.

Although cleanliness has a direct and scientifically proven relationship to health, this is not its only significance. As categories, cleanliness and dirtiness are almost as subjective as beauty and ugliness. The value of these definitions, which exist primarily in the eye of the beholder, is that they provide us with a means of sorting out our experience and of imposing order upon the world. A classic definition of dirt is that it is matter out of place: dirt is the label we attach to what we perceive as disorder, a state that is often regarded as threatening. Some semblance of reason is given to our apparently irrational fears by labelling dirt and disorder as unhygienic and the source of disease, a connection which is by no means always proven. According to the anthropologist Mary Douglas, who has discussed these matters at length in her book *Purity and Danger:*

'In chasing dirt, in papering, decorating, tidying, we are not governed by anxiety to escape disease, but are positively re-ordering our environment, making it conform to an idea. There is nothing fearful or unreasoning in our dirt avoidance: it is a creative movement, an attempt to relate form to function, to make unity of experience.'*

*Mary Douglas, *Purity and Danger*, Harmondsworth, 1970, p.12.

Evidently it is not purely a matter of personal taste, but is something derived from our culture. The process by which societies, as distinct from individuals, have established criteria of cleanliness is clearly complex and will repay historical as well as anthropological investigation.

Dirt, Disease and Anxiety.

There is good evidence that, in the late nineteenth and early twentieth centuries, people in Europe and America began to find dirt more alarming and to be increasingly anxious about cleanliness. Dirt could assume a terrifying character that it had never before had. But in spite of all the discussion about hygiene that took place in the early part of this century, it is impossible to say whether a greater dislike of dirt actually caused people to become cleaner. There is only the vaguest of objective evidence about standards of cleanliness at different times in history. The single fact that Louis

'Lysol' Advertisement, 1918. Advertisements for disinfectants and cleaning products are one indication of greater anxiety about hygiene in the early twentieth century. From *Ladies' Home Journal*, April 1918, p.110.

XIV is alleged never to have washed in his life now seems so extraordinary that some change must have taken place in accepted standards of personal hygiene. Equally, the widespread introduction of baths and bathrooms into houses from the late nineteenth century, while it may not have made people any cleaner (for it is not evidence that they washed more often), was a sign that they cared more about cleanliness. Many other changes point to the same conclusion. Thus, the widepread replacement of browns and reds by white in interior decoration from the end of the nineteenth century at least in part reflected a wish to see greater cleanliness in the home, but again, it does not indicate that life was objectively any cleaner.

Although it is probably impossible to give conclusive reasons why cleanliness came to matter so much more in the early twentieth century, some ideas are suggested by Mary Douglas. In *Purity and Danger*, she expresses the idea that anxieties about pollution arise when the external boundaries of a society are threatened, or when the lines defining the internal relationships in a culture are threatened, or when dangers arise from internal contradictions within the morality of the culture.* If we follow her theory, we might expect the rapid social change and disintegrating social boundaries that came with the increasing political power of the working class to be behind the middle-class preoccupation with bodily, domestic and public cleanliness in the early part of this century. Even if it is impossible to prove that the fetish for hygiene was caused by bourgeois fears of losing social and political authority, there are enough signs of strong class prejudice in the movement for greater hygiene to suggest some relationship. It seems not implausible that a regimen of cleanliness and order should have been adopted by the middle class as a means of resisting social upheaval and of providing some psychological security against it.

From the 1890s, almost everywhere in Europe and America, steps were taken to improve habits of hygiene. The pressure for reform was strongly middle-class in character, coming from professionals and social reformers. Their attention extended into many departments of life, from dress to methods of dusting, from the problem of alcoholism to the feeding of infants, from sexual practices to the design of dwellings; home, shop, factory, school, railway carriage and street all received meticulous consideration. The reformers seem to have succeeded, without great difficulty, in persuading the majority of the middle class to share their belief that hygiene and health lay at the root of all social problems.

The initial aim in improving standards of hygiene was to reduce the number of deaths from infectious diseases. In this respect, the campaign of the 1890s and early 1900s was a continuation of the public health movement of the 1840s and 1850s, but although the motives were the same, the means of achieving them had changed. In the mid century, public health reform had concentrated on sanitary improvements that involved state or municipal action: the improvement of drainage and water supply, and the demolition of slums. By the 1890s, better water and drains had significantly reduced the incidence of typhoid and cholera, but other diseases, particularly tuberculosis, occurred, if anything, more frequently, while the high rate of infant mortality was a universally recognised problem. It was to these problems that health reformers turned their attention in the 1890s.

*Douglas, pp.146-147.

In the mid nineteenth century, the most widely accepted explanation for the occurrence of disease had been the miasmatic or zymotic theory, which attributed it to a process of spontaneous combustion that was supposed to occur in foul, stagnant air. According to this theory, the best way of preventing disease was to make sure that there was constant ventilation everywhere. By 1890, however, the zymotic theory was in the process of being superseded in scientific circles (though not yet more widely). The work of Louis Pasteur and Joseph Lister in the 1860s had established the basis for a germ theory, and in the early 1880s, the bacilli of typhus, cholera and tuberculosis were identified. The discrediting of the zymotic theory meant that fresh air and ventilation were no longer the prophylactics that had been supposed. Health reformers therefore transferred their attention to anything that might carry germs: to flies, dirty clothing, unwashed hands and, above all, to dust; everything that might be described as dirt was now linked with the transmission of disease.

Because most of the newly identified carriers of disease were beyond the scope of state or municipal action, there was no means by which direct public intervention could bring about lasting improvements. As cleanliness of houses and bodies depended upon individuals, the only means of reform was through education.

Up to this point, there was nothing in the movement for hygienic reform that a reasonable person could disagree with. It is only in the means employed to establish the new standards of hygiene that the controversial nature of the movement becomes apparent. From the 1890s, a wide variety of measures were introduced to encourage a more responsible attitude towards the prevention of disease. Schools began to teach hygiene, schools of motherhood were established, notices prohibiting spitting were displayed in public places, organisations like Women's Institutes and the Boy Scouts spread propaganda about cleanliness, and health visitors were added to the staff of local authorities and public health departments to carry the message of hygiene into people's homes.*

*On schools of motherhood, see A. Davin, 'Imperialism and Motherhood', *History Workshop Journal*, no.5, Spring 1978, pp. 9-56; on schools of household management, see A. Moll Weiss, *Les Ecoles Ménagères à L'Etranger et en France*, Paris, 1908; Heller describes the various measures introduced in Switzerland to educate the public in higher standards of cleanliness. A system of teaching hygiene to Boy Scouts is described by E.Y. Tilley, *Healthy Man Badge for Boy Scouts*, Glasgow, 1923.

The whole movement was strikingly middle class in outlook. Health and hygiene may have been matters for all classes, but the way in which the reformers treated the issues was entirely different for the working class and for the middle class. The reformers were concerned to teach the working class new habits and new ways of life, without which they believed that all other attempts at social reform, whether in housing or education, would be negated by the continuing likelihood of epidemic diseases. Apart from the obvious humanitarian impulse, the middle-class interest in the hygiene of the proletariat also reflected the material consideration that less illness and death amongst the working population would increase the abundance of labour and therefore lead to greater wealth. Beyond these conscious and rational motives, there was perhaps an unconscious desire to teach habits of order and cleanliness to the working class in order to establish some control over the way of life of a part of society by which the bourgeoisie felt threatened. By contrast, the presentation of hygiene for the middle class was more of a voluntary affair, often associated with vitality, relaxation and sport.

In campaigning for improved standards of cleanliness, the reformers used one or both of two sets of arguments. One appealed to reason and was based upon scientifically proven facts about

Housewifery Lesson, Morden Terrace School, London, 1908. From 1882, all London schoolgirls were taught domestic work. This is a practical exercise in cleaning and polishing.

disease and bacteria. The other was wholly emotive and relied on arousing feelings of anxiety and guilt about dirt. On the whole, the arguments based upon scientific logic were less effective than those which appealed to emotion, mainly because the rational arguments fell foul of prejudices about social class, whereas the emotive arguments did not. Ultimately, however, none of the arguments rivalled design as a means of implanting the idea of the importance of cleanliness. Only when advertisers, designers and manufacturers began to make use of the imagery of hygiene did the general public fully assimilate the lessons which the hygienists had been teaching.

One area on which the reformers had concentrated was the teaching of hygiene in schools, and something of the flavour of their campaign can be found in the way that domestic subjects were taught in London schools around the turn of the century. From 1882, all girls in London Board Schools had been given some instruction in basic cookery and housework to equip them for domestic service (their most likely occupation upon leaving school) as well as to prepare them for future marriage. Because existing school buildings lacked adequate accommodation for teaching domestic subjects, special centres were built, and the amount of teaching was increased during the 1890s. A formal syllabus was drawn up for a three-year course in cookery, laundry and housewifery that was introduced in 1898. It emphasised that the theoretical aspects of these subjects were to be taught and that girls should learn the scientific principles underlying the activities

*Final Report of the School Board for London, 2nd edition, revised, London, 1904, p.122-126.

as well as merely the practice of them.* Nevertheless, in spite of the emphasis upon scientific knowledge, it is clear from the text-books and examination papers that much of the teaching was very dogmatic and designed to condition the girls in responses for which there could be no 'scientific' justification. Among the exact information about the nutritional value of foods and the causes of diseases in one textbook, the following passage occurs in a section entitled 'The Evils of Disorder':

'. . . nothing conduces to peace and ease of mind more than tidy surroundings. Disorder can only be avoided by daily routine and the deliberate determination not to have the routine interfered with unless in exceptional cases, as illness. If the time which should be spent in washing or turning out a certain room is passed with a gossiping neighbour, the whole of the day's work will be upset and the work of one day will be put on to the next.'*

*M.M. Burgess, Health, London, 1914, p.53.

In the girls' examinations, the mixture of scientific detachment and emotional conditioning is particularly apparent. Fairly typical were the following questions from an 1893 examination on the theory of housework:

—What is the proverb about cleanliness?
—Describe how you set to work to clean a bedroom, and give any reasons for the order in which you set about doing so.
—In dusting a room, how do you make sure that the dust is really removed?
—Of what substances does dust usually consist?
—Why is it unwholesome, and in what diseases would it be danger-ous to breathe the dusty air?*

*Joint Committee, School Board of London, City and Guilds of London Institute, and the Drapers' Company, 'Manual Training Classes: Theoretical Examination in Housewifery, 21 January 1893', (SBL 1423, Greater London Council Records Office).

Similar domestic economy curricula were introduced around the same time in other countries.* In most cases, there was the same combination of social values and moral responses taught without distinction from scientific and rational principles.

*See Heller; Moll Weiss, 1908.

Opposite:
Learning to bathe an infant,
Childeric Road School,
London, 1908. The lesson is
being given on a doll.
Equipment for laundry lessons
hangs on the wall behind.

In practice, the logic of the hygienists often conflicted with their social prejudices. On the basis of scientific rationalism, there was an optimum hygienic solution for every aspect of life, whether dress, housing or working environments; strictly adhered to, the hygienists' principles should have made these equally applicable to all classes, but the general determination of the bourgeoisie to preserve visible signs of class distinction meant that these principles were almost invariably compromised. One example of inability to overcome class prejudices was in railway carriages. Because these were potentially unhealthy places, their design and furnishing came under severe criticism from hygiene reformers, as in the following passage written by a French doctor in 1907:

'Varnished wood, hardened leather, with rounded angles in the corners to prevent dust traps that defy cleaning, are what one ought to find in cabs, buses and railway carriages.

'But custom, perpetuating the traditions of apparent luxury . . . has decided otherwise . . . The seats and furnishings of carriages are in cloth or velvet; and as if these materials were not enough to retain dust, they are luxuriously upholstered in such a way as to multiply the corners inaccessible to cleaning done with even the best will . . .

'Certainly there would be no comfort in these first class carriages for the well-to-do without, for example, thick carpets; but these only aggravate, by their dangerous filthiness, the general insalubrity of the surroundings.

'It is enough on a clear, sunny day to observe what happens in a carriage on the entrance of a passenger, and especially of a lady passenger, to get an idea of the dirtiness of such a carriage, said to be luxurious.

'Each step of the passenger on the carpet, each movement, whether putting down the suitcase, or sitting down, is the occasion for a cloud of dust to arise from the surface touched . . .

'And as it must be supposed that convalescents with contagious skins, people with colds, flu, and above all tuberculosis are lodged in these compartments, one can easily deduce the qualities of the air that are going to nourish, for a greater or lesser length of time, the newly arrived passengers.'*

*Dr J. Héricourt, *L'Hygiène Moderne*, Paris, 1907, pp.171-173.

Ideally, the improvement of railway carriages would have meant the replacement of all dust-retaining surfaces and materials by wood, linoleum, American cloth or leather.

However, the difficulty in applying the hygienists' principles was that in all European countries railway companies provided different classes of passenger accommodation. (In the United States, railways had originally operated with only one class, but the widespread introduction of Pullman cars in the late nineteenth century meant that in practice they also had two classes.) Railway policy was to provide progressively more uncomfortable accommodation in the lower class carriages to discourage those who could afford expensive tickets from buying cheaper ones. The result was that, although first class was the most comfortable, it was also the least hygienic, while the spartan seats and bare floors of the third and fourth classes met the hygienists' requirements most closely. Here it was possible to keep the floors uncarpeted and to cover what upholstery there was in American cloth rather than conventional upholstery fabric. First class accommodation,

A. Solomon: *First Class – The Meeting*, oil painting, 1854.

*On the social distinctions in railway carriages, see C.E. Lee, *Passenger Class Distinctions*, London, 1946, and C. Hamilton Ellis, *Railway Carriages in the British Isles from 1830 to 1914*, London, 1965, pp.63-65.

on the other hand, remained relatively unaffected by hygienic arguments: carpets, curtains and soft upholstery – all dust-retaining materials – continued to be used, with only slight changes to eliminate the most unhygienic parts of the decor.* Although the logic of the hygienic principles was to abolish all differences in accommodation in favour of a single optimum design, such a reform would have conflicted with the policies of the railway companies and the social prejudices of passengers. In the face of such prejudices, the 'scientific' arguments of hygiene and cleanliness had to give way and be compromised.

First class railway compartment, Great Western Railway, 1911. Comfort, without regard for hygiene. The buttoned upholstery, carpet and numerous mouldings came to be regarded as hazards to health.

A. Solomon: *Second Class – The Parting*, oil painting, 1854. Solomon uses the customary contrast between the plushness of the first class carriage and the sparsity of the second class to bring out the poignancy of his subject.

First class railway compartment, Great Western Railway, 1937. Twenty six years later some concessions to hygiene had been made in the elimination of the buttoning and the mouldings, but the retention of dust-absorbing fabric upholstery shows that comfort still mattered more to railway companies and their passengers than the logic of the hygienists.

Bathroom, 28 Ashley Place, Westminster, London, c.1895. The first plumbed-in baths in the houses of the well-to-do usually had wooden surrounds. The decor of the room often did not differ greatly from that of the rest of the house.

Hygienic rationalism again came into conflict with established social conventions as a result of the introduction of baths and bathrooms into working-class homes. In Britain, plumbed-in baths had begun to be installed widely in middle-class houses from the 1880s, but they remained virtually unknown in working-class houses until the 1920s. Most of the early baths and bathroom fittings were designed as if they were pieces of furniture, with porcelain baths and basins encased in mahogany cabinets, sometimes of quite elaborate design. In appearance, bathrooms were not greatly different in character from other rooms in the house; indeed, in some cases, baths were installed in the dressing rooms of houses that had not previously had bathrooms. Around the turn of the century, though, the whole conception of the bathroom and the design of its fittings changed. Bathrooms acquired great importance in the war on dirt and disease, and conditions of

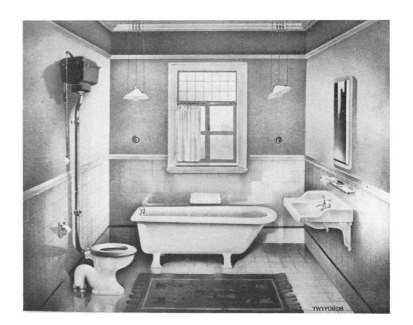

Twyfords, J7 Bathroom, 1911. Conforming to the view that bathrooms should meet higher standards of hygiene, sanitary ware manufacturers started to make all their baths free-standing in the early 1900s. From Twyfords 1911 catalogue.

Harmsworth's Household Encyclopaedia, vol.I, 1923, p.240.

absolute hygiene were expected in them. As *Harmsworth's Household Encyclopaedia* put it,

'There is no room where cleanliness and neatness are more necessary . . . No bath should be fixed except in such a way that every part, underneath or at the sides, can be easily got at and cleaned. Woodwork, whether as a rim to the bath or as a casing around it, is to be avoided at all costs . . .'*

These strictures were reflected in the design of baths, which from around 1900 were no longer installed with cabinetwork around them, but stood free on legs.

In early twentieth-century Britain, the possession of a bath, in a bathroom, was regarded as a major sign of middle-class status. Somerset Maugham wrote in 1922 that 'the matutinal tub divides the classes more effectively than birth, wealth or education.' However, baths were by then already beginning to appear in working-class homes in Britain. The new houses subsidised by the State from 1919 all had baths, many with separate bathrooms. The baths were generally of white-enamelled cast iron, standing on legs – virtually the same utilitarian, hygienic objects as were being installed in middle-class homes.

By 1930, fixed baths were sufficiently common in working-class homes to have lost their exclusively middle-class image. However, attempts were made to preserve the bath as a mark of class distinction. One way of doing this was through myths about the uses to which baths were put (the British coals-in-the-bath myth had variants in other countries – in Switzerland, it was rabbits in the bath), and the other was through the middle class seeking a new image for its own bathrooms. In the new designs for fittings that appeared around 1930, baths and washbasins were often coloured and their extremities were concealed behind panels, walls were tiled, and a whole range of matching accessories was supplied to make a harmonious bathroom. Unlike the bathrooms of previous decades, and those supplied in working-class houses, which had an ill-assorted assembly of fittings, the

167

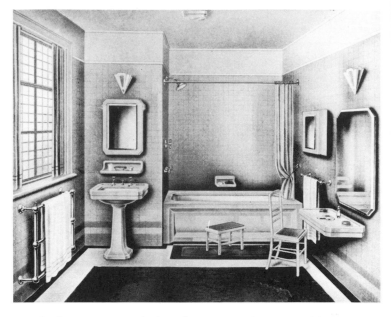

Twyfords bathroom suite, The Adamant, 1935. By the 1930s, hygienic all-white bath fittings were considered too like the bathrooms in state housing to be attractive to the middle classes, and manufacturers introduced coloured fittings in suites of co-ordinated design.

*This discussion of bathrooms is based on M. Swenarton, 'Having a Bath', in *Leisure in the Twentieth Century*, Papers given at the Second Conference on Twentieth Century Design History, London, 1977, pp.92-99.

new bathrooms were designed as a complete ensemble and emphasised comfort and beauty as well as hygiene. These bathrooms enabled their owners to see them as different in nature and even in function from those in working-class homes, thus preserving something of the value of the bath as a mark of class difference in the face of the hygienists' logic that every home should have one.*

Because rational, scientific arguments presented such difficulties, the hygienists turned increasingly to methods that exploited guilt. However, before guilt could be brought into play, cleanliness had to be transformed from a physical problem into a moral one. Attempts to do this through education tended to be clumsy, and at times ludicrous. Thus, an English school textbook, *Fighting Dirt*, by Ernest Hood, published in 1916, set out to present hygiene in an amusing and simple manner. Its premise was that the allies of disease, which were dirt, flies, breathing through the mouth, spitting, impure air and darkness, could be identified with the forces of evil. Through the allegory of warfare, hygiene was presented as a constant battle, with the body as a fort always in danger of attack by enemy germs (represented in the illustrations by German soldiers). Only by constant vigilance against the forces of disease could the body survive and be victorious.

The hygienists built up anxiety about cleanliness by teaching that every trace of dirt was a potential source of disease. This easily accepted notion was misleading since dirt and disease are not strictly comparable: dirt is a personal value, not an absolute, whereas disease and germs do have a verifiable physical existence. Once dirt was identified with disease, nothing short of absolute cleanliness could pass as satisfactory. In a book on household management published in France in 1906, Augusta Moll Weiss wrote about the housewife's duty to cleanliness:

'An object may be said to be clean when it is free from all stains and all dust. To struggle against dust, to remove it, whether from the surface of the body, from furniture or clothes, whether by cleaning the floors or renewing the atmosphere, is to do the work of the hygienist, fulfilling one of the most essential tasks of the housewife. The desire for material order must end up becoming a sort of reflex action, and even more the desire for cleanliness must end up becoming a real *need*. Disorder and lack of cleanliness should cause a sort of *suffering* in the mistress of the house.'*

*A. Moll Weiss, *Le Livre du Foyer*, 2nd edition, Paris, 1912, p.11.

Put in these terms, the condition of total cleanliness was comparable to a religious state of grace, and just as unattainable. Yet, within twenty or thirty years of the publication of Moll Weiss's book, her attitude towards cleanliness had become widely accepted. Housework and cleaning did gain enormous emotional significance, while every trace of dirt and every impure smell became grounds for guilt and anxiety. As R.S. Cowan has written, 'cleaning the bathroom sink was not just cleaning, but an exercise for the maternal instincts, protecting the family from disease.'* The slightest deviation from perfect cleanliness was a cause for social anxiety, since the invisible passage of germs could put the health of the family, companions and even the entire nation at risk.

It seems most unlikely that a few hours a week of school time, plus a few books and magazine articles could have been responsible

*R. Schwartz Cowan, 'Two washes in the morning and a bridge party at night: the American housewife between the wars', *Women's Studies*, vol.III, no.2, 1976, p.151. See also R. Schwartz Cowan, 'The "Industrial Revolution" in the Home: Household Technology and Social change in the Twentieth Century', *Technology and Culture*, vol.XVII, no.I, January 1976, pp.1-23; and 'Microbes and Housework', chapter 5 of B. Ehrenreich and D. English, *For Her Own Good, 150 years of advice to Women*, London, 1979.

Clean your refrigerator with Old Dutch every week. This is of utmost importance, especially in the summertime when foods spoil so easily — so many health troubles are caused by food contaminated in an unclean refrigerator.

Old Dutch safeguards your refrigerator with

Healthful Cleanliness

an important health protection

Old Dutch Cleanser — Chases Dirt

The most important thing you can put into your refrigerator is *Healthful Cleanliness*. You need it to keep food pure and wholesome. The surest way to keep the refrigerator sanitary, fresh and sweet is to clean it regularly with Old Dutch.

Old Dutch is a natural cleanser whose basic ingredient, "Seismotite," is of distinctive character and efficiency. Through the microscope you see it as thousands of flaky, flat-shaped particles. There is nothing else like it for removing dirt. With the visible uncleanliness it takes away impurities you cannot see. Old Dutch chases all dirt, none is left behind!

Old Dutch doesn't scratch. This drawing of a highly magnified Old Dutch particle shows how these particles, like tiny erasers, remove the dirt by a clean sweep without scratching. Safest for all cleaning because it contains no grit.

Grit scratches. This drawing of a highly magnified gritty particle shows how grit scratches. Scratches not only mar the beauty of surfaces, but are lodging places for dirt and often dangerous impurities. Avoid harsh, scratchy grit.

Old Dutch Chases Dirt — Protects the Home

The Symbol of Healthful Cleanliness

Advertisement for Old Dutch cleanser, 1928. Advertising took up the gospel of hygiene and preached it more effectively than the rational arguments of hygienists. From *Ladies' Home Journal*, July 1928, p.39.

for such widespread hygiene fetishism. There must have been other reasons, and amongst the possible causes we should consider the effects of design and advertising. From about 1920, the design of a very disparate range of articles and complete environments began to embody ideas of cleanliness, while the advertisements for the same products warned of the consequences of neglecting health and cleanliness which ranged from emotional rejection by loved ones to social ostracism, illness, death and national downfall. The design of the products themselves embodied the same message of obligatory cleanliness. In an appliance like Loewy's 'Coldspot' refrigerator, the pristine whiteness and seamless finish ensured that the slightest stain would clamour for instant removal. The Coldspot's appearance, like that of innumerable other appliances and artefacts, was a continual reproach to slovenly ways, an object lesson in cleanliness. In a world filled with such images and forms, ponderous and time-consuming instruction in the virtues of domestic cleanliness ceased to be necessary.

Healthy Design: Images of Cleanliness

As design has not always been used to convey ideas about standards of cleanliness, it is worth investigating how this function has been developed. The belief that design, rather than, say, prayer, custom or morality, might contribute to health originated in the eighteenth century with attempts to find ways of reducing mortality in prisons and hospitals. Observing that patients nursed in draughty barns and tents stood more chance of recovery than those nursed

WALES' AMERICAN SCHOOL CHAIRS.

No. 1.

These chairs are plain and substantial. Each chair is based upon a single iron pedestal, which is secured to the seat of the chair at the top, and to the floor of the school-room at the foot. The center-piece of the chair-back descends directly into the foot of the iron pedestal, intersecting the back of the seat as it passes, in such a manner as to form a *back stay*, thereby producing in the chair, as a whole, the greatest possible degree of firmness and strength.

No. 2.

American School Furniture, c.1850. The child's health and posture determined the designs: the chairs were graded in size so that there was always a chair just the right height for the child's feet to rest on the floor without the muscles of the thighs pressing on the front edge of the seat. The backs were to rise above the shoulders, and the chairs were fixed close to the desk so that the back was always supported. From H. Barnard, *School Architecture* 5th ed., New York, 1854, p.350.

No. 2 represents an improved school desk for two scholars.

*Sir John Pringle, *Observations on Diseases of the Army in Camp and Garrison* 2nd edition, London, 1753, pp.104-106. The effects of ideas of hygiene upon hospital design are discussed in J.D. Thompson and G. Goldin, *The Hospital: a Social and Architectural History*, New Haven and London, 1975; and A. Forty, 'The Modern Hospital in England and France: the Social and Medical Uses of Architecture', in A.D. King (ed.), *Buildings and Society*, London, 1980. The application of the same ideas to prisons is discussed in R. Evans, *The Fabrication of Virtue*, Cambridge, 1982, chapters 3 and 4.

*J.R. Tenon, *Mémoires sur les Hôpitaux de Paris*, Paris, 1788, pp.160-167.

*H. Barnard, *School Architecture*, 5th edition, New York, 1854, pp.341-379, and E.R. Robson, *School Architecture*, London, 1874, pp.359-402.

*F. Nightingale, *Notes on Hospitals*, London, 1859, p.16.

*H.C. Burdett, *Hospitals and Asylums of the World*, London, 1893, vol.IV, p.26.

in conventional buildings, certain doctors argued that a copious flow of fresh air was likely to make buildings healthier.* If hospitals could be designed to be naturally self-ventilating, it was supposed that the buildings could themselves become instruments of cure, independent of the treatment provided within. The influence of this principle extended beyond the design of hospitals to such institutional buildings as schools and prisons, and to working-class housing. For all of these, designs were developed during the nineteenth century that were both self-ventilating and intended to have a beneficial effect on the health of the occupants.

Some authorities extended their arguments from the designs of building to furniture and utensils. For example, in 1788, the French surgeon J.R. Tenon stated in his great treatise on hospitals that properly designed hospital beds could be a means of cure, and he gave eight pages to the form of the ideal bed.* In similar discussions about school desks in the following century, it was held that certain designs would contribute to good posture and healthy physical development, while others would have the opposite effect.* These discussions set important precedents for the principle that design might affect health.

The early hospital reformers had regarded cleanliness as important but secondary to good ventilation and not until the middle of the nineteenth century did it begin to rank equally. Some responsibility for this can be attributed to Florence Nightingale, whose work of nursing the sick and wounded of the Crimean War had made her a national heroine. On her return to England in 1856, she devoted herself to improving the quality and status of nursing. Because she had seen at Scutari that the hospital environment had a marked effect upon patients' chances of recovery, she became strongly committed to the improvement of hospital buildings. Amongst her other requirements, she placed great stress on the design of buildings that were easy to keep clean, and extended the principle to furnishings and utensils for the hospital or sick-room. For instance, she wrote:

'For all eating, drinking and washing vessels, and for other utensils, the use of glass or earthenware is superior to that of tin or any other metal, on account of its greater cleanliness. Notwithstanding the greater amount of breakage and of expense, glass or earthenware is therefore best whenever possible. Some kinds of tin vessels cannot by any amount of cleaning be freed from an unclean smell.'*

Florence Nightingale's influence extended far outside the hospitals, and it is common to find her instructions to nurses on cleaning methods repeated in late nineteenth-century household manuals. She believed that things should be seen to be clean. The discovery that germs were the cause of disease gave some scientific basis for Florence Nightingale's prejudice against dirt, and demands for absolute cleanliness in hospitals became more emphatic. Strong preferences began to be shown for pure white utensils and sanitary fittings which could be made visibly clean. The great authority on hospitals, H.C. Burdett, wrote in 1893 of water closets that: 'The whole should be white, and no ornament of any kind should be permitted.'*

Attitudes like these entered everyday life through the influence of doctors, sanitary reformers and hygienists; once acknowledged, they created the basis for an entirely new standard of judgement

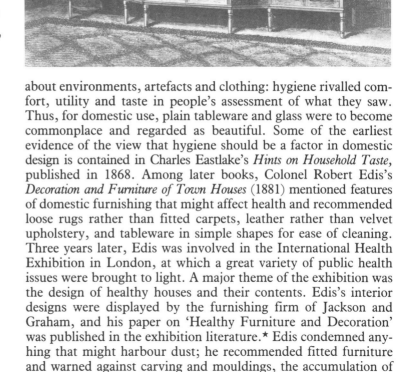

Sideboard, designed by R.W. Edis, made by Jackson & Graham Ltd., 1884. Exhibited at the International Health Exhibition, this piece demonstrated Edis's ideas about hygienic furnishings by fitting close to the ceiling and standing off the floor. From S.E. Murphy, *Our Homes and How to Make them Healthy*, 1883, p.345.

*Robert Edis, 'Healthy Furniture and Decoration', *Health in the Dwelling*, vol.I of *International Health Exhibition Literature*, London, 1884, pp.287-365.

about environments, artefacts and clothing: hygiene rivalled comfort, utility and taste in people's assessment of what they saw. Thus, for domestic use, plain tableware and glass were to become commonplace and regarded as beautiful. Some of the earliest evidence of the view that hygiene should be a factor in domestic design is contained in Charles Eastlake's *Hints on Household Taste*, published in 1868. Among later books, Colonel Robert Edis's *Decoration and Furniture of Town Houses* (1881) mentioned features of domestic furnishing that might affect health and recommended loose rugs rather than fitted carpets, leather rather than velvet upholstery, and tableware in simple shapes for ease of cleaning. Three years later, Edis was involved in the International Health Exhibition in London, at which a great variety of public health issues were brought to light. A major theme of the exhibition was the design of healthy houses and their contents. Edis's interior designs were displayed by the furnishing firm of Jackson and Graham, and his paper on 'Healthy Furniture and Decoration' was published in the exhibition literature.* Edis condemned anything that might harbour dust; he recommended fitted furniture and warned against carving and mouldings, the accumulation of useless ornaments and the use of fluffy, dust-retaining fabrics. His designs for the exhibition included fitted furniture with tops that reached to the ceiling to avoid dust traps, and several pieces that stood on legs to make it easy to dust underneath.

Edis's ideas about furnishing were fairly representative of progressive taste in the 1880s, and others shared his preference for simplification in the interests of hygiene. Of all the items of furniture discussed, few received as much attention as the bedstead. Because the sleeper would be oblivious to the condition of the air, the greatest risks to health were thought to occur in bed. In the late nineteenth century, it was bedrooms in which hygiene was thought to matter most and in which dust-retaining surfaces and materials were to be most strenuously avoided. Because the strictest application of these principles was required in bedsteads, the simplest designs were favoured. Under no circumstances were there to be any drapes, and the preferred materials were polished oak, cast iron or brass. Iron bedsteads, which had been in production since the 1830s, had always been popular because of their cheapness and non-absorbency (which meant that they would not harbour noxious miasma), but the fact that their spare form would not collect much dust brought them new popularity in the 1880s and 1890s.

By the end of the nineteenth century, much of the more *avant-garde* furniture incorporated hygienic features, such as the minimum of relief ornament, but the reasons were primarily moral and aesthetic. Only after about 1910 did hygiene begin to be a widespread determinant in the design of furniture and other artefacts. This was nowhere more apparent than in office furniture; office desks stood on legs to make cleaning beneath them easier, and one of the main arguments for steel furniture in offices was the ease with which it could be cleaned. In the 1920s, the pursuit of absolute cleanliness appeared also in the more advanced designs for domestic furniture. Chromed steel and glass were welcomed not just because of their associations with machines, but also because they could easily be kept clean, and, above all, could look absolutely spotless.

Another area much affected by notions of hygiene was dress. This had been discussed by health reformers and doctors since the early nineteenth century, when tight-lacing had been much criticised, but it received much greater attention in the 1880s and 1890s. The new theories of healthy costume coincided in many respects with the *avant-garde* taste for 'artistic' dress in the 1890s. Healthy costume aimed to avoid all constriction: stays and corsets were not to be worn, nor were shoes and boots with pointed toes, and it was recommended that all clothing should be suspended from the shoulders, not from the waist, thighs or knees. (The introduction of the liberty bodice in 1908, following a run of patents for shoulder suspenders, made it possible to put this principle into practice).* Some dress reformers specified that clothing should be light, not more than seven pounds in weight, and there were views on the best materials to use.*

*E. Ewing, *Dress and Undress*, London, 1978, p.119. For suspender designs, see British Patents: 19,956, 9th April 1900; 7,155, 24th March 1902; 351, 6th January 1903; 12,884, 4th June 1907.

*S.M. Newton, *Health, Art and Reason*, London, 1974.

Oak Bedstead, c.1880. Beds with drapes were much criticised for their unhealthiness, and plain iron or oak bedsteads greatly preferred. This one, in oak, was recommended as simple enough to be copied by any village carpenter. From Lady Barker, *The Bedroom & Boudoir*, 1878, p.32.

As with the other kinds of design influenced by hygiene, the principles put forward at the end of the nineteenth century did not have much effect on dress at the time. Rational dress was never worn by more than a tiny aesthetic and socialist minority, and it was not until the 1920s that concepts of hygienic dress widely affected women's clothing, and the accumulation of propaganda against the evils of corsets and tight-lacing (demonstrated by diagrams of deformed rib cages) provided a justification, if not an explanation, for the 'twenties style of loose-fitting, waistless clothes that very obviously hung from the shoulder.

Another effect of the desire for greater cleanliness was the development of a multiplicity of preparations, appliances and gadgets – not just domestic plumbing, baths and washbasins, but also deodorants, washing-machines and vacuum cleaners. The history of the vacuum cleaner is a good example of the commercial applications of the phobia against dirt, and of the way appearance and styling were affected by the imagery of hygiene.

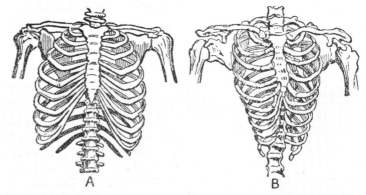

A. NATURAL CHEST.   B. CHEST DEFORMED BY TIGHT CORSETS.

Baby Daisy hand-operated bellows vacuum cleaner, 1908. The suction pipe connected to the plate at the side. One of many manual vacuum cleaners marketed around 1900.

*The main sources on the history of the vacuum cleaner are Siegfried Giedion, *Mechanization Takes Command*, New York, 1948, pp.548-549, 582-595; and S. Giedion, 'Vacuum in the Home', *Technology Review*, January 1947, pp.157-160. In his book, Giedion discusses many other aspects of the mechanization of hygiene and cleanliness.

Héricourt, p.153.

The vacuum cleaner was first conceived in the United States.* In 1860, a patent was taken out for a machine that both brushed and sucked dust, and within the next few years a number of similar devices were patented, although none was put into commercial production. It was not until the 1890s that the first vacuum cleaners were put on the market. By this time, there was good reason for wanting a device to replace the duster and broom: the fear of germ-laden dust had begun to settle in people's minds, reinforced by strong propaganda against the evils of dry dusting. For example, a French doctor wrote in 1907:

'Dry sweeping and dusting are homicidal practices: they consist of taking dust which has been lying on the floor and on the furniture, mixing it in the atmosphere, and causing it to be swallowed and inhaled by the inhabitants of the house. In reality, it would be preferable to leave the dust alone where it was.'*

People were taught to sweep with used tea leaves to catch the dust and to dust only with a damp duster. It was logical, then, to develop instruments to remove the lethal dust without making it enter the atmosphere. Early vacuum cleaners from around the turn of the century were hand or foot operated, and must have been laborious to use and rather inefficient. Even so, the very large number of designs suggests that manufacturers found a strong demand.

Mobile Compressed Air
Cleaner, France, 1903.
Operated by companies who
offered a cleaning service, the
machine was parked in the
street outside. Although this
machine worked by compressed
air, blowing dust into the bag,
others worked on a vacuum.
From *La Nature*, 5th December
1903, p.24.

Far more efficient than the manually operated bellows cleaners
were the machines with a power-driven vacuum pump. These
were developed simultaneously in England and France from about
1902. Powered either by electricity or by paraffin engines, they
were large and were operated by companies who hired them out
with a team of operatives. They were used principally for large
buildings, such as department stores and theatres, but they were
also occasionally hired by individuals for domestic cleaning. An
alternative to the mobile vacuum plant was a permanent installation
with an outlet leading to each room. Systems of this kind were
installed in the Frick Building in New York in 1902 and shortly
afterwards in the House of Commons in London; permanent
installations for domestic use were advertised in the United States,
although their cost must have restricted them to the very wealthy.

Around 1905, several individuals began quite independently to
develop small, portable electric-powered vacuum cleaners, which
could be used regularly by a domestic servant and would be relatively cheap. A succession of patents were take out from 1908 for
such machines, and by 1909 there was an electric-powered vacuum
cleaner on the market in the United States, with revolving brushes
and a fan to create suction. Development continued rapidly, and
by 1914 there were several models on the market in Britain,
some working by suction alone, while others also had revolving
brushes. By 1916, the period of rapid development was over, and
the American Hoover Suction Sweeper Company started to manufacture a design that remained basically unchanged for the next

twenty years. Several other companies went into production with designs of their own around the same time.

In selling vacuum cleaners, manufacturers were quick to emphasise their hygienic properties. The arguments for vacuum cleaners as labour-saving appliances were not particularly convincing: Christine Frederick, an American household efficiency expert, had shown in 1920 that vacuum cleaners saved little time, though they did the job more effectively.* Consequently, it was as instruments of hygiene that vacuum cleaners were generally advertised. The advice that Christine Frederick (who had become a marketing consultant to domestic appliance companies) gave to the British electrical goods industry in 1927 on how to sell vacuum cleaners was to stress their hygienic qualities and to use the familiar anxiety-inducing arguments to drive the message home. Having explained the faults of old-fashioned cleaning methods, she continued:

'The principle behind all new cleaning methods is not scattering but *absorption of dust*. This new principle is exemplified in the many dustless and specially treated dustcloths and mops, but reaches the height of perfection in the electric suction cleaner. This electrical appliance, whatever the specific model, extracts dust, holds it, absorbs it, actually removes it. Thus we see that the use of a vacuum cleaning method is based on an entirely different method and a much higher standard of room and home

*C. Frederick, *Scientific Management in the Home: Household Engineering*, London, 1920, pp.156ff.

Below:
Advertisement for portable electric vacuum cleaners, 1914. These were among the first effective domestic vacuum cleaners. Note that it is a servant using the lower machine: at its price, only the upper middle class would have been able to afford the machines. From M. Lancaster, *Electric Cooking, Heating, Cleaning etc.*, London, 1914.
Right:
Hoover 700 vacuum cleaner. This machine, marketed throughout the 1920s, was similar in form to the model introduced in 1916.

Revolution in House Cleaning.

THE 1914 SURPRISE.

Since the body of this book went to press, we have introduced two new Models of Electric Suction Cleaners, the

" ECONO "

and the

" CLEVELAND,"

that form the last word in domestic home cleaning.

"ECONO" Electric Vacuum Cleaner.

The **" ECONO "** Model has been designed to meet the requirements of those who desire a smaller, lighter and cheaper machine than our famous **" SANTO,"** which it resembles in appearance.

Only 18 in. high and 11 in. in diameter, weighs only 23 lbs

UNIVERSAL MOTOR.
AUTOMATIC LUBRICATION.
METAL SUCTION HOSE.

Guaranteed for Twelve Months

Price Complete with Accessories.
£15 15s.

The **" CLEVELAND "** Model is the **Lightest, Cheapest and Simplest** electric Vacuum Cleaner on the Market.

It is sold at the price of a Hand Cleaner.

Every part Standardised and instantly replaceable.

Guaranteed for Twelve Months.

Price **£6 15s.**

Complete Set of Accessories **36s.** extra.

"CLEVELAND"
Electric Vacuum Cleaner.

Welcome the Eureka Man

- he brings new standards of home sanitation

Advertisement for Eureka vacuum cleaner, 1928. The copy to this advertisement played on the dangers of dirt and suggested that as well as taking matter (dirt) out of the home, it brought something (hygiene) to it. From *Ladies' Home Journal*. October 1928, p.209.

cleanliness. It is based in fact on a very superior principle of hygiene: freedom from dust and germs, and ultimate disease.

'Now we have found the "universal ideal" behind the vacuum cleaner! We see that it is much larger, much more far reaching than asking the housewife to exchange a hand broom for a power sweeper. It is asking her to accept a higher, safer, more desirable health standard for her entire family. What housewife could refuse to accept such an offer, and even skimp and save if need be, to purchase the device that would bring more health into her home? If the facts are put before her in this vivid and commonsense way, any housewife will recognise the dangers which scattering dust, soot and germs mean in the household, particularly in the household with children.'*

Electrician, 30th September 1927, pp.396-397.

Although it was easy for salesmen and advertisers to emphasise the benefits to health and hygiene offered by vacuum cleaners, the design of the machines themselves did little to convey this impression to customers. The pistol grip of the Electrolux model marketed during the 1920s bore the symbol of the rod of Aesculapius, but the iconography was probably too subtle to have meant much to most customers; what was required was much more dramatic visual evidence that the vacuum cleaner did what it was said to do. Most of the early models were designed in a spirit of technological rationalism, in which each of the elements – motor, fan, nozzle and dust bag – was clearly identifiable as a separate part, as was the case with, for example, the Orion. An

Handle of Electrolux vacuum cleaner, c.1928. The butt bears the rod of Aesculapius, symbol of medicine and health.

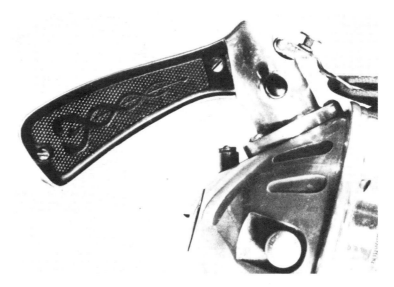

Vacuum cleaner, c.1925. In the design of most early electric vacuum cleaners, there was no attempt to conceal the different parts of the machine.

Hotpoint 500 vacuum cleaner, 1937. In this machine, the aluminium casing of the brushes was continued to form a cover for this motor, which can be seen underneath occupying exactly the same position at the rear as it had in earlier models. The extended aluminium shell over the motor was purely for styling reasons, and added to the weight and cost of the machine.

exception to this pattern was the standard Hoover model, in which brushes, fan and motor were encased within a single form.

Around 1935, the appearance of vacuum cleaners began to change dramatically. The immediate reason for these changes was that manufacturers were anxious to increase sales, and were making use of the recent discovery of motor car manufacturers that consumption could be encouraged by the introduction of new designs to make old models seem obsolete. In the new designs of vacuum cleaners, the protuberances of the earlier machines disappeared, and the works were encased in smooth, sleek shells of cast alloy. In the Hotpoint 500 of 1937, for example, the mechanism was almost unchanged from earlier models, but the casing which shone with cleanliness, concealed the untidy works from view. In the same spirit, Hoover had employed the industrial designer Henry Dreyfuss to redesign their basic model. After twenty years, the original Hoover model no longer looked different enough from the designs of other manufacturers, and it was extremely heavy and cumbersome to use. The new model 150, introduced in 1936, used magnesium alloy castings and moulded bakelite to make it considerably lighter, while its low streamlined form distinguished it from competitors and, with its smoothness, increased its appearance of hygiene. Dreyfuss himself emphasised that he had tried in the design to tie up all the parts in one harmonious

*K.O. Tooker and F.L. Pierce, 'The Hoover One Fifty', *Modern Plastics*, vol.14, November 1936, pp.32-33.

whole.* Most subsequent vacuum cleaners have reworked the basic design principles of the Hoover 150: lightness (much helped by the use of plastic components) and cleanliness in appearance.

There had been little technical development in domestic electric vacuum cleaners since their introduction around 1910, but the visual change in them was so great that the early designs now seem quaint and archaic. New designs were introduced partly to bring down the price of the machines by reducing the costs of material and components, and partly because the lighter machines were more marketable. Once there was no opportunity for technical development, manufacturers turned to appearance and styling as a means of competing with their rivals, adopting imagery calculated to reinforce the message already being put across by their advertising and salesmen. In some cases, the pursuit of new imagery in the designs caused manufacturers to contradict their other aims. The Hotpoint 500, for example, used rather more metal than earlier models, and as a result was actually heavier. Such are the paradoxes of design.

A similar story of the commercialisation of cleanliness could be told with many other products: washing-machines, gas and electric cookers, and detergents. In every case, the product was designed, developed and marketed with the object of creating opportunities for greater cleanliness, an aim to which no reasonable person could possibly take exception. It was precisely the reasonableness of the aim, often conveyed so well by the design, that made it so effective as a marketing technique, for it put people under a compulsion to buy the product.

It would be wrong to suggest that the development of an aesthetic based upon cleanliness has been a one-sided affair, promoted exclusively by manufacturers, for the image of cleanliness has been sought just as earnestly by consumers. The idea that cleanliness might be beautiful took hold with such force that every new product that purveyed an appearance of hygiene was felt by consumers to be fulfilling a genuine need: far from being hard to adapt to, cleanliness was an aesthetic that satisfied many desires.

On the whole, commerce had more success than the hygienists themselves ever had in realising higher standards of cleanliness. Health education in schools, and in schools of motherhood, was a cumbersome instrument of reform, and the paternalistic class attitudes it incorporated made it as likely to prejudice people against greater hygiene as to convince them of its necessity. Much more effective were new products and appliances, particularly when these were designed in an aesthetic which appealed so strongly to people. Vacuum cleaners, soap powders and washing machines all created new opportunities for higher standards of cleanliness

Hoover 150 vacuum cleaner, 1936. This design by Henry Dreyfuss, superseding the 700 model, was an attempt to 'clean up' the form, as well as make the machine lighter.

Sally Blane, 1929 Wampas Baby Star and "Starlet" of the R. K. O. Studios, Hollywood, finds it so easy to remove spots with Energine that she sees no good reason to ask for help.

Beauty Must be Spotless

THERE can be no blemish to perfect beauty. The smallest visible spot on a garment spoils the whole ensemble. Nobody knows this better than the actors and directors of America's great screen productions.

That's why *Energine* is used almost exclusively and in large quantities by those who have charge of the costly movie wardrobes.

Energine leaves no ring—no clinging odor—simple directions now on every can. A very small amount on a cloth removes spots quickly, easily, completely.

Energine cannot possibly injure the most delicate skin or daintiest fabric because it is pure —contains no acid, alkali or caustic. *Energine*, used constantly, maintains the original appearance and prolongs the wear of finest garments.

For twenty-five years *Energine* has been used successfully by millions of people who have

learned that nothing takes its place.

Energine removes dirt and grease spots from every kind of fabric— dresses, hats, scarfs, suits, coats, neckties, gloves and shoes.

Druggists everywhere sell *Energine* 35c for 10 oz. can. 60c for a 20 oz. size. Slightly higher prices abroad. Insist on *Energine!* No substitute does as well.

Largest Selling Cleaning Fluid in the World

Advertisement for cleaning fluid, 1929. Ultimately, it was advertisers and manufacturers rather than health reformers who most successfully taught the public to worry about hygiene. From *Ladies' Home Journal*, May 1929, p.246.

and made neglect of cleaning all the more blatant and inexcusable, particularly as they were backed up by norms of design that made every stain and speck of dirt stand out. Although it was the hygiene reformers who had wanted to identify dirt as a cause of suffering that could be alleviated only by cleaning, it was commerce and manufacturing industry that turned the idea into reality.

8. Electricity – the Fuel of the Future

Though they serve the same function, there is all the difference in the world between the two electric cookers illustrated opposite. The Magnet, manufactured in 1914, is a massive cast-iron structure, ornamented with polished mouldings; today, it looks more like a safe than an electric cooker. The top, also of polished iron, has two boiling plates and a grill plate set into it; beneath, there is an oven. The only means of controlling the temperatures of the plates and the oven is by three-way switches, which reduce the current to a half or a quarter. By comparison, the English Electric cooker, manufactured in 1961, is a flyweight. Made of stove-enamelled, pressed-steel panels with rounded corners, the cooker depends for its visual qualities on smoothness and whiteness and on the neatness of the joins. The boiling rings are of a type that heats up rapidly, while the oven and one of the rings have thermostatic switches that can be preset to any temperature. Above the rings is an illuminated control panel with rather more extensive instrumentation than was offered on the Magnet. Arguments about hygiene do to some extent account for the visual and technical changes between the two cookers, but they are by no means the full explanation.

A historian of technology might attribute the differences between the two cookers to technical developments in the fifty years between the dates of manufacture: the invention of more efficient means of converting electricity into heat, of better switching mechanisms, and of new methods of forming metal. What this account does not explain is why the inventions should have been made in the first place, or why they should have been applied to the design of electric cookers. Technical innovations do not happen of their own accord: they occur only when somebody sees that there is advantage to be gained from them, and they are applied only when it is in someone's interest to do so. Certainly they cannot be explained simply by reference to the advance of scientific knowledge, an approach represented in the 'march of progress' view that is found all too often in histories of technology. The essential changes are not only that the English Electric cooker was made by different manufacturing methods and incorporated new technology, but that it embodied a set of ideas that were not to be found in the older cooker. To understand those ideas we need to turn to the history of electricity itself.

Between the dates of these two cookers, and particularly between the two world wars, electricity production in Britain grew substantially. The growth in demand came predominantly from domestic consumers, who turned to electricity not only for lighting but also for heat, for cooking, for cleaning carpets and for washing and ironing clothes. These new uses were encouraged by the marketing efforts of the electricity supply industry, which profited from the extra revenue and took a great interest in the development of appliances.

Electricity Supply in Britain

*The main sources of information about the history of electricity supply in Britain are H.H. Ballin, *The Organisation of Electricity Supply in Great Britain*, London, 1946, and L. Hannah, *Electricity Before Nationalisation*, London, 1979.

Below:
Magnet electric cooker, 1914. A massive appliance with only rudimentary controls.
Right:
English Electric 2034 electric cooker, 1961. Designed by the Design Research Unit. A more compact cooker, with a clean finish and thermostatic controls.

In Britain, electricity was first generated for sale in 1881.* The pioneer public supply, at Godalming in Surrey, was used exclusively for lighting, but the enterprise did not survive for long. The Electric Lighting Acts of 1882 and 1888 established legal arrangements for the production and supply of electricity, and by the early 1890s, a number of supply undertakings were selling electricity. Because the Acts had made it illegal to export electricity across local authority boundaries, the undertakings were all local, and the majority of them were run by municipalities. Almost the entire demand for electricity resulted from lighting, whether for the streets, for public and commercial buildings or for homes. The cleanliness and brilliance of electricity compared with gas made it easy to develop the demand. It soon became clear, though, that the sale of electricity exclusively for lighting caused serious problems in the economics of production. As the demand for lighting is limited to the hours of darkness, particularly the evenings, the necessary generating capacity remained idle for a large part of each day. To explain the relationship between the actual demand and the potential demand that could be serviced, Colonel Crompton, the engineer for the Kensington Court power station, introduced the term

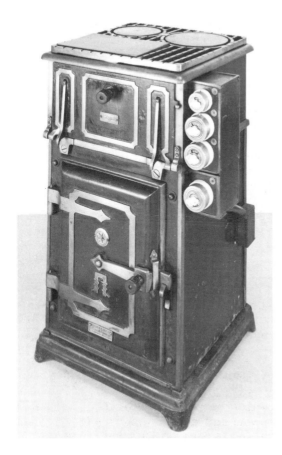

'load factor' in 1891. This is the ratio between the actual amount of electricity supplied during a period of time – a day, week or year – to the amount of electricity it would have been possible to supply at maximum output throughout that period: in theory the highest load factor would be 100%, which would be virtually impossible to achieve in practice. At present, the British national load factor is just below 60%.* The load curve for the Kensington Court station showed that even in December, the month of greatest demand, the load factor was only about 20%, a level that was typical of stations supplying electricity for lighting alone.

*United Kingdom Department of Energy, *Digest of United Kingdom Energy Statistics*, 1980, Table 73, p.103.

Such low load factors concerned the industry because of their effects on the economics of production. There are two components in the cost of producing electricity: the running costs of fuel and wages, and the capital costs of the plant, generating sets and supply cables. Until recently, the capital cost has been the larger of the two, and it continues regardless of the amount of electricity generated. To meet all its customers' demands, an electricity supplier has to install sufficient generating capacity to meet the peak load, even though the plant may have to stand idle for long periods when there is no demand. In the Kensington station in 1890, with an annual load factor of only 13%, the plant was idle 87% of the time. Had the industry ever developed a satisfactory method of storing electricity generated outside the peak, the uneven demand would not, of course, have been a problem.

Low load factors wasted capital and made the electricity that was produced extremely expensive, as the entire cost of the plant had to be covered by a very small total sale of electricity. Unlike ordinary commodities, for which the cost could be reduced by increasing the demand and selling more, increased demand for electric lighting would only make the situation worse, since the increase would invariably occur at the peak and require still more generating capacity. The answer to the problem lay in improving the load factor by building up a demand for other uses of electricity throughout the day. The search for alternative uses was to become a major theme in the history of electricity supply.

Building Domestic Load

In his presidential address to the Institute of Electrical Engineers in 1895, Colonel Crompton outlined some of the ways in which the demand for electricity could be diversified. Principal among the possible uses of power were factories, traction for trams and trains, and cooking, heating and other domestic purposes.

'We not only desire to have the output of our generating station more evenly distributed throughout the 24-hour day, so as to fill up the valleys and reduce the peaks of our daily diagram, but we also wish to improve the summer diagram as compared with the winter one . . . The great disparity between our winter and summer loads is due to our geographical position, and will always exist so long as the major part of the energy we supply is for lighting purposes, and the obvious remedy is to encourage its use for motive power and for heating and cooking; and to me at the present time it appears a far easier matter to educate the public to the advantages of using electricity for heating than to induce them to use motive power to any considerable extent. For this reason I have persistently advocated the perfecting of electric heating and cooking appliances.'*

Journal of the Institution of Electrical Engineers (JIEE), vol.XXIV, 1895, p.10.

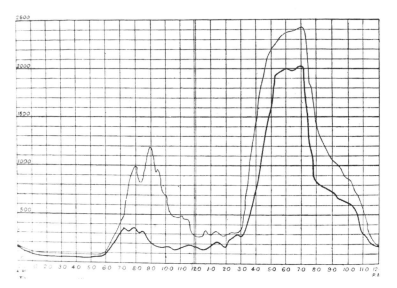

Load factor curve, Kensington Court Power Station, over 24 hours. The thick line was for 6th November, 1890; the thin line for 2nd December, 1890. From *Proceedings of the Institute of Civil Engineers*, vol. cvi, 1891, p.7.

The initiative for domestic applications of electricity thus came from the supply side of the industry, and although domestic use took several decades to reach the scale Crompton had envisaged, it continued to be much discussed by electrical engineers. Contrary to Crompton's anticipation, the industrial and traction uses for electricity were the first to develop and, by 1900, were already beginning to bring about an improvement in load factors.

For several reasons, domestic load increased much more slowly and, even in 1914, was still negligible. The high price of electricity and the considerable cost of wiring a house restricted the clientele to the well-to-do, and even those who could afford the expense were dissuaded for such reasons as incomprehension and fear of electricity, and the fact that it compared badly as a form of domestic energy with gas, which was much more widely available.

However, the domestic use of electricity was so attractive to supply engineers because of its likely effect upon load factors that it was well worth their while to try and overcome the drawbacks. Both industrial and traction loads had the disadvantage that they had their own peaks, the industrial load during weekday mornings and afternoons, the traction load on weekday mornings and evenings. Although they helped produce a very much more even load curve than lighting on its own, neither use produced much demand for electricity at night or at weekends. Worse still, industrial and traction uses combined with lighting to produce an even higher peak load in the late afternoon of winter weekdays. Domestic demand for electricity was expected not only to add a more even load throughout the day and the week, but also, if anything, to peak at times when other demand dropped. Electricity consumed when people got up in the morning and cooked their breakfasts would precede the peaks of traction and industrial power, while the midday dip in industrial power would be filled by the cooking of lunch; cooking and heating in the evenings and at weekends would also occur outside periods of industrial demand. Electric fires used for occasional heating on cool summer evenings would help fill the seasonal drop in demand, but were not expected to add to the winter peak, since it was anticipated that electricity would always be too expensive to use for continuous heating.

*See especially the following papers and the ensuing discussions: W.R. Cooper, 'Domestic Electricity Supply (including Heating and Cooking) as Affected by Tariffs', JIEE, vol. XLII, 1908-09, pp.26-48; H.W. Handcock and A.H. Dykes, 'The Present Aspect of Electric Lighting', JIEE, vol.XLIV, 1909-10, pp.57-73; H. Gray, 'Electric Heating as Applied to Cooking Apparatus', JIEE, vol.XLVII, 1911, pp.249-263; T.P. Wilmshurst, 'Commercial Aspects of Electric Cooking and Heating', JIEE, vol.LI, 1913, pp.180-194.

During the years 1905-14, a great deal of attention was given by supply engineeers to the potential of domestic demand and its likely effects upon the load factor, and to the development of appliances, without which there could be no domestic consumption of electricity. Cooking and space heating, both heavy consumers of current, were thought to provide the most promising means of building up domestic load. Engineers who believed in the future of domestic demand (and by no means all of them did) recognised that to attract consumers to electricity, cookers and heaters needed to be reasonably efficient and, above all, to demonstrate a superiority over gas.*

Anticipating a rapid growth in domestic consumption, a number of entrepreneurs began to make electrical appliances in the years before 1914. Most of the appliances were produced by hand-craftsmanship, and as there were many manufacturers and few domestic consumers, it is likely that only minimal quantities were made of any design. By 1914, however, an enormous variety of

Electric potato peeler, 1914. Although clearly made for the catering trade, this and other electric-powered machines were recommended for domestic use. From M. Lancaster, *Electric Cooking, Heating, Cleaning, etc.*, 1914, p.286.

Advertisement for Magnet electrical appliances, 1914. This shows the very extensive range of small electrical appliances already available by 1914. From M. Lancaster, *Electric Cooking, Heating, Cleaning, etc.*, 1914.

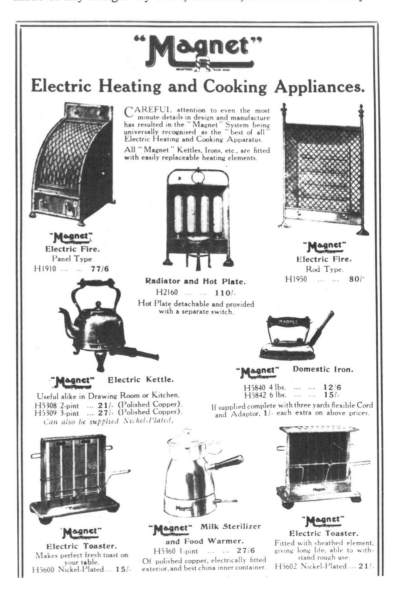

Electric breakfast, 1914.
Electric coffee pot, toaster and
egg-boiler in use. The
attraction, to supply engineers,
of the electrically-cooked
breakfast, was that it used
power at a time of low demand.
From Mrs Lancaster, *Electric
Cooking, Heating, Cleaning,
etc.*, 1914.

*Maud Lancaster, *Electric
Cooking, Heating, Cleaning etc.,
being a Manual of Electricity in
the Service of the Home*, London,
1914, gives a very full account
of the domestic electrical
appliances available in 1914.

*See discussion to W.R.
Cooper's paper in JIEE
(1908-09).

*C.R. Belling, 'Electric Fires
and Cookers', *Electrical Review*,
vol. 108, 19th June 1931,
p.1048.

appliances were available for anyone who could afford them; indeed, almost every type of appliance known to us today could be obtained.* There were not only electric cookers and heaters, but kettles, toasters, dishwashers, washing machines, vacuum cleaners, mixers, potato peelers and knife grinders. Uses of electricity which improved the load factor were particularly favoured. So, for example, 'electric breakfasts', which fell outside the main load period, received strong publicity. Some of the appliances originated in the United States, which, partly because gas supplies had never developed to any extent, had advanced further in the domestic uses of electricity, but many of the appliances were British designed and made. On the whole, as electricity supply engineers frequently complained, the standard of design was not high.* In some cases, such as certain domestic clothes washing machines, the appliances were manual models to which an electric motor had been attached. Some electric cookers had been made by installing electric elements in the cast-iron carcases of gas cookers, while those that were purpose-built often looked very much like gas cookers.* Even where, as in the case of electric fires, the product was not a direct substitute for a manual or gas appliance, there was rarely much about the designs to indicate their specifically electrical nature, and the level of efficiency was generally unspectacular. The extravagant claims that were sometimes made for the luxury of the all-electric home were hardly justified by the appliances themselves, which could not in any case be put to more than occasional use because of the high price of electricity. By 1914, then, the electric house looked feasible, but the actual proportion of households using electricity was too small to make much difference to the load.

World War I was a prosperous time for the electricity industry, since it was called upon to supply power for many of the wartime industries. As shift and, in some cases, continuous working gave very high load factors, there was little reason for the supply industry to concern itself much with domestic consumers. However, peacetime once again confronted the industry with the problems of

Electric fire, c.1910. Despite the elegant brasswork, the electrical nature of this product was not exploited in the design.

*B.R. Mitchell & H.G. Jones, *Second Abstract of British Historical Statistics*, Cambridge, 1971, p.71.

*The development of domestic consumption of electricity is discussed in Hannah, chapter 6; and in D.A. Wilson, 'The Economic Development of the Electricity Supply Industry in Great Britain, 1919-1939', Ph.D. thesis, University of Loughborough, 1976, chapter 5.

uneven demand and low load factors. Domestic demand resurfaced as the solution to the industry's problems, but so, too, did the same obstacles to its development, and the fact that no more than 6% of British homes were wired for electricity by 1918 prevented any rapid expansion of supply.

In spite of these drawbacks, the domestic consumption of electricity did rise from about 7 kilowatt hours (kWh) per head of population in 1920, to 128 kWh in 1939 and to around 770 kWh per head in 1961. Of all the categories of electricity sales – domestic, industrial, commercial, street lighting and traction – it was domestic sales that increased the most: the proportion of electricity generated that was sold to households rose from 8% in 1920 to 27% in 1939 and to 41% in 1963, figures which fulfilled the ambitions of the early twentieth-century electrical engineers.* The most spectacular growth, in terms of proportional increase in domestic sales, came between the wars. Although this time has been described as a golden age for the industry, since the potential for expansion was so great, considerable obstacles had to be faced in building up domestic demand.*

Of the obstacles, the high price of electricity was the most serious. The problem had long been recognised as circular: high prices discouraged domestic demand, but the only way to lower costs was to improve load factors, which could only be done by increasing domestic demand. Many engineers argued that the best solution was some form of tariff that would not penalise good customers who consumed large amounts of electricity, but at the same time would not result in losses from supplying households that consumed very little. As tariffs which had a high charge per unit discouraged any increase in consumption, the ideal involved a substantial fixed charge and a low unit price. This system, the 'two-part tariff', was widely recommended; by 1939, it had been adopted by most undertakings across the country. Not only did the two-part tariff promote electricity sales, but, during the inter-war years, the relation between the fixed charge and the running costs was such that, if anything, large consumers who used electricity for cooking and heating were slightly subsidised by the many small consumers who used electricity only for lighting.*

*Hannah, p.200.

Even so, electricity continued to be more expensive than other kinds of fuel. In the 1920s, it was generally too expensive to be considered as the sole means of heating and cooking, and even after substantial price reductions in the 1930s, it still remained generally more expensive than other forms of energy. With no price advantage over other fuels, electricity was most likely to attract new consumers through the merits of the appliances that utilised it. The design and efficiency of electrical appliances therefore became an important element in the promotion of domestic electricity sales. As one supply engineer said in 1922:

'In my view there are two conditions necessary for successful domestic load building, i.e. cheaper current, and cheap and good appliances . . . The best propagandist is a satisfactory service, which cannot be given without reliable appliances.'*

*J.E. Nelson, JIEE, vol. LXI, 1922-23, p.201.

The second problem in building up domestic demand was distribution and wiring. There was no point in offering electricity at even the lowest of prices if there were only a few households in a position to buy it. Between 1918 and 1939, however, the extension of mains supply to both new and existing houses meant that the proportion of households connected to the mains rose from 6% to about two thirds. Commercially, a particularly important factor was the amount of electricity each household could potentially consume. Quite a high proportion of the households wired during the inter-war years were equipped only for lighting. More households had one 5 amp socket into which an electric iron might be plugged, but probably only at most one third of all homes that were wired had more than two electric sockets, and they were principally newly built houses in the upper price bracket.*

*Hannah, p.208; Alan A. Jackson, Semi-Detached London, London, 1973, p.145; D.A. Wilson thesis.

The third obstacle to the development of domestic demand, fear of electricity, was not as trivial as it might appear. There are enough stories of superstitions about electricity to make it clear that for many people electricity was far from a natural form of energy. One case, known to the author by hearsay, was of two old ladies who anxiously kept plugs in all the electrical sockets to prevent the electricity leaking out; another old lady was said to be terrified by the installation of even an electric bell lest the workman be killed in the process. In another case, at a country house where a private generating set was installed, the owner was so apprehensive of the unpredictable powers of electricity that he refused to allow a potential of more than 50 volts. Even in the United States, a case was reported in the 1930s of a woman who refused to use a modern

*C.R. Gibson, *Electricity as a Wizard*, London, 1929, p.146; the house concerned was Ston Easton Park, Somerset; Margaret G. Reid, *Economics of Household Production*, New York, 1934, p.254.

*Quoted D.A. Wilson thesis, p.169.

electric cooker on the grounds that it was 'just too spooky' and preferred her wood-burning range.* Ridiculous though such stories may sound, the electricity industry took these fears seriously, recognising that they were one of the major obstacles to the development of domestic demand. Speaking at the general meeting of the Electrical Development Association in 1934, the chairman said: 'One of the greatest bugbears to be contended with in the development of electricity [is] the haunting spectre of fear.'*

To some extent, fears and prejudices could be overcome by education and by rational explanations of the physics of electricity. However, since the fears themselves were partly irrational (and even now are to be found in people who have had the opportunity to learn the rudiments of electricity), no amount of reason could entirely overcome them. A more effective approach was therefore to try replacing the popular idea of electricity as a dark, invisible and lethal force by a more positive image of it as a miraculous source of energy that would take away all the troubles of the world. Propaganda about electricity made much of its being a uniquely 'modern' fuel, and descriptions of electricity promised unheard-of benefits that it would bring. For instance, in the *Electrical Review* in 1924, it was said that:

Electrical Review, vol.94, June 1924, p.928.

'. . . with the coming of electricity a new era has dawned. One of the great powers of nature has been tamed and harnessed and trained to the service of man, making life clean, wholesome and simple.'*

Millenarian accounts of the all-electric age were common, as in the following quotation from the 1920s:

'Of all the gifts that electricity brings, almost the greatest is the relief from the burden of mechanical, monotonous, everlasting toil. Just as our factories have become organised to turn out their product rapidly and efficiently by electrical machinery controlled by man, our homes will be transformed to operate smoothly with the aid of electricity, so that the labour involved in cleaning, in heating, in cooking and in washing and other domestic tasks will be performed by an electrical deputy. The energy thus released can be devoted to the enjoyment of home life, to education, to the cultivation of music and art and the other beneficent recreations for which a measure of freedom is essential. Leisure will cease to be a monopoly of the well-to-do and will extend until it becomes a common possession.*'

*A.G. Whyte, *The All-Electric Age*, London, 1922, p.228.

Electricity was held to promise a bright, clean, efficient, cheerful, toil-free world; it would make real the visions of Utopias and science fiction. Electrical millenarianism flourished best in prose and films, but the industry did its utmost, through advertising, exhibitions and show houses, to convince the public that electricity was indeed the fuel of the future. Its principal agent was the Electrical Development Association (EDA), an organisation set up under the Electricity Act of 1919 and financed by the supply undertakings. From 1926 onwards, the EDA became heavily involved in the development of domestic demand, and electrical millenarianism, though of a restrained form, played a significant part in its publicity. In the late 1920s, the EDA was publicising electricity with slogans like 'To Electricity belongs the Present and the Future', and 'Science's Greatest Gift to the World

Electrical Development Association poster, 1927. Part of the electricity industry's attempt to improve the image of electricity.

*EDA publication no. 611, *Service Book of Advertising Blocks*, 1927.

– Electricity'. In 1927, the EDA mounted a campaign to promote the domestic use of electricity under the slogan 'For Health's Sake – Use Electricity', supported by posters which illustrated a genie-like spirit and promised to carry out all the uncongenial tasks of the world.* The emphasis on the benefits that electricity would bring, and on its liberating effects, have been recurrent themes in its advertising, but at no time were they more apparent than in the 1920s, when the problem of overcoming superstitious ideas about electricity was at its greatest.

It was also hoped that millenarianism would divert attention from electricity's other drawbacks – its high price and lack of superiority over its great rival, gas. The gas industry had the advantage of having been in business very much longer than electricity. Gas had been available in towns in Britain since the 1850s, and the majority of urban houses were supplied with it by the 1900s. The electricity industry therefore had to win its customers away from gas, which was not easy as there was little doubt about

Creda electric cooker, 1933. The first model to be marketed with a thermostatically controlled oven, eleven years after 'Regulo' ovens were introduced for gas cookers.

the superiority of gas for domestic heating and cooking in the 1920s. Gas was cheaper, with more efficient and better designed appliances. For instance, the boiling plates on electric cookers were notoriously slow and wasteful of heat compared to gas rings. The introduction in 1922 of a thermostatic control, the 'Regulo', for gas ovens gave gas cookers a decided advantage over electric cookers, in which the oven temperature had to be regulated by observation of a thermometer on the oven door and adjustment of the three-heat switch. Thermostatic controls were not introduced for electric cookers until 1933, and even then they were fitted only to the more expensive models. There were thus good reasons why the electricity industry chose to draw attention away from its present weaknesses and instead to emphasise, often in rather unspecific terms, the great benefits that electricity would bring about in the future. For the gas industry, there were great advantages in competing with a fuel that depended so heavily on unfulfilled prospects, for it could offer its own qualities as actual and immediate. The gas industry was able to make much of the contrast between the Utopian visions projected by the electricity industry and its own capacity to offer all its benefits in the present. One advertisement, from a publication of 1930, ran as follows:

'The Dream Come True
A labour-saving home for every woman now
Politicians, social workers, novelists, and journalists continue to paint for us rosy pictures of a future when all houses will be so well equipped with labour-saving devices that we shall just sit round pressing buttons while Robots do everything. But these things are always in the future . . . What the modern practical young housewife wants is not a House of the Future – which never comes, but a House of Today – a home fitted now with clean, economical labour-saving equipment, not a vague dwelling fitted at some future date with appliances not yet invented. The gas industry is making such happy, labour-saving homes possible *today* in every part of the country, among rich and poor alike.'*

*British Commercial Gas Association advertisement in Mrs. R. Noble, *Labour Saving in the Home*, London, 1930, p.i.

It was statements such as this that exposed electricity's dependence on ideas and potential rather than present realities in its appeal to domestic consumers.

It is clear that had every consumer acted with rational economic instincts, the growth in electrical demand between 1920 and 1939 would have been nothing like as great as it was. The high cost of electricity and the fact that electricity was no more efficient than gas for cooking and heating meant that consumers who chose electricity must have been influenced by other reasons than the pursuit of value for money. One such reason was that it was said to be a progressive and liberating source of energy with unlimited future potential. Ultimately, whether or not people gave credence to these claims depended upon what they thought of the appliances that harnessed the energy. The future of electricity therefore depended on improving the design of electrical equipment.

Appliance Design and Images of Electricity

For the supply industry, domestic electrical appliances had to meet two fundamental requirements: to be efficient and as far as possible superior to gas appliances, and to convey the idea that electricity was the only modern form of energy. Until the 1930s, most electrical appliances satisfied neither requirement particularly well and gave rise to many complaints from the supply side of the industry.

Far from living up to the vision of electricity as a modern source of energy, the majority of appliances on the market in the 1920s looked ramshackle and clumsy. In an electric show house fitted out by Battersea Borough Council in 1927, the appliances that furnished the kitchen were cumbersome and distinctly old fashioned compared with the futurism projected by the EDA, on, say, the cover design of *Twentieth Century Cookery*, published around 1930. This brightly coloured post-cubist image of the modern electric age could not have presented a greater contrast to the dingy reality of the Battersea Electric House. The problem was to represent some of the qualities of modernity and efficiency represented on the cover of *Twentieth Century Cookery* in the design of appliances themselves.

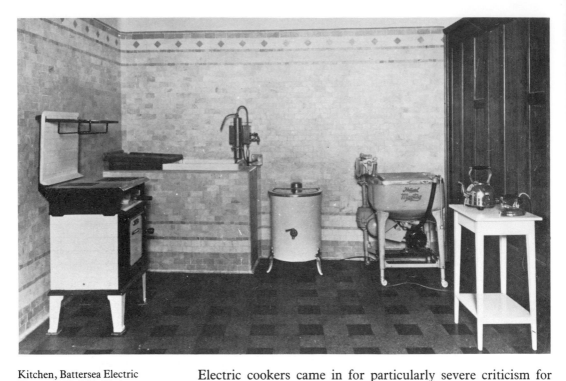

Kitchen, Battersea Electric House, 1927. This kitchen may have been well equipped, but the appliances were awkward and cumbersome.

*W. Wilson, JIEE, vol. LXIV, 1925-26, p.314.

*Political and Economic Planning (PEP), *The Market for Household Appliances*, London, 1945, chapter 3, para.115. On the history of the appliance manufacturing industry, see T.A.B. Corley, *Domestic Electrical Appliances*, London, 1966.

*G. Routh, *Occupation and Pay in Great Britain 1906-60*, Cambridge, 1965, p.104. The prices of appliances are derived from those quoted in catalogues and press advertisements.

Electric cookers came in for particularly severe criticism for their anachronistic design, which slavishly imitated that of coal or gas ranges. A speaker at the Institute of Electrical Engineers in 1926 complained that ' . . . oven designers are copying an older apparatus the features of which are dependent upon its having to be stoked with coal and placed so that its hot hob can be accessible for cooking utensils.'* Such backwardness in design was not calculated to lead consumers to believe that electricity was an advanced and superior form of energy.

There was little that supply engineers could do about the design defects of electric appliances. Supply undertakings were forbidden by law to do anything but generate and distribute electricity, and the only financial connection between them and the appliance manufacturers occurred when they bought appliances for hiring or retailing to their customers. They had no more influence over the manufacturers than any ordinary retailer, and the supply industry as a whole was able to exert pressure on manufacturers only through the EDA.

For their part, the appliance manufacturers had had no great incentive during the 1920s to improve their designs. Throughout the decade, the number of consumers was too small to offer much prospect of mass sales, and the variations in voltage between different undertakings made it difficult to achieve economies of scale in manufacture. The practice adopted by some undertakings of hiring appliances in order to promote electricity sales was said to make them poor customers for improved designs, since they would be required to scrap all their existing stock.* As a result, standards of design were low, and the appliances were very expensive. In the 1920s, when the average income of managers and professional men was between £500 and £700 a year, electric cookers cost upwards of £30, a vacuum cleaner around £20, and an ordinary electric fire about £3.*

20TH CENTURY

COOKERY

Cover of *Twentieth Century Cookery*. Published by the Electrical Development Association, c.1930. The image of modernity that the EDA wished to present contrasted strongly with the appliances actually available.

It was not until the early 1930s that appliances began to get cheaper and manufacturers started to pay serious attention to appearance and efficiency. The most important reason why they became more interested in innovatory design was that, as electricity prices began to fall, they foresaw the prospect of a mass market, which would justify a greater outlay on design. There was good reason to think that designs fulfilling the idea already implanted in people's minds by the EDA and others of electricity as the 'modern' fuel, were most likely to attract customers. The selection of 'modern' imagery was also encouraged by the example of American manufacturers, several of whom set up subsidiary companies and factories in Britain in the early 1930s. The more advanced state of the American electricity industry, combined with the earlier discovery by Americans of the commercial value of 'modern' imagery, caused their products to embody explicit images of progress which were imitated by British manufacturers.*

*See J.L. Meikle, *Twentieth Century Limited*, Philadelphia, 1979, pp.10-18.

Above:
Ferranti copper bowl electric fire, Type 1, c.1910. One of Ferranti's early electrical appliances.
Right:
Ferranti parabolic reflector fire, 1929. This fire offered a theoretically efficient distribution of heat. This model had a Georgian surround.

One of the earliest and best-known instances of the radical improvement and redesign of an electrical appliance (in this case an exclusively British product) was that of the Ferranti reflector fire. Dr S.Z. de Ferranti was a man of wide interests and abilities who had been concerned with all sides of the electricity industry. In 1890, at the age of 26, he had conceived an ambitious scheme for supplying electricity to the whole of London from a power station at Deptford which was to have been much larger than any other station planned at the time. Although the station was built, it ran into difficulties and never became the success that was intended. Before World War I, Ferranti had been manufacturing

RADIANT HEAT
IN THE OFFICE

Electricity now brings into the office a radiance hitherto unavailable.

The Ferranti Fire projects clean heat where it is required and, as everybody knows, feet warm, head cool is the desirable condition, especially in the office.

The glowing heat of the Ferranti Fire is grateful and comforting two to three yards away.

electrical appliances, among them electric fires. In the mid-1920s, he returned to the development of domestic load and investigated possible improvements in the design of electric water heaters and space heaters.*

*Hannah, pp.10-12; manuscript notebooks of Dr Ferranti, held by Ferranti Ltd, Holmwood, Lancs.

In theory, any electric fire gives 100% efficiency in the conversion of electricity into heat, but there may be big differences in the distribution of heat. Improvements in the design of electric fires did not therefore affect overall efficiency, but simply the way in which the heat was distributed. Reflector fires had been in existence since before World War I, and Ferranti turned his attention to ways of increasing the efficiency of the reflector to radiate a larger proportion of the heat. His solution, a parabolic reflector with a thin wound-wire heating element lying along the focus, shed a warming glow over a large area and helped overcome one of the common criticisms of electric fires: that they gave little visual evidence of heat. Ferranti started to manufacture the fire in 1929 and offered several versions of the basic form, one with a plain surround and another with Georgian trim. In 1931, he introduced a model that could be set into a fireplace, as well as a smaller and cheaper portable model. The Ferranti fire became something of a classic of design in Britain in the 'thirties and was praised enthusiastically by Nikolaus Pevsner in 1937 in his book *An Enquiry into Industrial Art in England*.

Ferranti's publicity for his fire made much of its scientific design:

'The remarkable radiation efficiency of the Ferranti fire is obtained by the scientifically correct application of a well-known principle in the projection of heat . . .'*

The Ferranti Fire, publicity booklet, n.d., p.14.

But as important as its radiant efficiency was its appearance, which, as well as being discreet and tasteful, also had some of the 'modern' and technological qualities attributed to electricity.

During the 1930s, other manufacturers became increasingly aware of the importance of appearance in electrical appliances. Discussing the market for electric fires in the *Electrical Review* in 1934, A. Curwen asked:

Far left:
Illustration, Ferranti publicity booklet, c.1930, showing the parabolic reflector fire in use.
Left:
Berry Magicoal electric fire, The Sundown, 1925. Simulated and electric fires were a longstanding way of giving a familiar form to the invisible source of energy.

'How are we to create this demand for electric heaters? First we must improve their design until they impress by their very appearance – they must symbolise electricity. This is the age of the unorthodox, and I feel that if fire manufacturers departed somewhat from accepted designs, they would find a better market for their products.'*

Electrical Review, vol. 114, 9th February 1934, p.188.

The appearance of most early electric appliances had taken the form of the object whose function they most closely followed. Electric cookers looked like gas cookers, which in turn imitated coal ranges, and from early in their history many electric fires had simulated coal or log fires.* These 'traditional' designs arose partly from the unimaginativeness of manufacturers and their designers, but partly from the belief that such familiar appearances would help overcome prejudices against electricity. However, as a result of comments from others in the electricity industry, manufacturers became aware of the discrepancy between the traditionalism of their products and the modern image for electricity that the industry and the EDA were trying to promote. From the early 1930s, the designs began to change in ways that met with the

*See A. Forty, 'The Electric Home', Unit 20 of Open University Course A305 *History of Architecture and Design 1890-1939*, Milton Keynes, 1975, p.60.

Creda parabolic reflector fire on tubular steel stand, 1935. A 'modern' design for an electric fire.

*JIEE, vol. LXXII, 1933, p.137.

Below:
HMV Bruton electric fire, 1939. The double parabola of the reflector improved the distribution of heat, and the extensive use of chrome had connotations of contemporary car styling.
Right:
HMV Lincoln electric fire, 1955. The fins, intended to reflect radiant heat over an even wider area, again gave the fire a 'modern' form.

approval of the supply side of the industry. For instance, R.B. Matthews, an engineer who had complained in 1927 about the design of electric fires, found himself able to say of them in 1933, that 'Since [1927] . . . there has been a remarkable improvement, and in many cases there are striking departures from previously accepted principles.'*

Though electricity is invisible, colourless and no more good than bad, the properties ascribed to it were that it was clean, silent, instantaneous, modern and revolutionary. To symbolise these qualities, manufacturers and designers employed 'modern' design, based on the 'Art Deco' style, on the style of the European Modern Movement, or on features derived from automobile styling. Chromium plating and streamlining became the clichés of electrical product design from the early 1930s. Ferranti's fire had made use of some of these features: the chromed surface of the parabolic reflector created its visual effect as well as diffusing heat. Subsequent appliance designs were more aggressively 'modern': for instance, a smaller version of the parabolic reflector fire rested on a chromed tubular steel support that owed much to the furniture designs of the German architect Marcel Breuer or to those of the English firm of PEL; when Walter Gropius, a celebrated pioneer

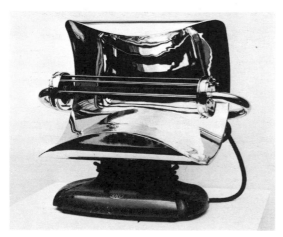

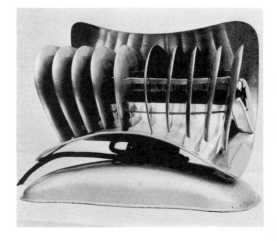

*D. Sharp, T. Benton & B.C. Cole, *PEL and Tubular Steel Furniture of the Thirties*, London, 1977; R.D. Best, *Design and be Damned* (unpublished typescript), p.136.

Sunbeam electric mixer, c.1958. The automobile-derived motifs gave this appliance an up-to-date image.

*H. Dreyfuss, *Designing for People*, New York, 1955, p.80.

Advertisement for electricity, 1980. Electricity can only effectively be marketed through its appliances, and to draw custom, these must be (or appear to be) technologically advanced. In this advertisement, the modernity of the cooker is implied by contrasting it with an obviously antiquated model. From *Company*, August 1980, pp.66-67.

of Modern Movement architecture, came to England in 1934, he chose a fire of this design for his own use.* Although many electrical appliances continued to have a highly traditional appearance, it was designs such as those of the HMV electric fires, with their strong references to contemporary car styling, that projected an image of electricity as the modern, progressive and liberating source of energy.

After World War II, appliances continued to be an important part of campaigns for the domestic sale of electricity, again with designs that conveyed to consumers the image of electricity as the most up-to-date form of energy. Appliances manufactured in the 1950s incorporated the latest features of styling, like the electric mixer with the car headlamp motif at the front and space-ship fins at the rear. Likewise, the English Electric cooker described at the beginning of the chapter contained features (particularly the control panel) that were redolent of the future. Designers have acknowledged that they intentionally used references to cars and aeroplanes in order to convey ideas of progress and modernity. The American industrial designer Henry Dreyfuss wrote in 1955 that the impetus for the changes in the design of modern kitchens had been brought about:

'. . . by two things that had nothing to do with cooking a meal or taking a bath – the automobile and the airplane. Actually, the auto and the plane have become symbols of the nation's scientific imagination and a vital part of its psychology, establishing trends and influencing people in everything they buy.'*

In the marketing of electricity, emphasis on the technological futurism of appliances remains important – a 1980 advertisement for electricity featured a cooker, the great efficiency and advanced features of which were brought out by its utter dissimilarity to the older cooker standing by it.

Although the symbolism used to express modernity and the future has changed over time as images have been superseded, the idea that electricity will put one into the twentieth, or indeed the twenty-first century has been a constant feature of the design of electrical appliances. This technological futurism, while by no means confined to electrical products, can be explained in them

Beauty and the beast.

Thankfully, cookers have changed just a little since that particular beast left the showroom. Especially electric cookers.

Elegantly styled with precise fingertip controls, and superbly finished with tinted glass and gleaming stainless steel... they're beautiful to behold.

Yet it's not only their looks that have changed. It's the way they cook too. Thanks largely to a host of superb features that would make your present cooker turn green with envy.

Like double ovens. And money-saving dual-circuit grills and dual-circuit rings. Custom hobs. Stay-clean oven linings. Digital clocks.

So that's a new electric cooker – a better choice all round. Call in at your Electricity Board shop soon. And make a fairytale come true.

Meanwhile, send for our Good Looking Cooking book by writing to Dept. C.H, The Electricity Council, 30 Millbank, London SW1P 1RD.

The new electric cookers are better insulated. Sothey not only cook better, they are valuable energy-saving money too.

COOK ELECTRIC
Clean and simple

by the particular problems the electricity industry had in making its colourless, odourless, invisible, dangerous and expensive form of energy attractive to the public. The design of appliances has been one means by which people have received favourable ideas about electricity and formed the desire to use it despite all their prejudices and objections.

Wireless Sets

*A. Briggs, *The Golden Age of Wireless*, London, 1965, pp.6 and 253.

*PEP report, 1945, chapter 6, para.155.

Wireless sets were the first pieces of electrical equipment to be owned on a mass scale in Britain. In 1922, when broadcasting began, there were 36,000 licences for receivers, in 1931 there were 4.3 million, and in 1939 there were 9 million, enough for almost every member of the population to have access to a set.* Radio sets were the most popular electrical appliances; the next most widely owned was the electric iron, of which there were estimated to be 6.5 million in Britain in 1939.* Wireless sets were also among the first electrical appliances to use futuristic design, and, although styles have changed, the same basic imagery has continued. However, radios, unlike other appliances, used little or no current from the mains, and the electricy supply industry did not have the same cause to be interested in their commercial development. The reasons for the introduction of futurist design in wireless sets lay elsewhere and had to do with the ways in which radio as a medium was thought to appeal to the public.

When broadcasting was introduced in the 1920s, it was a novelty without parallel and without precedent. Broadcasting brought sounds of the outside, public world into the home much more vividly and immediately than the gramophone, and the unfamiliarity of this experience occasionally had surprising effects on listeners. The wireless set also provided most people's first experience of owning a piece of modern technology and thus carried great weight as a symbol of scientific progress, putting them in touch with changes that they were told that technology would bring in all areas of life. Because of its great potency as a symbol of what life in the twentieth century would offer, radio became one of the most popular metaphors for the changes that technology would bring about in everyday life. It is hardly possible for us today to appreciate the impact of radio, because we have become so used to technical innovation and the claims made for it. The closest comparison might be with the pocket calculator, which has enabled

Burndept IV Wireless Receiver, 1924. Most early wirelesses were presented as pieces of technical apparatus.

*For a fuller discussion of wireless cabinet design, see A. Forty, 'Wireless Style: Symbolic Design and the English Radio Cabinet 1928-33', *Architectural Association Quarterly*, vol.4, Spring 1972, pp.23-31.

everybody to possess a product of the silicon chip technology which we are told will transform the world out of all recognition.

The design of the appearance of wireless sets went through three distinct stages.* In the years immediately after broadcasting began, the rate of technical development of wirelesses was very rapid, and significant improvements were continually being made in the design of receivers. Customers' attention was focused on the innovations, and they would look for sets incorporating the latest improvements. In these conditions, the buying public was relatively unconcerned about what the receivers looked like and was more interested in how many and what type of valves each model had. In appearance, the earliest sets tended to be rude assemblies of diodes, capacitors and resistors, a form that was in its own way extremely striking but reflected the almost total pre-occupation of both manufacturers and public with the technical properties of the apparatus. Some superior models were housed in cabinets, but these, like the one made by Heal's for George V, were not mass-produced and tended to be custom-made by cabinet makers who were independent of the wireless manufacturers.

In the late 1920s, wireless-making was a boom industry: hire purchase meant that even relatively poor people could buy radio sets, and it was generally upon radio sets, rather than the cookers and heaters that the electricity industry was so keen for them to buy or hire, that they spent what spare money they had. The wireless, after all, gave pleasure, whereas other electrical appliances only promised efficiency, and even that was doubtful and at a price. In these favourable conditions, the wireless industry grew very fast, and as long as the rate of technological innovation continued so rapidly, much of each manufacturer's appeal to the market depended upon his being able to offer a better set than his rivals. However, around 1929, as the rate of technological advance began to slow down, the superheterodyne receiver offered by one company was no longer very different from that made by any other.

Wireless set designed by Sir Ambrose Heal for George V, 1924. In mahogany, with mother-of-pearl inlay depicting a whispering shell transmitting radio waves and a conch shell receiving them. Apart from this discreet symbolism, this cabinet was not recognisable as a radio when the doors were closed.

In the second stage of development, manufacturers, unable to compete with each other by technical innovation, turned to other means, notably the design of cabinets, to which little thought had been given previously, except in the most expensive sets. The problem that faced manufacturers was what cabinets should look like. There seemed good reason to believe that customers would rather not furnish their living rooms with pieces of obviously scientific apparatus, but what were the alternatives? Most manufacturers began to market their sets in wooden cabinets, which were still usually designed and made by outside firms of cabinet makers and generally resembled other pieces of furniture. But the more far-sighted were not satisfied with these designs. There were complaints that wirelesses could not be distinguished from other pieces of furniture; stories circulated of guests mistaking the radio set for the cocktail cabinet. Some manufacturers therefore began to consider whether there might not be better ways of housing wireless sets, ways that would perhaps fit people's expectations of radio more closely.

The problem of the best way of housing wireless sets centered around people's ideas of radio. Although radio was extremely popular, the sounds and voices that it brought into the home could be very disturbing. Early broadcasts exploited radio's unprecedented realism, and listeners were encouraged to sit in a darkened room so that their imaginations would heighten the illusion of reality. The effect of one of the first successful radio plays, Richard Hughes's *Danger*, was to make listeners feel that, like the characters, they were trapped underground in a mine.*

Yet radio's dependence on convincing its audience that they were listening to reality also made it very confusing. Were listeners really to think that they had Stanley Baldwin or the Hallé Orchestra sitting in their living rooms? Clearly they were not, but the less they believed this to be true, the less they were likely to enjoy radio. The dilemma has been even more of a problem with television, and most people avoid thinking about it by assuming most of the time that what they see on television is reality itself. Listeners in the 1920s and 1930s could at times be very credulous; the outstanding instance of how they could be duped occurred in the United States when Orson Welles's version of H.G. Wells's *War of the Worlds* was broadcast, and thousands of people who had turned on their sets during the programme fled from their homes, convinced that the Martian invasion was actually happening.

In reconciling the illusory reality of broadcasting with its actual artificiality, there was a good deal to be said for the furniture approach to radio cabinet design, since it helped to assimilate the unfamiliar medium into people's homes. A cabinet which harmonised with the domestic furnishings at least helped to make the monstrous unreality of radio seem part of everyday life. Some manufacturers took this approach to its limits, concealing their sets inside articles of furniture which served other functions, like the radio easy-chair illustrated on p.12. Others took a less bizarre course, but kept to the notion that their sets should appear as furniture. This approach, however, did not fulfil the popular idea of radio as the symbol of future progress: it was supposed to represent everything that living rooms, and lives, lacked; sets that simply imitated what was already there could not fully satisfy people's expectations. The solution adopted by one firm, Murphy,

*V. Gielgud, *British Radio Drama*, London, 1957, p.20; reference to the problem of the confusion caused by radio was made by M. Muggeridge, *The Thirties*, London, 1940, pp.44-45.

Above:
Advertisement for the Murphy A-3 receiver, cabinet designed and made by Gordon Russell, 1931. One of the first cabinets that was unmistakably a radio, but which was also designed as contemporary modern furniture. From *The Wireless and Gramophone Trader*, 16th May 1931.

Right:
Pye radio receiver, 1930. Pye radios were sold in cabinets that were essentially pieces of modern furniture. They were distinguished by the sunburst motif on the loudspeaker grille. From *Wireless and Gramophone Trader*, 18th October 1930.

*G. Russell, *Designer's Trade*, London, 1968, pp.147-154; and N. Pevsner, *An Enquiry into Industrial Art in England*, Cambridge, 1937, pp.103-105.

which manufactured good quality sets in the medium price range, was to have cabinets that were still furniture, but recognisably modern. Murphy went to one of the leading designers of modern furniture, Gordon Russell, who produced a design that incorporated features from contemporary furniture without being derivative of some other article and was instantly recognisable as a radio set. In people's homes, these cabinets would almost invariably have looked more modern than the other furnishings. For the next twenty years, Murphy continued to have their cabinets designed and made by Gordon Russell, maintaining throughout the principle that the wireless, as a modern invention, should be housed inside a case of modern design that was also a piece of furniture and therefore gave the alien and confusing sounds of radio a place in people's homes.*

Throughout the 1930s, the majority of other manufacturers adopted a similar policy and sold their radios in cabinets that were essentially pieces of furniture, though not all of such tasteful appearance. Some, like Murphy and Pye, laid great stress on the quality of cabinet design, in the belief that sophistication and modernity were likely to attract customers.

The convention of housing wirelesses in cabinets that were identifiable as pieces of furniture gave radio an image which, while it might have been convenient, was not particularly true to its nature. One firm that did not follow the convention was E.K. Cole Ltd., which sold wirelesses under the brand name of Ekco. Cole was responsible for initiating what can now be recognised as the third stage of radio cabinet design, in which the imagery of technological futurism (as distinct from the raw technology that was evident in the Burndept receiver of 1924) was introduced to

Old couple having tea with Pye radio in the background, c.1935. The radio stands out as the most modern piece of furnishing in this interior.

provide the basis for the design. Although its technical development slowed down around 1930, radio continued for the following decade to be the most universal and available symbol of social change based upon technical progress. People still expected radios to move with the times and characterise the future. This expectation, originally fulfilled by constant improvements in the circuitry of receivers, was transferred into the design of radio cabinets. Cole discovered the potential for visual design to achieve this effect through circumstances connected with the production rather than the sale of wirelesses. Because of problems with the manufacture of wooden cabinets, the firm decided in 1930 to start making cabinets in bakelite.* This was a recently developed thermosetting plastic which promised to be a very cheap material for cabinets, provided that enough sets were sold in each design to cover the cost of the moulds. For its first two bakelite cabinets, Ekco employed a traditional furniture designer, and the results looked very much like imitation wooden cabinets. The firm then became dissatisfied and decided to employ a designer associated with the Modern Movement, in the hope that something more appropriate to the material might be achieved. Ekco approached the architect Serge Chermayeff, who already had a reputation for his modern furniture, and the set he designed went into production in 1933 as the AC64. Although this design could still have been constructed in plywood, it made rather more of the qualities of bakelite. In the following year, Ekco invited several 'modern' architects to submit designs in competition, and chose to put those by Wells Coates and Serge Chermayeff into production.

*Pevsner, 1937, pp.105-107; also W. Landauer, 'Plastics', *Trend*, vol.1, 1936, pp.75-91.

Below:
Ekco 313 Radio, 1930. Ekco's first experiment in moulded plastic cabinets. Although moulded in bakelite this design could equally well have been made in wood. From *Wireless and Gramophone Trader*, 1930.

Centre:
Ekco M25 radio receiver, bakelite cabinet, 1932. Designed by J.K. White. Although more 'modern', this cabinet was still similar to wooden ones.

Wells Coates's design, the AD 65, was unlike Chermayeff's designs in bearing no resemblance at all to furniture. Not only would it have been impracticable to make it of wood, but its circular form with chromium plated grille, prominent tuning dial and conspicuous knobs conveyed the impression that it housed a piece of unequivocally modern technology.

Where the Burndept receiver of 1924 had been technological in appearance, but not particularly modern, Wells Coates's AD 65 combined an evocation of technology with modernity. Unlike the earlier set, it gave the impression that the experimental stage was over and that it belonged instead to a world that would be made harmonious and comfortable by reliable and smooth-running technology. In its combination of technological sophistication with futurist imagery, the AD 65 was an achievement not previously realised in any radio cabinet design. As long as the use of valves required receivers to be fairly large, the convention of designing radio cabinets as furniture continued, but the introduction of transistors after World War II made great reductions in size possible and revived the problems of what a radio set should look like. As the majority of sets became portable, furniture ceased to have any relevance to cabinet design. Manufacturers cast around for other solutions, and made use, for example, of the forms of light hand luggage. By the 1960s, the majority were using the same set of ideas, though through different imagery, as had been developed by Ekco in the 1920s, and radios began to appear in the form of conspicuously modern objects of technology. Even if not all designs had pretensions to such technical sophistication as the black-anodised boxes of the 1970s, the tendency to adopt advanced scientific imagery has been fairly widespread.

The technical developments in wireless design since the 1950s have been minimal, but manufacturers have persisted in making radio sets look as if they were breaking the frontiers of science. Their attachment to this image led to the innumerable designs that imitated the appearance of the apparatus developed for the space programme. This self-conscious futurist symbolism has continued despite the fact that radios are no longer the only pieces of electronic technology in popular possession, nor even, since the

Ever Ready Sky Countess
portable transistor radio, 1959.
The advent of the battery-
powered transistor demanded a
new image for the cases: many
manufacturers chose to imitate
light hand luggage.

development of the silicon chip and its use in pocket calculators,
the most advanced. The effect has been to prevent radio from
taking a respectable place in history by trying constantly to convince
us that it belongs to an age that we are only just on the brink of
entering.

The use of imagery to make products appear 'ahead of their time'
has been a recurrent and at times thoroughly monotonous feature
of twentieth-century design. The reasons are not hard to see for the
appeal is exactly the same as that on which all millenarian religions
have been based. The attractions of a future from which all present
ills will have been eliminated are overwhelming; furthermore it is
emotionally very much easier to live in the past or the future than
it is to live in the present. The discovery by twentieth-century manufacturers that one of the most effective ways to stimulate the desire
for commodities was to suggest that they were the key to a clean,
harmonious and comfortable way of life would have come as no
surprise to any nineteenth-century revivalist preacher. What,
however, would have been a surprise was the entirely novel way
in which designers were able to make inanimate objects convey
this message without the assistance of words or pictures. The
success of design in using the imagery of science and technology
to convey a vision of a future free from discomfort and anxiety
has been one of the stranger phenomena of twentieth-century
society.

9. Labour-Saving in the Home

One of the claims made for electricity was that it would save work in the home. Publicity issued by the Electrical Development Association during the 1920s frequently promoted this idea, as in this quotation from an EDA pamphlet:

'What is the stroke of magic which for the last few years has been transforming household tasks, formerly so burdensome, into a part of the daily routine cheerfully undertaken by mistress or maid? Watch the keen interest of women in domestic labour aid appliances at any Home Exhibition. You will discover that the little electric motor is largely responsible for this welcome change. Indeed, Electricity comes as a timely solution of the servant and other problems, which threatened to disturb that most potent factor in civilisation – THE HOME; Electricity provides the modern housewife with a perfect servant – clean, silent, economical.

'What used to be the labour (hard labour) of hours is now accomplished almost without effort in a matter of minutes.'*

*'Chats' about Electricity, Electrical Development Association pamphlet no.422, 1925, p.5.

The idea that machines could turn housework from laborious drudgery into a few minutes' pleasure was not specific to electric

NO LONGER *tied down by housework*

Spring-clean with **ELECTRICITY**

EDA publicity, 1928. Electricity advertising went in for extravagant claims.

appliances, but exploited by manufacturers of all kinds of other household products and gadgets. Yet how could this absurd and impossible idea ever have been made to seem real, especially in a century when, more than ever before, women were expected to take pride in and labour over exactly the same work that was to be eliminated? The willingness of rational people to believe that appliances could remove work from the home was made possible only through a whole set of ideologies about housework, and to a large extent it was domestic appliance design that was responsible for making housework seem what it was said to be.

Mythologies of Housework

*A. Oakley, *Housewife*, London, 1974, pp. 52-53. The following discussion of the sociology of housework is based heavily on the same book.

Most modern housewives would rather see themselves as successors to the mistresses of middle-class nineteenth-century homes than to working-class wives of the same century.* Although doing their own housework makes modern housewives more like working-class women of the past than like middle-class women whose housework was done for them by servants, this gross self-deception helped housewives to suppose, as most have been inclined to do, that what they are engaged in is not really work at all, but some other kind of activity.

One of the most fundamental reasons why people have not regarded housework as work in the same sense as typing letters in an office or packing cartons in a factory has been to do with the conflicting domestic demands placed upon women. In Western societies in the early twentieth century, it came to be assumed that the only way for women to achieve fulfillment and recognition as women was by being successful in the rôle of housewives and mothers, an assumption that only began to be questioned openly in the 1960s. For the greater part of this century, despite the contrary standards that applied in wartime, both sexes took it for granted that women should derive pleasure from doing housework and looking after homes and families – a straightforward ideal, but one which the actual nature of housework rendered impossible. Because housework has been rewarded, not with money, but with the allegedly superior currency of emotional satisfaction, it is easy to think it is different to other work. Nevertheless, judged by the standards usually applied to other sorts of work, housework compares rather badly, for it is laborious and isolated, the hours are long and the work is unending.

There was a danger that if the negative aspects of the work became too obvious, they would detract from the pleasure that women were expected to derive from housework, and interfere with its unusual system of reward. Society and housewives themselves avoided these contradictions by resisting making comparisons between housework and other kinds of work, a dissociation which came about much more naturally if housework was not thought of as work at all. The nature of housework as a duty has been reconciled with the expectation that it should also be a voluntary expression of love through the idea that it is not actually work, an idea that has been represented endlessly through advertising, the media, stories in women's magazines and the design of kitchens and domestic appliances until it has acquired the force of 'common sense'.

A second reason why housework was dissociated from other kinds of work had to do with what was thought of as its demeaning nature. Although in some quarters housework was represented as the most worthwhile and rewarding of activities, the very same tasks of cleaning, cooking, washing and mending, when done by servants in the homes of the nineteenth and early twentieth-century middle class, had been regarded as lowly and undignified. So much was domestic service looked down upon that young women in service would usually try and conceal the fact that they were 'skivvies' from any potential male admirer for fear that the knowledge would cool the man's interest.[*] When, as happened in the early part of the twentieth century, increasing numbers of women who aspired to middle-class status found themselves having to do the same work as servants, it was natural that they should want to distinguish housework from servant's work in order not to be degraded by it. Rather than pretending that housework was not work at all, another strategy was to make it into a 'craft' and, through the development of higher standards, to endow it with the status of a profession, which was the purpose behind organisations like the Good Housekeeping Institute.

*C.V. Butler, *Domestic Service, an Enquiry by the Women's Industrial Council*, London, 1916. pp. 13-40; M. Powell, *Below Stairs*, London, 1968, p.79.

Because of its associations with servants, domestic work had come to be regarded as improper for middle-class women as early as the mid-nineteenth century. For instance, a surgeon's wife wrote in 1859: 'I must not do our household work, or carry my baby one: or I should lose caste. We must keep a servant.'[*] Only 'progressive' or eccentric people could risk ignoring the convention that middle-class households needed to keep at least one servant. As long as the supply of servants was sufficient, this convention presented no problems, but difficulties arose in the early part of the twentieth century because of the rapidly increasing number of aspirants to middle-class status. A rough indication of the change can be seen in the growth in the number of salaried workers from about 1.7 million in 1911 to about 2.7 million in 1921.[*] Though these people, paid monthly and wearing a suit to work, might have regarded themselves as middle-class, the fact that there had been no corresponding increase in the number of domestic servants meant that their wives were compelled to do their own housework. This was demeaning and interfered seriously with their claims to belong to the middle class. Aspirants to this status therefore found the mythologies surrounding housework particularly attractive: the idea that housework was not work removed one of the main barriers to social advancement by obscuring the reality of the domestic tasks they found themselves still having to do.

*Quoted in T.M. McBride, *The Domestic Revolution*, London, 1976, p.18.

*A.L. Bowley and J. Stamp, *The National Income, 1924*, Oxford, 1927, pp.11-12.

The Myth of the Mechanical Servant

The pretence that housework was not work could seem more convincing if there were some alternative to the servant, a substitute which could appear to do the laborious and degrading parts of her work. Thus an additional myth was created about housework, the idea that domestic appliances were replacements for servants. This idea has had a compulsive attraction both to housewives and to manufacturers of domestic appliances. The myth that the work once done by servants has been taken over by gadgets and machines has been repeated so often that it has acquired the authenticity of historical truth. But persuasive though this line in advertising has been, it hardly needs to be said that appliances and servants are not interchangeable, since a large part of domestic work in cooking, cleaning and childcare consists of tasks that cannot be automated.

You set it and forget it...

no filling
no emptying
no scrubbing
no wringing
no clouds of
steam

BENDIX
SOAKS · WASHES
RINSES THREE TIMES
DAMP-DRIES CLOTHES
DRAINS & SWITCHES OFF

.. all by itself !

BENDIX
automatically
**gives you time to do those
things you want to do**

Write for full particulars to:
**BENDIX HOME APPLIANCES, LIMITED,
ALBION WORKS, KINGSBURY ROAD, BIRMINGHAM, 24**

★ Over half a
million British
housewives
use BENDIX
Automatic
Washers in the
home or at
their local
"Launderette"
every week

Advertisement for Bendix washing machine, 1955. The advertisement was optimistic about the freedom it would bring to the housewife. From *Daily Mail Ideal Home Book*, 1955, p.118.

*Oakley, p.7.

Advertisements have tended to exaggerate the extent to which appliances could take over entire tasks: for example, the 1955 advertisement for the Bendix washing machine implied that it could appropriate the entire task of domestic laundry (though only, it turned out, to leave the housewife free for another form of domestic work). Similarly, the manufacturers' illustrations of cookers, with ovens brimming with roasts, soufflés and other dishes while smartly dressed women stood idly by, suggested that these were magical cooking machines with the capacity to deliver ready-cooked meals by some process of immaculate conception.

Although appliances do reduce the amount of labour involved in particular domestic tasks, it is significant that since they have become widespread, they have not been used to bring about any overall reduction in the time spent on housework. There is evidence that during the period when domestic appliances became common in Britain, women spent not less but more time on housework: in 1950, a survey of full-time housewives surveyed showed that they spent an average of 70 hours a week on housework, and another survey in 1970 showed an average of 77 hours.* What seems to have happened is that appliances lightened the burden and saved time in certain tasks, but also made it possible to achieve higher standards. Thus the time saved was spent on doing the same job, or other jobs, more often or better.

The labour-increasing consequences of labour-saving devices had been noticed in the United States as early as 1930, when an article in the *Ladies' Home Journal* argued:

'Because we housewives of today have the tools to reach it, we dig every day after the dust that grandmother left to a spring cataclysm. If few of us have nine children for a weekly bath, we have two or three for a daily immersion. If our consciences don't prick over

*Ladies' Home Journal, May 1930, p.30.

vacant pie shelves or empty cookie jars, they do over meals in which a vitamin may be omitted or a calorie lacking.'*

Domestic economy experts also observed and commented on the labour-increasing effects of appliances. Thus, Hazel Kyrk, whose book *Economic Problems of the Family* was published in America in 1933 wrote:

'In household production too, as elsewhere, we have shown a tendency to use the time freed by labor-saving machinery not for more leisure, but for more goods or services of the same general character. The invention of the sewing machine meant more garments, for a time garments on which there was an enormous amount of sewing – tucks, ruffles and so on. The invention of the washing machine has meant more washing, of the vacuum cleaner more cleaning, of new fuels and cooking equipment, more courses and more elaborately cooked food.'*

*Hazel Kyrk, *Economic Problems of the Family*, New York, p.99.

The failure of appliances to bring about any savings in the time spent on housework was not a consequence for which the appliances themselves could be blamed. It is clear that the compulsion to use them to achieve higher domestic standards was the result of the 'conscience' referred to in the *Ladies' Home Journal* article or, in other words, the general expectation that twentieth-century women should take trouble in looking after their homes and families to the highest possible standard.

Despite all this, appliances have continued to be described as 'labour-saving', and the idea that they are substitutes for servants

Publicity photograph, American electric cooker, 1961. No mess, no sweat – the cooker, it seems, produces meals on its own.

"Which shall it be?" The overworked woman in unsightly attire, or the attractive woman in neat attire who keeps her self-respect because she uses an electrical cleaning service?

Publicity photograph for Hoover electric vacuum cleaner, 1927. Significantly, the advantages held out for the vacuum cleaner were not that it saved time, but that it enabled the housewife to dress neatly while cleaning the carpets. From *The Electrician*, September 1927.

has been repeated with monotonous regularity. The unlikely equivalence between people and machines was made to seem real in a fabric of stories about the departure of servants and their replacement by appliances that were published between 1910 and 1930 in magazines and household manuals. The following story, 'I Am Glad my Servant Left', appeared in the *Ladies' Home Journal* in 1918:

'My maid left to go into Munitions work . . . I've been thinking, and I'm glad she's gone! I have gone to the bottom of why I don't like housework, and conclude it is because I have never had the right thing to work with at the right time. I recall that "there are always tools to work with for those who will", and on the other hand that "a poor workman loses his tools". I figure that what I save on clothes this year will balance the increased cost of food and what I save on the maid's wages I can put into working conveniences and still be to the good.'*

Ladies' Home Journal, November 1918, p.28.

The author went on to list the many appliances, among them a vacuum cleaner, an electric knife-sharpener, a dishwasher and a washing machine, that enabled her to enjoy life without a servant.

In this story, the cause of the servant's departure had been the war, but different versions of similar events had appeared before

1914, each with the moral that it was possible to live more comfortably and more economically by substituting a few appliances for the labour of a servant. In a book called *First Aid to the Servantless*, published in Britain in 1913, the author, Mrs J.G. Frazer, gave a fictional account of how Mr and Mrs Smith, having sacked their maid Imogen, were able to live a very much more agreeable existence with the aid of a few appliances, such as a vacuum cleaner, a washing-up machine, an electric boot-cleaner, some improvements to the fixtures of the home and some re-organisation in their lives Another book with the same message was Randal Phillips's *The Servantless House* (1920). With investment in a few appliances and some changes in domestic fittings, such as wooden rather than brass stair rods, chromed rather than brass taps, and drainage racks in the kitchen, Phillips argued that it was possible to live not only more comfortably but also more cheaply without servants. He appended a set of accounts to show that where the total cost of a servant was £90 a year, including wages and board, a mere £40 would buy a number of lasting labour-saving improvements and still leave money in hand out of the year's expenditure.

Such stories and arguments all suggested that the appliances were indeed servants in another form. This might be seen as nothing but a harmless poetic fiction which no one seriously believed. Even so the myth has had enough influence for it to be mistaken for the truth in almost all histories of domestic appliances and domestic labour, as in the discussion of 'labour-saving' appliances in *The Oxford History of Technology*, which begins as follows:

'The First World War was a watershed in social habits and conditions and greatly affected the design and adoption of household objects. During and after the war servants effactually vanished for ever – and in any case comparatively few families were left who could have afforded them.'*

*G.B.L. Wilson, 'Domestic Appliances', chapter 47 in *A History of Technology*, edited by T.I. Williams, vol.VII, part 2, Oxford, 1978, p.1135.

The author goes on to assume that appliances were developed to replace the absent servants. This account disregards several facts. In the first place, domestic service far from disappeared in Britain after 1918: although many servants left service during the war, the number in employment by 1921 had returned almost to pre-war levels. Domestic service remained common in Britain until 1939; only then did it disappear for good. The decline in domestic service was a long-term process that took place over about fifty years, between 1890 and 1940. In 1891, the year in which the greatest number was recorded, there were approximately 0.24 servants per household in Britain; by 1911, the figure had dropped to 0.16, and the decline over the next twenty years was more gradual, to 0.14 servants per household in 1921, and to 0.12 in 1931.*

*Calculated from Great Britain, *Census Reports*, 1891 to 1931.

It is clear that the decline was not precipitated by World War I and that in the period between 1911 and 1939 the process was slow and gradual. Since there was a fairly rapid increase in the ownership of domestic appliances in the inter-war years, quite out of proportion to the decline in servant numbers, it would appear that appliances were manufactured and bought for other purposes than simply to provide substitutes for servants.

Another objection to the 'servant displacement' theory is that most of the early appliances were designed for use by servants. Until the 1930s, virtually the only people, at least in Britain, who

*G. Routh, *Occupation and Pay in Great Britain 1906-60*, Cambridge, 1965, pp.64, 104.

could afford to buy domestic appliances were also those who employed domestic servants: in the early 1920s, the average income of professionals and managers lay between £500 and £700 per annum and even people of this class would have been hard-pressed to afford a vacuum cleaner for £20 or a washing machine for £25.* Manufacturers were well aware that their principal customers were sufficiently well-off to employ servants, and in Britain in the period just before and just after World War I this was acknowledged in manufacturers' advertising, which frequently showed appliances being used by servants (illustrated on p.177). Indeed, it could be argued that far from replacing servants, appliances actually halted the decline in their numbers. The grounds for supposing this are that towards the end of World War I, when there was alarm among the middle class that the temporary shortage of domestic servants might become permanent, ways began to be sought of making domestic service more attractive. The reluctance of women to go into service was attributed in part to the sheer laboriousness of the work, and it was therefore supposed that better designed houses and more labour-saving appliances would entice working-class women into domestic service. The Women's Advisory Committee of the Ministry of Reconstruction reported as follows in 1919:

'We are convinced that much of the dissatisfaction and discomfort felt by workers and employers arises from preventable waste of labour and bad general conditions which could be remedied. Domestic workers will not take pleasure in their work so long as much of it consists in constantly carrying by hand for unnecessary distances, often up and down stairs, considerable weights of water, wood and fuel, of tending heating and cooking apparatus undesirably wasteful of labour, and of the larger cleaning processes which could be better effected by outside workers furnished with mechanical appliances. One evil is the prevalence of antiquated house planning and labour wasting fittings and appliances.'*

*Ministry of Reconstruction, Women's Advisory Committee, 'Report on the Domestic Service Problem', Cmd. 67, *Parliamentary Papers*, 1919, vol.29, p.28.

The introduction of appliances, combined with the installation of hot water systems, could certainly relieve some of the burdens of domestic work, even if they did not actually induce working-class women into service. Certainly, employers believed that well-equipped homes were more likely to attract servants, since advertisements for domestic posts in London newspapers in the 1930s often included such terms as 'labour-saving house' or 'labour-saving appliances'.

Although manufacturers gave their products such names as the Daisy or the Betty Anne (both vacuum cleaners) to suggest that the appli ice was a substitute for a servant, and although household manuals and magazines frequently drew the public's attention to the economics of exchanging a servant for some labour-saving appliances, there were probably few households in which this transaction actually occurred. In general, at least in Britain, the class that had been able to afford servants before 1914 was still able to do so after the war, while those without the means before the war remained in the same position afterwards.

The myth of the mechanical servant furnished people who had never employed a servant, and were never likely to, with the illusion of a substitute at least as good as a servant of flesh and blood. It allowed housewives to believe that what they found themselves doing was not really work at all. In reality, nobody could have been entirely taken in by the idea that washing machines or vacuum cleaners were really substitutes for servants, but the illusion helped quell any uneasiness that people might have felt about their status in society and made it possible for almost all housewives, of all classes, to believe that they were the successors to the servant-employing mistress of the nineteenth-century house.

The Aesthetics of Housework

The styling of appliances has always depended in part on the users for whom they were intended. Initially, it was only small appliances, likely to be used directly by their owners in their living or dining rooms, such as electric kettles and toasters, that were designed with much attention to their appearance. There was no reason for 'below stairs' appliances for cleaning and cooking to match the standards of elegance found in the drawing room. Many of the appliances intended for use by servants resembled industrial equipment. The similarity was not seen as needing to be concealed; an Electrical Development Association pamphlet of 1924 specifically mentioned that there were domestic mixers 'designed like the dough mixers of modern bakeries, but in miniature form.* While it would be an overstatement to suggest that the form of such appliances was wholly determined by the class of labour for which they were intended, it would at least be true to say that as long as they were made principally for use by servants,

*'Chats' about Electricity, p.6.

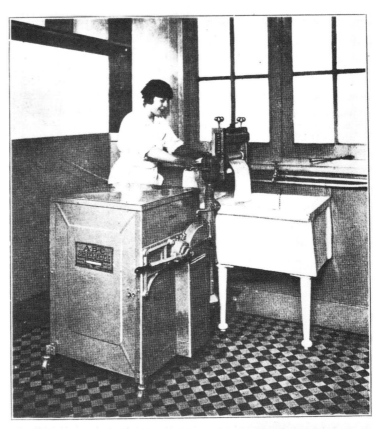

Electric washing machine, c.1920. Early domestic electrical appliances were generally expected to be used by servants, and resembled industrial plant. From A.G. Whyte, *The All Electric Age*, London, 1922.

ANOTHER FORM OF ELECTRIC WASHING MACHINE AND WRINGER
The motor operating the washer and wringer is started and stopped by the handle at the side of the machine.

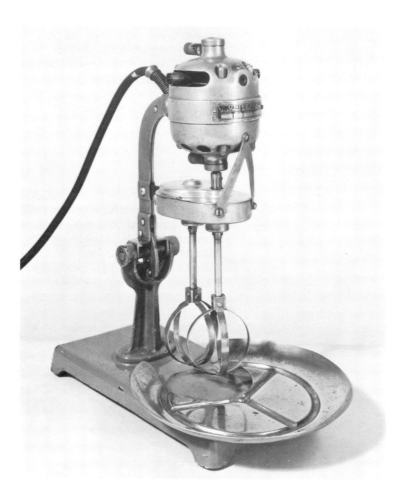

Domestic electric food mixer, c.1920. An appliance of essentially industrial appearance.

it did not matter greatly to the people who bought them if the appliances were heavy, clumsy and crudely assembled.

Clearly, the most important requirements of design were that the appliances should be efficient in operation, easy to use and quickly assembled or dismantled. From the 1930s onwards, these were the principal criteria of good appliance design, and, particularly during the 1950s, many improvements were made along these lines. However, manufacturers were well aware that appearance and styling could also contribute towards making the public believe in the labour-saving potential of their products, an important consideration once they started to expand their market by appealing to the servantless middle class. In the 1930s, when domestic appliances began to be mass-produced, the most potent metaphor for efficiency was the factory. Just as the imagery of the factory was employed extensively to suggest efficiency in offices, housewives were encouraged to achieve efficiency in the home by planning their domestic duties as if they were tasks in an industrial routine. Much was made of the potential of scientific management techniques for rationalising work in the home: two American texts, both published in 1915, Mary Pattison's *The Business of Home Management* and Christine Frederick's *Household Engineering*, were the earliest and best known of numerous books and articles in which it was shown how the breakdown of domestic tasks could lead to more efficient housework.* Diagrams of movements

*Household efficiency is discussed in D.P. Handlin, *The American Home*, Boston 1979, chapter 6; and Gwendolyn Wright , *Building the Dream, A Social History of Housing in America*, New York, 1981, chapter 9.

in the kitchen, after the manner of F.W. Taylor's analyses of labour in the factory, indicated supposedly optimum kitchen layouts. The analogy between the home and the factory in these books and many later writings was strengthened by frequent references to the kitchen as a workshop and to domestic appliances as tools. For instance, according to one domestic manual:

'No man in a factory would be expected to produce good work without proper tools, but the housewife often tries to do her work with totally inadequate equipment . . . She must, therefore, make sure that her home is run easily by using care in choosing tools.'*

*Odham's Household Management Illustrated, n.d. [c.1950], p.161.

These analogies between the home and the factory also influenced design. Manufacturers deliberately styled their appliances in forms reminiscent of factory or industrial equipment of the time to emphasise the labour-saving efficiency which they claimed for their products. For example, the first model of the British Kenwood food mixer, introduced just after World War II, closely resembled industrial catering equipment of the period, and many other appliances manufactured between the 1930s and the 1950s showed similar imagery.

Making a domestic appliance look like a piece of factory equipment might have been a good way of making it seem efficient, but in other respects it was an extremely bad marketing device, particularly when, in the 1950s, appliances began to be bought by people who actually spent a large part of their lives working in factories. The presence in the kitchen of an object that looked like a machine tool not only militated against notions of the home as a place separate from work, but also made housework look disturbingly like real work, a comparison that everyone was anxious to avoid.

It is noticeable that during the 1950s appliances that resembled industrial equipment began to get unfavourable comments in the press, whatever their functional or operational merits, and by the end of the decade it had become something of an insult to describe a

Efficient (a) and Inefficient (b) Kitchen Plans, 1920. The application of Taylorism to the kitchen was an attempt to bring the efficiency of the factory to the home. From C. Frederick, *Scientific Management in the Home: Household Engineering*, London, 1920.

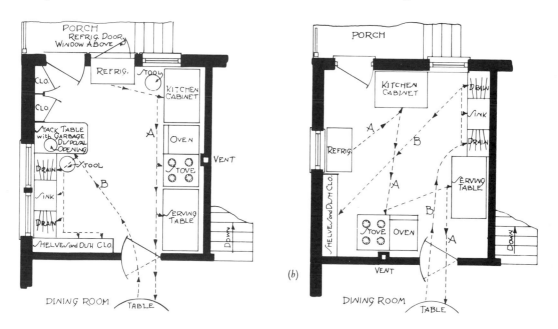

Kenwood domestic food mixer, A700, 1948. The design was a scaled-down version of catering mixers.

*L. Bruce Archer, 'Electric Food Mixers', *Design*, no.125, May 1959, pp.41-43.

domestic appliance as looking industrial. This, for instance, was *Design* magazine's criticism of the Kenwood mixer in 1959:

'The full, rounded curves of the power head, looking more like porcelain than metal, and the thick parallelism of the column emphasise the heaviness of the machine. Add the old-fashioned black-on-white paintbrush script of the maker's name, and the general effect is closer to hotel kitchen machinery than to the modern domestic interior.'*

The pioneer of a new kind of styling for domestic appliances was the German firm of Max Braun. Although long-established as an electrical manufacturer, Braun did not start making domestic appliances until the 1950s. The two principal designers employed

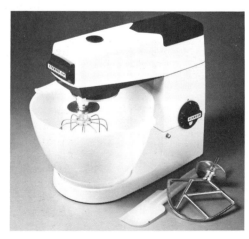

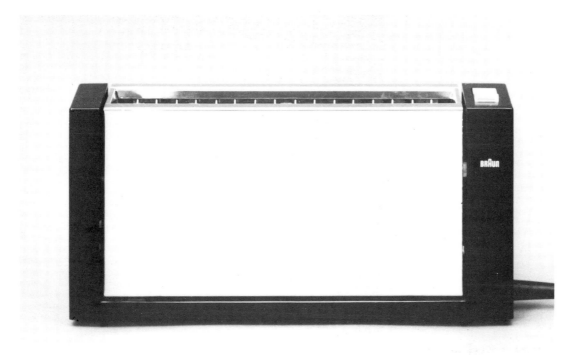

Braun electric toaster, HT1, 1961, designed by Reinhold Weiss. Braun introduced a new aesthetic for domestic appliances, distinguishing them from office or factory equipment.

*R. Banham, 'Household Godjets', reprinted from *New Society* in *Arts in Society*, edited by P. Barker, London, 1977, pp.164-169; see also 'Design Review, Braun', *Architectural Review*, vol.131, 1962, pp.344-348.

Far left:
Braun electric kitchen machine, KM2, 1957. This design, with its delicacy and crispness, departed from all previous mixer styling.

Left:
Kenwood chef mixer A701, 1960, designed by Kenneth Grange. Other manufacturers followed Braun's example in restyling their products.

*Archer in *Design*, no.125, p.44.

by Braun, Hans Gugelot and Dieter Rams, both associated with the Hochschule für Gestaltung at Ulm, developed a standard of appearance that departed radically from all previous appliance design. Braun products appeared in discreet, smooth, grey and white boxes, designed on proportional systems and had a purity of form that was recognised by the intellectual élite as being derived from the classical tradition.* The forms had a more immediate marketing attraction in being unlike industrial equipment. The appliances, though robust, were so elegant and delicate in their finish that they were more like finely-worked sculpture than anything that belonged in the office or the factory. For example, the base and powerhead of the food mixer, designed by Gerd Muller and put on the market in 1957, were housed beneath a virtually unbroken skin, ornamented only by the coloured plastic of the control knob and area above the beater socket, and by the crisp lettering: it was quite unlike other mixers on the market at the time, which used imagery that was mostly derived from cars, spaceships or factories (see illustration on p.199). The styling of Braun products suited the deceits and contradictions of housework well, for their appearance raised no comparisons with machine tools or office equipment and preserved the illusion that housework was an elevated and noble activity. When *Design* magazine compared the Braun mixer with other makes, it acknowledged the machine's unique capacity to satisfy the expectations of housework. 'Only the Braun', it wrote, 'appeared to have been designed with a woman, a kitchen sink, and a crowded shelf in mind.'*

Other manufacturers rapidly followed Braun's example and modified the design of their products along the same lines, even if they did not take the aesthetic to such virtuous lengths of purity and refinement. For example, Kenwood, whose original mixer had been compared unfavourably with the Braun, redesigned their machine in 1960 to incorporate some Braun-like characteristics: the power-head and base were fitted into a single monolithic form, and the styling was crisp and hard-edged, with the separate elements of the machine expressed by coloured plastic mouldings.

Commercial sense developed a standard of appearance for domestic appliances which succeeded in making even more vivid the illusion of housework not being work. Unlike advertising, television or fiction, whose messages were always transitory, the physical presence in the home of appliances of specifically domestic appearance was a continuing confirmation of the special nature of housework.

Consumer-oriented Design

It might be asked how manufacturers came to represent the mythologies of housework so closely in the design of appliances. Their success might suggest that they and their designers had become exceptionally well attuned to consumer's sensibilities. Certainly, they tried hard during the 1950s to understand better what consumers wanted and to incorporate their understanding more perfectly in design. Indeed it became something of an axiom in the 1950s, at least in the United States, that the consumer's values lay at the heart of all good design. For example, one American industrial designer, David Chapman, stated in 1957:

'I am convinced that the search for successful product development does not start with a study of manufacturing processes, merchandising techniques, cost accounting or analysis of competitive merchandise . . . the industry must get to the roots of the problem and study people and their way of living.'*

*Quoted in 'Overseas Review', *Design*, no.104, August 1957, p.43.

But although increasingly sophisticated market research may have made designers better able to understand people's wants, increasingly sophisticated techniques of persuasion, described so vividly by Vance Packard in *The Hidden Persuaders*, were making manufacturers more adept at convincing their customers that the products being offered had been designed exactly to match their desires. It is therefore almost impossible to say to what extent the needs that consumer-oriented design satisfied were felt independently, rather than being the products of persuasion.

If we consider the following statement made in 1957 by Arthur BecVar, head of appliance design at General Electric in the United States, we can see how he was advancing ideas that he and many others probably believed to be true but which were also very useful in convincing the public of their need for domestic appliances:

' . . . more emphasis is placed on home and family living . . . larger families and lack of servants have necessitated as many automatic helpers in the home as possible. By his investment in mechanical servants, an individual can show how he is providing for his family.

'The woman's rôle in our society has become increasingly complex with the triple responsibility of raising a family and running a home, holding a job, and keeping up with outside activities. She is more active in civic, social and national affairs than ever before. She is caught in a maelstrom and needs all the technological help which a technological society can give her. Yet with all these forces

Design, no.104, p.46.

pulling her in different directions, she still wants to retain the role of creative home maker – but without unnecessary drudgery.'*

BecVar described the conditions of modern domestic life in terms that superficially seem accurate, and certainly corresponded in part to what most people thought. Yet the analysis was also misleading: while he acknowledged the conflict between domestic and external rôles, he overlooked the much more fundamental conflicts in the purely domestic rôle of the housewife, where the work was meant to be the expression of love but actually consisted of unrewarding and unending tasks. BecVar's stress upon housewives' wishes to participate in outside activities was calculated to make the purchase of domestic appliances irresistible; had he chosen to recognise other conflicts experienced by housewives, he could not have offered such a straight-forward solution.

Consumer-oriented design was highly selective in what it chose to express of consumers' ideas and beliefs, with a strong tendency to relate only to those problems of consumers' lives that the product concerned stood a good chance of being able to banish. Naturally, it was very much easier to banish false or mythical problems rather than real ones.

The way that the design of manufactured goods invariably contains all sorts of ideas has been a major theme of this book. Yet the process by which design incorporates these ideas is by no means direct, although manufacturers would sometimes like us to believe that it is and that they act only as neutral agents, transmitting through their products ideas that we are all said to hold. In practice, however, manufacturers filter and distill these ideas and add some of their own, all with the intention of making their products seem more desirable. Hygiene and labour-saving have both mattered to a lot of people in this century, but as represented in domestic appliances, they have been modified, added to and subtracted from in ways that manufacturers supposed would suit their commercial ends. In the way it transforms ideas and beliefs, successful design is like alchemy: it fuses together disparate ideas from different origins, so that the form of the completed product seems to embody only a single idea, which comes across as so familiar that we find ourselves supposing it to be exactly what we ourselves had always thought.

Wherever the ideas embedded in manufactured goods come from, they are just as important in design as the more objective factors such as the price of labour or the availability of materials. The rôle of ideas, other than purely artistic ones, has not usually been given much weight in discussions of design. When it has been acknowledged, the ideas have generally been referred to as influences, a description that belittles their importance and fails to make clear how central they are. Without the existence of certain ideas about the nature of domestic life and the part that appliances might play in it, none of the products discussed in this chapter could have been designed. Despite the existence of capital, labour, machines and materials with which to make them, and a market to sell them to, it is only ideas that have allowed any of the products to progress beyond a shapeless heap of raw materials. The capacity of design to create form occurs only through the conjunction between ideology and material factors: if either is absent, the union cannot take place.

10. Design and Corporate Identity

Of all the ways in which design can influence the way we think, the only one to have been acknowledged widely has been its use to express the identity of organisations. Empires, armies, navies, religious orders and modern corporations have all used design to convey ideas about what they are like both to insiders and to the outside world. Thus, as the Romans conquered successive nations and races and incorporated them within their Empire, buildings in recognisably Roman, rather than local style, helped to impress upon subject nations the supremacy of Roman law and government, while it also helped to ensure that Roman settlers in distant parts of the Empire did not forget their allegiance to Rome and become too closely identified with the native populations.

Several hundred years later, the new monastic orders of the early Middle Ages used architecture in a similar way to impress upon monks the supremacy of their order above purely local interests. Until the development of the Cluniac order in the tenth century, Christian monasticism had been cellular in organisation: the many individual monasteries all followed broadly the rule of St Benedict, but they were otherwise independent and, apart from acknowledging the authority of the Pope, belonged to no hierarchy. Gradually, in the tenth century, the abbey of Cluny became the centre of monastic reform, and its revised and more rigorous system of rule was introduced into many monasteries throughout Western Europe; Cluny became their spiritual head, dispensing rules and advice to other houses, and often providing them with abbots. Along with the new monastic ideal, the Cluniacs also carried with them a preference for a particular form of architecture, subsequently to become known as the Romanesque. Though there is no evidence to suggest that the Cluniacs intended their architecture to demonstrate the principles of their order in any particularly direct way, or that they were very dogmatic in its application, Romanesque became closely associated in people's minds with the abbey of Cluny.*

*Joan Evans, *Monastic Life at Cluny 910-1157*, London, 1931; and Joan Evans, *The Romanesque Architecture of the Order of Cluny*, Cambridge, 1938.

In the twelfth century, the influence of the Cluniacs was supplanted by a new monastic reform movement, the Cistercian order, centred on the abbey of Clairvaux. Like the Cluniacs, the Cistercians developed a preferred form of architecture, which was to be the basis of the Gothic style, and they disseminated this with considerable energy. New Cistercian houses were built according to a strict pattern, which was reproduced in all the countries where they established foundations. The ground plans were so similar that a monk from France visiting an abbey in England could immediately comprehend its layout and organisation; equally, the appearance of each abbey identified it as Cistercian. There were clear advantages in this architectural policy; it made Cistercian houses and Cistercian monasticism easy to distinguish from backward and unreformed monasteries, and it impressed upon the monks and abbots their allegiance to the order, whose authority extended across national and political boundaries. Any inclinations by particular abbeys to develop independent rules, or to secede from the order, were discouraged not only by the routine visits of monks from other houses in the order, but also by the enduring presence of the distinctive architecture of their buildings.*

*A.W. Clapham, *English Romanesque Architecture after the Conquest*, Oxford, 1934, pp.74-83.

Organisations which extend over a large geographical area, perhaps across different countries and languages, have always had difficulties in maintaining their cohesion. The problems were as great for the monastic orders of the Middle Ages as they are for multi-national companies today; the design policies of a company like IBM, which operates in many countries, have been developed to fulfill much the same purpose as early Gothic architecture served for the Cistercians, making the identity of the company apparent to the employees, and advertising the company's special characteristics to the public. Some of the ways in which design has been used by modern organisations to hold themselves together and to publicise themselves have been described by a corporate identity consultant, Wally Olins, in his book, *The Corporate Personality*, published in 1978.

The book is so informative that I need do no more here than summarise his argument. Design, he says, can be used to convey to people the shape and nature of organisations that might otherwise appear formless, either because of their geographical spread or because they have come into existence through the merging of many smaller organisations. Particularly for a large organisation, made up of many smaller companies, each of which may be better known to the public and to the stock market, design is a way of conveying their collective identity to the world; in helping the employees of the separate parts of a large company to recognise the identity of the whole, it can counteract the hostilities that often arise between those working for the different parts of conglomerates that have been created by mergers. Rather than simply adding to Olins's list of examples, the rest of this chapter will be taken up with considering the variety of problems that were resolved through the use of design in a single organisation.

London Transport: the creation of a public transport conglomerate

London Transport provides one of the best known and most often quoted case histories of corporate design. However, the way in which it has been discussed exemplifies the inadequacies of much design criticism and history, in particular the tendency to isolate design in a make-believe world of pure aestheticism. Little attention has been paid to why design was so important to London Transport, or what it was expected to do; and most of the discussion has been centred on the contribution of one man, Frank Pick. In the 1920s, Pick was the managing director of the company that ran most of London's buses and underground railways, and in 1933, he became the Vice Chairman and Chief Executive of the newly-formed London Passenger Transport Board, a post which he held until 1940. While Pick undoubtedly conceived London Transport's design policy, and much of the success in its execution was due to him, it would be wrong to suppose that the policy was

Ticket Hall, Euston underground station, photographed in 1924. A typical station entrance before the design reforms of the 1930s.

*Nikolaus Pevsner, 'Patient Progress One: Frank Pick', in his *Studies in Art, Architecture and Design*, vol.2, London, 1968, pp.190-209 (reprinted from *Architectural Review*, vol.XCII, 1942). For an earlier version of the argument developed in this chapter, see A. Forty, 'Lorenzo of the Underground', *London Journal*, vol.5, no.1, 1979, pp.113-119.

*C. Barman, 'Frank Pick', *Architectural Review*, vol.XCI, 1942, pp.1-2; and C. Barman, *The Man Who Built London Transport*, Newton Abbot, 1979.

motivated solely by his taste and his own aesthetic idealism. The descriptions that have laboured Pick's belief in the moral and regenerative powers of design and his support for 'modernism' have largely ignored the fact that he was the manager of a large and very complicated organisation, and everything he did about design or anything else had to satisfy commercial ends and to meet with the approval of the rest of the management. Although Pick believed, in the tradition of John Ruskin and William Morris, that design could raise human life to a higher spiritual level, his choice of designs was based upon what he judged would be good for London Transport. To separate Pick's interest in design from his role as a manager of London Transport, as Sir Nikolaus Pevsner's article about him did, is to sever design from the sinews of material life, a form of butchery too often performed by historians of the subject, generally to fatal effect.*

One of the few people to have acknowledged the commercial aspects of London Transport's design policy was Christian Barman, who was publicity manager in the 1930s and was responsible for the co-ordination of the design policy.* Yet even he does not make altogether clear how important design was in management, or exactly how it was used to deal with the problems that beset London Transport during the inter-war years. Those problems have been described very extensively by T.C. Barker and Michael Robbins in volume two of their *History of London Transport*. Like most historians, however, Barker and Robbins appear unaccustomed to thinking of design as having any relevance outside purely artistic, or technical spheres. That it might have affected the entire way in which the population of London regarded London

Ticket Hall, Southgate station, opened in 1933. The orderliness and unity of the design of this new station on the Piccadilly line extension contrasts sharply with the Euston entrance. The photograph is at night: in daylight the hall is lit naturally by the clerestory windows encircling the space.

Escalator Tunnel at Turnpike Lane station, opened in 1932. The spaciousness and dignity of the new stations on the Piccadilly line extension signified a new era in underground travel.

Transport and might have influenced the development of ideas about the size, shape and character of the city does not seem to have occurred to them, though from remarks in his writings it is clear that these possibilities had been appreciated by Frank Pick.

During the inter-war years, Londoners saw considerable changes in the appearance of their public transport. Underground station entrances which had been poorly lit, dark lobbies, like the entrances to hell, became open, bright and airy spaces. Escalators, lit by reflected light, replaced lifts at many stations. Beneath, the cavernous tunnels which had been lined with white glazed bricks like public

ODBEFHIJKLMN PQURSTVWCG QU WA &YXZJ

lavatories or workhouse reception wards, were refaced with square cream tiles that reflected a softer light and did not show the dirt so easily. The station signs were laid out in an orderly manner and were clearly distinguished from the posters lining the platforms by the red and blue roundel, which was the symbol of the Underground. Throughout the system, the same clear lettering was used for station signs, directions and information; the typeface, designed by Edward Johnston in 1916, became a distinctive mark

Station Furniture for London
Transport, incorporating
roundel and station signs, 1933.

Platform, Bounds Green station, in 1932. The improvements to station design gave the platform tunnel a smooth shell, improved the lighting, and clearly distinguished station signs from posters.

of the company and was in time extended throughout the system to identify all its property and all its publicity. The station furniture was a model of pure, simple design, as neat and orderly as the typeface. In the stations and outside them, posters in artistic styles otherwise rarely found outside Bond Street art galleries advertised the joys of travel by this efficient and orderly system. On the railways, the locomotives of the earlier trains were gradually eliminated and the motors installed under the floors of the carriages, to give more passenger space; pneumatic doors operated by the guard replaced passenger-operated doors and gates, while the interiors of the carriages became increasingly seamless in appearance, with flush surfaces, faired-in details, invisible bolts and screws, high-quality upholstery to specially commissioned designs, and special bulbous handholds to replace the earlier strap loops. Above ground, the motor buses changed during the 1930s from crude machines like orange boxes on wheels to sleek objects with every constructional detail concealed beneath shaped panels.

These changes took place gradually until, by 1939, the single most striking characteristic of London Transport was that all the parts – every station, bus, train, poster, seat and litter bin – were identifiable as the property of a single organisation. This is not a solution to transport design that can be taken for granted: other capital cities, though their rail and road services may be run by a single organisation, have not gone to such lengths to identify them as such.

The reasons behind London Transport's approach come from its history. Its origins lay in the many independent bus, underground railway and tram companies that developed in the latter part of the nineteenth century and the early twentieth century.*

*This summary, and most of the information about London Transport in this chapter are based on T.C. Barker and Michael Robbins, *History of London Transport*, vol.2, London, 1974.

227

Left:
Piccadilly line carriage in 1923. Relatively large amounts of dark woodwork and low lighting levels were characteristic of carriages before the design reforms.

Right:
ST Bus, 1929. The type of bus most widely used by the London General Omnibus Co. in the late 1920s.

Right:
RT Bus, 1939. The perfected version of the inter-war improvements in bus design; the RT bus was a vehicle of London Transport's corporate style.

Left:
Bakerloo line carriage, 1938. The new carriage designs reduced the amount of woodwork, made the more numerous handholds integral with the interior, and modified the carriage lighting.

The first underground railway in London, the Metropolitan, was opened in 1863, with a service between Paddington and Farringdon Street; in the succeeding forty years, new lines were built by other companies, creating a network of separate routes beneath London. A short period of rash speculation in the early part of this century made it clear that some of these lines had been very expensive enterprises and that they were none too profitable. By 1906, one group, the Underground Electric Railways of London (UERL), was on the brink of financial disaster, from which it was saved only by agreeing to co-operate with some of the other underground railway companies. The scheme began by offering through booking between any two stations on the network, which simplified travel and helped to increase traffic. In 1908, the companies agreed to publicise themselves collectively as a single Underground system, though they remained financially independent. However, in 1907, a new manager of UERL had been appointed, a man called Albert Stanley, who was to prove a most remarkable and able entrepreneur. Under his direction UERL succeeded by 1913 in merging fully with most of the other Underground companies. However, the underground had been suffering severely from competition by the newly developed motor bus. Recognising the great advantages and profitability of the bus, in 1912 the UERL

Two Dennis buses of the P.C. Co., 1924. The rivalry of independent bus operators, their buses identified by different liveries, was a feature of London's transport in the 1920s.

bought up the largest of the bus companies, the London General Omnibus Company (LGOC), and all but one of the smaller companies. Thus by 1913, UERL controlled most of London's transport, with the exception of the tramways, most of which were run by local government authorities.

During the 1920s, further acquisitions and development increased the size and the scope of the operations of UERL, but a number of newly formed independent bus companies, as well as the continued independence of the Metropolitan Railway and of the local authority trams, prevented the combine from establishing a monopoly of London's transport. Lord Ashfield (as Stanley had been created in 1920) was convinced that a public transport business in London could be a commercial success only if it were a monopoly administered by a single management, with the entire fare revenue from all forms of public transport at its disposal. Because it proved impossible for the UERL to establish a monopoly by means of the customary commercial processes of takeovers and mergers, only government intervention could bring about what Ashfield believed to be necessary. Through a somewhat surprising alliance between Ashfield and Herbert Morrison, the Minister of Transport in the 1929 Labour Government, a scheme was agreed upon which would transfer the ownership and management of all London's buses, trams and railways (with the exception of those owned by the main line railways companies) to a new single authority. The result was the creation in 1933 of London Transport, under the control of the London Passenger Transport Board (LPTB), a body which was neither a nationalised industry, since it continued to have equity stockholders, nor a normal public company since the stockholders had no voting rights. Lord Ashfield was made chairman of the LPTB, and, since the UERL combine constituted by far the largest part of the new London Transport, its interests and former staff dominated the management. The LPTB continued in existence until 1948, when it was fully nationalised along with the rest of the rail and road services in Britain.

London Transport was created through the amalgamation of 165 companies that had once been separate and independent. Of these companies, 73 had already been merged with the UERL combine before 1933, but the remaining 92 had to be incorporated into London Transport in 1933.[*]

*F. Pick, 'Organisation of Transport with Special Reference to the London Passenger Transport Board', *Journal of the Royal Society of Arts*, vol.84, 1936, p.207; Barker and Robbins, p.283.

Historically, London Transport was therefore a conglomerate, which had to establish for itself a distinctive identity that would successfully contain all its disparate parts, a problem that had already faced the UERL combine in its takeover and merger activities. However, UERL had not troubled itself too much about using visible means to unify all its separate activities and there was nothing about the appearance of one of the LGOC's buses to indicate that it belonged to the same organisation as a District Railway train. Although some attempts were made in the 1920s to give the UERL combine a corporate identity, it was not until the formation of London Transport in 1933 that a comprehensive design policy was energetically pursued.

Design Unifies the System.

With hindsight, one can see two distinct reasons for London Transport's corporate design policy. One concerned internal organisation and labour relations; the other was to encourage people to travel more.

The task of integration faced by the LPTB in 1933 caused difficulties for several years, as it depended not only on managerial changes and technical reforms, such as the standardisation of equipment, but also on transferring employees' allegiance from former independent companies to the Board.[*] To avoid labour disputes, the Board took great trouble to unify the wage scales of its employees[*] and to remove all trace of the identity of the former independents, discarding their separate operating rules, schedules and liveries in favour of a uniform identity for London Transport.

*London Passenger Transport Board, *Fifth Annual Report*, London, 1938, para.10.

*LPTB, *Fifth Annual Report*, para.27. See also H.A. Clegg, *Labour Relations in London Transport*, Oxford, 1950, pp.17-18 and pp.32-36.

Bus conductor's winter uniform, 1933. When the various independent companies were merged with the LGOC in 1933, new uniform designs helped smooth the process of unification.

A strong design identity encouraged the staff to see themselves as the employees not of a once independent company that had been taken over but of a unified London Transport.

Encouraging more travel involved the transformation of the popular perception of public transport from a daily inconvenience into a comfortable experience and the means to a fuller and richer life. While faster journey times, better schedules and greater comfort might be appreciated by those who travelled regularly on particular routes, the problem was to tell those who did not about the improvements that were being made. Fast journeys are transient experiences that are quickly forgotten, but buildings, trains and buses are lasting and are the signs by which transport systems are known to people. If these things could be designed to be obviously rational, efficient, and co-ordinated, they would speak the same message about the services they provided. The attention given to the design of stations, buses, trains, publicity and even seemingly insignificant objects like bus stops and ticket machines all contributed to the image of a planned and co-ordinated system.

Most of the stations that were built on the various suburban extensions to the underground lines between 1923 and 1950 had certain features in common. Many of them were designed by the architect Charles Holden, who was responsible for the development

Ticket Hall, Northfields station, 1933. The clerestory lighting system extensively used by the architect, Charles Holden, for the new Underground stations served to light the stations internally by day, and advertise them externally by night.

Top deck interior of RT bus, 1939. The almost seamless finish was one of the most successful examples of London Transport's pre-war design policy.

of the formula that was used, with variations, in different places. Instead of the dark, cavernous interiors of the older stations, Holden designed the new stations where possible with a double-storey-height interior space, which was illuminated with natural light by clerestory windows. During the day, light from the windows filled the booking hall, while at night the interior lighting illuminated the windows so that they shone out into the darkness, beckoning to travellers. Inside the stations, the booking kiosks, ticket machines, station bookstalls, light fittings, passenger barriers and fire-fighting equipment were all designed to harmonise with each other. It was a principle enunciated by Pick and observed by Holden and the other architects employed by London Transport in the inter-war years that every element should bear a visual relation to everything else. The order and harmony of details was calculated to lead the passenger to think that nothing had been left to chance and that, by analogy, the system as a whole was designed and managed with the same thoroughness. The stations designed in the 1930s were the most concentrated examples of this philosophy, but the same principle was applied to the design of London Transport's other property, in particular its trains and buses. The first bus to be designed for the LPTB, the RT, introduced in 1939, became famous for its stylishness and its reliability. Although modelled on the STL bus designed for the LGOC and introduced in 1932, the RT greatly surpassed the earlier model in the quality of its detail. The structure was concealed beneath panels, every screw and bolt was hidden, and every angled joint rounded; the light bulbs were set into the ceiling to form a row of exactly hemispherical protrusions, the window winders were elegantly formed,

Underground Poster, 1924, designed by E. McKnight Kauffer. Underground posters used avant-garde art to stimulate off-peak travel.

and the upholstery was covered in fabrics of abstract patterns designed by *avant-garde* textile designers. A single object could hardly go further in conveying the impression of order, harmony, integrity and attention to detail than the RT bus.

The fact that the same design features were common to the Underground stations and to other buses was likely to contribute to the passenger's sense that London's transport was indeed a system. Although the stations built for the Underground extensions in the 1920s and 1930s were not all exactly the same, they had the same materials and finishes, and had the booking kiosks and barriers laid out on the same principles, giving passengers a sense of familiarity and recognition wherever they went. While many older stations remained unchanged, the effect of the new stations was to make it seem to the public that the Underground railways were no longer a disparate and unplanned agglomeration

THE COLNE RIVER AT UXBRIDGE BY TRAM

LGOC Poster, 1925, designed by E. McKnight Kauffer. Advertising was particularly directed at promoting leisure time travel to the countryside, on outlying routes, the least economic parts of the system.

*F. Pick, lecture at London School of Economics, 26th February 1934, *Transport World*, vol.75, 1934, pp.119-123, quoted in Barker and Robbins, p.288.

of lines but that they had become part of an orderly and centrally planned system.

As well as conveying the system's orderliness, design also communicated its modernity. The adoption of conspicuously modern design by London Transport in the 1930s was not motivated simply by Pick's liking for the style, but by the fact that it conformed to the image of London Transport as advanced and progressive. A characteristic of Pick's management was his extensive use of statistics and his belief that the management of a transport system was a scientific matter. Pick boasted that:

'The whole atmosphere in which the work is carried on and the whole attitude towards the circumstances of the problem have been changed. It is a noteworthy gain to have placed the study of traffic and the determination of its problems upon a scientific footing.'*

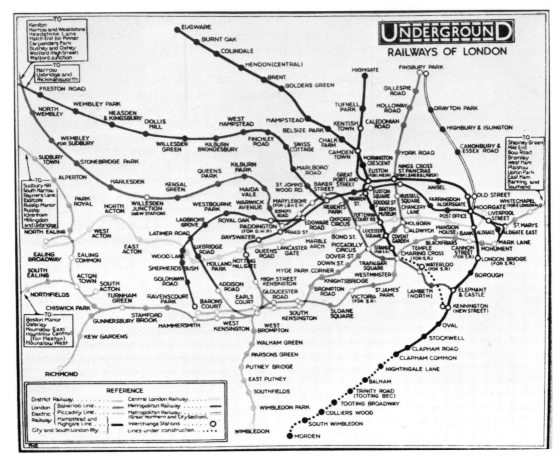

Underground Map, 1924. The stations are in their geographically correct positions.

The adoption of modern (and therefore scientific and functionalist) design was complementary to the management's ideals for the organisation, and it provided a way of telling the public about these otherwise invisible changes.

The earliest use of self-consciously 'modern' design in the Underground had appeared on the posters used to advertise the system. The use of pictorial posters to advertise travel was already established in Britain by the first years of the century, and the Underground was simply following the example of other railway companies when it started to advertise in the same way around 1906. However, during World War I, the Underground began to publish posters that made use of imagery and motifs from *avant-garde* art; posters designed, most notably by Edward McKnight Kauffer, to represent the benefits and joys of travel used artistic devices that would at the time have been quite unfamiliar to most people, and would have signified the underground electric railway as uncompromisingly modern.

As Christian Barman has written, the purpose of these posters was in 'persuading people to make journeys it had not occurred to them to make.'* However, because travel is only a means to an end, they did not advertise the services themselves, but they drew people's attention to things that they could do as a result of making a journey. The posters therefore publicised London's assets and attractions: places to visit, such as Hampton Court or Greenwich, London's West End shops, its theatres and cinemas and, above

*Barman, 1979, p.31.

all, the surrounding countryside. The advertisements aimed to encourage people to travel on the under-utilised parts of the network, the off-peak services, and the outer suburban routes. It is hard to say precisely how effective they were, though, by 1938, a considerable proportion of traffic was being generated by this kind of travel. It was estimated that one third of all journeys were for purposes other than travelling to work, and since almost all of these journeys took place outside the peak travel periods and so added nothing to the capital cost of providing the services, they represented an important part of London Transport's total revenue.*

*LPTB, *Fifth Annual Report*, para.80.

At the same time, the advertisements drew attention to the diversity of London and suggested the opportunities it offered, changing people's perceptions of the city from merely a place of dismal labour to a metropolis offering unlimited resources for every pursuit.

However, of all the means by which the UERL combine or London Transport changed people's ideas about the capital, none was more lasting and influential than the Underground map. So effective was this strikingly simple and legible map, introduced in 1931, that its representation of London has become one of the most widely accepted mental images for the city. Yet for all its clarity, it is highly misleading; unlike the previous maps, which represented the stations in their correct geographical positions, the new map not only reorganised the lines along horizontal, vertical or 45 degree axes, but also enlarged the distance between the stations in the central area, and reduced that between the stations in the outer area. The result was to make London look very much smaller than it actually is, as the outlying areas seem deceptively close to the centre. While this had the virtue of making the map very easy to read, it also, by making the distance between the suburbs and the centre look so small, induced people to undertake journeys they might otherwise have hesitated to make. Not only does the

Underground Map, 1931. The first of the new schematic maps, which enlarged the central area relative to the outer area.

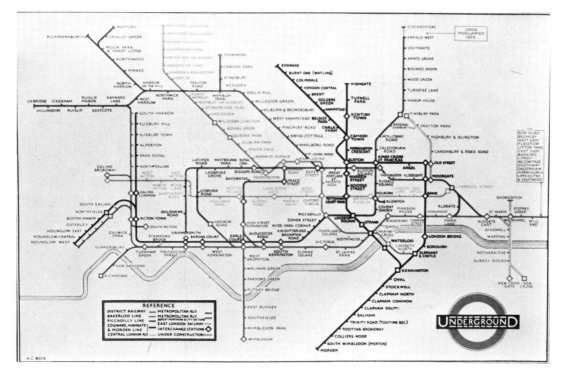

237

map distort the actual length of the journeys, making a trip from, say, Ruislip to Leytonstone seem very much less formidable than it actually is, but it also makes some of the other obstacles in such a journey seem considerably less significant than they really are. In particular, the arrangements for changing from one line to another are represented on the map by a standard symbol which obscures the true nature of the difficulties involved at some stations. Although improvements were gradually made in the connections between the lines as stations were rebuilt, the legacy of a system that originated as a series of separate lines run by independent companies continued, and still continues, to make itself felt. The difficulties involved in changing from, say, the Northern to the Circle line at Kings Cross, involving two escalators, staircases and some hundreds of yards walking, do not appear in their full enormity on the map. In giving the semblance of order and method to a series of railways that were not originally conceived as a system, the Underground map has been remarkably successful, at the cost of some deception. It is impossible to say to what extent London Transport's design policies excited people's appetite for travel, but there seems every reason to believe that by making travel seem easy, effortless and enjoyable, they contributed to the very substantial leisure traffic.

Before World War II, London Transport was in a more favourable position than it has since enjoyed; it had acquired monopoly powers, and the expansion of the suburbs created a growing demand for transport, while car ownership had not yet begun seriously to erode the traffic figures. During this period, considerable improvements were made to the quality of the services, which were unified within a system. But it was a system that no individual could perceive as a whole, for it was impossible to see more than one part of it at a time. It was highly desirable, though, that people should be aware of the changes, both for London Transport's public and political reputation, and for the sake of attracting passengers. The unified design policy, by identifying every object, bus stop, station sign, or train as belonging to the Board, and bearing a visible relation to every other piece of the Board's property, succeeded in communicating the presence of a system that was more than the sum of its parts.

The use of corporate design to consolidate the results of mergers and takeovers has become rather familiar in the last thirty years, but at the time when Pick first contemplated such a programme in the early 1930s, nothing as ambitious had ever been attempted. London Transport's use of design to establish its unity remains outstanding for its results. All too often, corporate identities have ended up looking like cheap off-the-peg suits that do not properly fit the organisation within; but London Transport's design identity was nothing if not a very high class piece of tailoring. Because so much attention was paid to making the design represent the aims of the organisation, and so much care was taken in fitting the identity to the design of each individual object, the result conveyed the impression of thoroughness and complete integration. Although today dilapidation, makeshift repairs and demoralisation among the staff have eroded the force of the vision, it is still occasionally possible, standing on a suburban Piccadilly Line platform, to glimpse how a progressive style applied consistently throughout the system created an organisation with which every employee could identify with pride.

11. Design, Designers and the Literature of Design

Compared to most works on the history of design, this book has referred very little to individual designers. Although the development of design as a specialised activity requiring particular skills was described in the first two chapters, this has been a book about design rather than about designers and their careers, ideas and theories. It is worth considering here why so many other books claim to be about design, but turn out to be concerned largely with the lives and works of individuals.

Much time and effort has been put into identifying often obscure people and researching their careers, although such knowledge adds relatively little to the significance of their designs. It seems odd that the biographies of individuals should be considered a satisfactory means of explaining an activity that is by nature social and not purely personal. The history of architecture and design is full of attempts to make sense of buildings and objects through the careers, ideas and theories of known designers, and the approach is to be found even in works that are not specifically biographies. For example, in *Pioneers of Modern Design*, which appeared in its revised form over thirty years ago and must be one of the most widely read books on design, Nikolaus Pevsner's main purpose was to establish a historical pedigree for Modern Movement architecture and design. However, his method was based on the assumption that design could be understood satisfactorily by examining its products with reference only to the careers and published statements of individual designers. Yet there seems no particular reason why the often obscure and long-winded statements made by architects and designers should provide a complete or even adequate account of the buildings or artefacts they design. If political economy consisted only of the study of the economy in the light of the statements made by politicians, the subject would indeed do little to increase our understanding of the world. Clearly, it would be foolish to dismiss designers' statements altogether, but we should not expect them to reveal all there is to know about design. After all, they themselves are not the cause of design having become such an important activity in modern society, and we should not assume that they hold any superior knowledge about the reasons for its importance.

The emphasis on the person of the designer to the exclusion of all other considerations has been particularly marked in the way that manufactured goods have been displayed in museums and exhibitions. For example, in 1979, the Arts Council of Great Britain mounted a large exhibition at the Hayward Gallery in London under the title 'Thirties' in which specimens of British art, architecture and design of the 1930s were displayed. Most of the artefacts on

*Arts Council of Great Britain, *Thirties, British Art and Design Before the War*, London, 1979.

*For a longer critique of the treatment of design in the 'Thirties' exhibition, see M. Swenarton, 'Should We Stop Exhibiting Design?', *London Journal*, vol.6, no.1, 1980, pp.112-115.

*Giedion, p.628.

show had evidently been selected for their conformity to a style believed to be that of the decade, and the information on the captions gave the name of the designer, the name of the manufacturer, the date of the design, and the name of the present owner. The only additional information provided in the catalogue was a short biography of every designer named.* From these pieces of information, the visitor to the exhibition would naturally conclude that what was most significant was who designed each object. The absence of all other information, such as the original price of the products displayed or the market for which they were intended, or how they were advertised, or some facts about the manufacturer, made it difficult for the public to see that the designs were not only expressions of the designers' creativity, but also embodied ideas and material constraints over which they had no control. As it was, the very existence of many of the objects was made to seem primarily due to the creative powers of the designers.*

A likely cause for the stress that Pevsner and others placed on individuals is the relative safety of this as a method compared to the perils encountered in trying to treat design in terms of what it does rather than who did it. The outstanding attempt to deal with design at a social rather than an individual level was *Mechanization Takes Command*, published in 1948, in which Siegfried Giedion tried to show how design was determined by certain extremely general dominating ideas. The problem about Giedion's approach was the status of these ideas: in his book they hang like vast clouds suspended above society, overshadowing everything beneath, a simile that is reinforced by his frequent references to ideas being 'in the air'. Where, though, did these 'ideas' come from? How could they, as Giedion implied, possibly have an existence independent of human consciousness and affect all people at any one time? For example, Giedion opened his account of the development of bathing and bathing apparatus in the nineteenth century with the statement, 'The nineteenth, that century which looked so much to other cultures, awakened to the idea of regeneration'.* How, though, could such an idea exist prior to the awakening of consciousness and outside people's heads? As a proposition, it seems most unlikely, but, as it can be neither proved nor disproved, it is also useless for the purposes of historical enquiry. Giedion's model of social consciousness cannot be counted among the many good points of *Mechanization Takes Command*, and this is a serious fault, for so much of the book's historical analysis relies on the general ideas that are said to determine design. Although Giedion's purpose, to investigate the relation between design and societies, was admirable, the shortcomings of his model of society and the defectiveness of his schema for relating ideas to materiality were all too obvious. The effect has been to deter others from following him in the pursuit of his original enquiry, and encouraging them to keep to the relative safety of studying the empirically verifiable connections between what designers think and what they do.

There have also been some more positive reasons why the identity and careers of designers have been researched so energetically. Designed objects have begun to be collectors' items and thus to hold some of the same status as works of art: signs of this were apparent at the 'Thirties' exhibition, where the display tickets identified the owners, many of whom were antique dealers. Products by recognised and acclaimed designers have attracted substantially

AEG Electric kettle, 1909, design by Peter Behrens, photographed in an antique shop in the 1970s. By virtue of being the work of a well-known designer, this product acquired a value it would not otherwise have had.

*Select Committee on the Copyright of Designs, Minutes of Evidence, *Parliamentary Papers*, 1840, vo.IV, paras 105, 388, 752, 755, 3616-18.

higher prices than anonymously designed objects. The electric kettles manufactured by the German firm of AEG at the beginning of this century, because they were designed by Peter Behrens, are now bought and sold at prices above those of other electric kettles of the same date, which must rarely realise more than their value as scrap. The creation of a market in designed goods, and one in which the works of known designers are more highly valued, provided one motive for establishing identities. The need for accurate attributions has long been recognised in the art market and partly explains why *catalogues raisonnés* and biographical monographs figure so large in art history, but the same process has only recently begun to be felt in the history of design.

This still does not explain why the activity of design has been treated as existing in the relationship between the mind of the designer and the form of the object designed. Of the two possible reasons for this tendency, the more superficial lies in the tendency of designers, when asked about design, to describe what they do. Designers who have written about their work have described the creative steps they have taken, their ideas about form, the constraints under which they have operated and their methods of working. Yet while such accounts are not meant to mislead, their effect is often to obscure the fact that design involves more than just the work done by designers and to create the fallacious impression that the designers themselves were solely responsible for the results. Although designers prepare designs, the responsibility for carrying them out rests with the entrepreneur; in the development of a manufactured article, it is normal for many preliminary designs to be prepared, from which one is chosen by the entrepreneur to be worked up for production.

This procedure was just as usual a century and a half ago as it is today, and, in every case, it has been the entrepreneur and not the designer who chose which design to put into production. When the calico print masters of Manchester in the 1830s sometimes had two or three thousand patterns prepared and printed perhaps five hundred*, they were acting in a way identical to the management of British Leyland when it rejected half a dozen different prototypes for the car which became known as the Mini Metro before approving the final design in 1978. The act of selecting the design to be manufactured is just as important a design decision as any performed by the designer, but it is one that he is not empowered to take himself, and that must be made by the entrepreneur. Many designers will admit that when they put up their first proposals, the entrepreneur chose a different design from the one they themselves favoured, and that it was the entrepreneur's choice and not their own on which development went ahead. It is the entrepreneur not the designer who decides which design most satisfactorily embodies the ideas necessary to the product's success, and which best fits the material conditions of production.

Because designers generally talk and write only about what they do themselves, design has come to be regarded as belonging entirely within their realm. This misunderstanding has reappeared in innumerable books and in the coverage of design in the press and on television. It has also, with more serious consequences, been taught in schools of design, where students are liable to acquire grandiose illusions about the nature of their skills, with the result that they become frustrated in their subsequent careers.

The second and more fundamental reason why so much has been made of what designers think and do has come out of an apparent paradox in their rôle. On the one hand, design is determined by ideas and material conditions over which designers have no control, yet, on the other hand, designs are the result of designers exercising their creative autonomy and originality. To put the paradox in the most extreme terms, how can designers be said to be in command of what they do, but at the same time merely be the agents of ideology, with no more power to determine the outcome of their work than the ant or worker bee? There is no answer to this question: it is a fact that both conditions invariably co-exist, however uncomfortably, in the work of design. The same apparent paradox occurs in all manifestations of culture: any painting, film, book or building contains ideas about the nature of the world, ideas which exist in other minds apart from that of the artist, author or designer, but which are mediated through his or her ability to conceive a form or means of representation. The paradox has been widely discussed, and there are have been numerous attempts to give a theoretical explanation.*

*For an introduction to the theoretical debates on the status of the artist in the production of culture, see Raymond Williams, *Marxism and Literature*, Oxford, 1977, and J. Wolff, *The Social Production of Art*, London, 1981.

For most designers, however, the solution to the problem lies not in theory, but in collusion with the myth of their own omnipotence and in wholly ignoring their rôle as agents of ideology. Although some designers do acknowledge that they are involved in the transmission of ideas over which they have no control and which they may not fully understand, it is more common to hear them describing their work as if they had overall power. Clearly, it is necessary for designers to believe, at least temporarily, in their own omnipotence in order for them to be able to create at all, but this does not mean, as they often assume, that everything they do is the result of their own conscious will and determination. The omnipotence is surely, like all such claims, a fantasy, but an attractive one: the myth of creative autonomy obliterates the problem of ideology as a determinant in design and releases designers from the uncomfortable prospect that they might be no more than actors in the theatre of history. That others, such as critics and historians, should have proved so attached to the myth is more surprising, and can only be explained by its accordance with the widespread assumption that, despite all evidence to the contrary, individuals are the masters of their own will and destiny.

Lucky Strike cigarette packet, 1940, before being redesigned prior to redesign by Raymond Loewy.

Lucky Strike cigarette packet, 1940, as redesigned by Raymond Loewy. The principal changes were to give the design a white ground, change the lettering and make both sides the same.

*Raymond Loewy, *Never Leave Well Enough Alone*, New York, 1951, chapter 12; and Raymond Loewy, *Industrial Design*, London and Boston, 1979, pp.218-219.

One example of a successful design will suffice to illustrate how easily a designer's own view of a job can make him appear omnipotent. The design of the Lucky Strike cigarette packet has not, to the best of my knowledge, been written about by anyone except the man who designed it, Raymond Loewy: it therefore provides a subject fresh for exegesis.* In 1940, American Tobacco decided for reasons which are not known that the packet in which their Lucky Strike cigarettes were sold needed to be redesigned. They took the job to Loewy, a Frenchman who had emigrated to the United States in 1919 and had established a successful industrial design practice in New York. The changes Loewy made to the Lucky Strike packet were in fact very minor, so minor that one wonders why he has drawn so much attention to them: he changed the ground colour of the pack from green to white, altered the lettering of the word 'cigarettes', and made both sides of the pack the same, where before only one side had borne the red target symbol. The new design was evidently judged a success by the manufacturers, as it has continued unchanged to the present.

In his autobiography, *Never Leave Well Enough Alone*, Loewy has described the characteristics that he thought made the design a winner. The elimination of the green simplified the printing, as well as dealing with the problem of the unpleasant smell given off by the green ink. The white ground made the brand symbol more conspicuous, and placing it on both sides made it always visible. The design was also meant to change the way people thought about the cigarettes, as Loewy described:

'. . . owing to its impeccable whiteness, the Lucky pack looks, and is, clean. It automatically denotes freshness of content and immaculate manufacturing.'*

*Loewy, 1951, p.148.

In the 1940s, of course, these signs did not serve the same purpose as they would now, since smoking was not then known to have any adverse effects upon health.

Loewy's account of the design and his reasons for its success made much of his own ingenuity and talent. Were we to accept this version and to take the single most important fact about the Lucky Strike packet as being that it was designed by Raymond Loewy, we should be following the routine of conventional histories of design. Yet for all its apparent credibility, there are large flaws in this version. While one cannot deny that skill and creativity went into the design, it seems hard to believe that only Loewy could have come up with the idea of a white cigarette packet, and once we admit the possibility that other designers could have achieved similar results, the case for attributing the design's success entirely to Loewy's personal creativity falls away. If there were others who could have produced it, some of the reasons for the design's success must have lain elsewhere than in the individuality of the designer. Suppose for a moment that we did not know who designed the packet. In this condition of ignorance, which is how we normally experience designs, we would have no choice in trying to understand the causes of the design's success but to consider what ideas it signified.

The potency of the Lucky Strike design might, for instance, be understood in terms of the problem perceived by manufacturers in the United States of creating a single national market out of the heterogeneous assortment of different races and nationalities that have become the country's citizens. The massive influx of immigrants to the United States in the late nineteenth and early twentieth centuries had created a population which strenuously wanted to be identified as American, but in which individuals were daily reminded by their tongues, diets and customs of their origins as, say, Chinese, Irish or Italian. They could identify themselves as Americans only if they had ideas of what Americanness was, and these ideas, to be acceptable to them, had to be compatible with their own ethnic or national identities. Great efforts were therefore made to establish an American ideal with which all races and creeds could identify. American culture is full of affirmations of what it means to be American, a characteristic that seems odd to non-Americans, but has been very important to the development and cohesion of the nation: Canada, with its militant French separatist movement, is a warning of the consequences of the failure to establish a satisfactory national identity. The ideas by which the American was distinguished seem vague and so extraordinarily general as to be very hard to question or refute. Their very flabbiness, however, is one of their great qualities, for it enables them to be shared by all Americans without undermining the self-image of any sub-group of Italians, Jews or Poles. The following description of the characteristics said to distinguish Americans is taken from a book published in 1933:

'What according to the American standard is rated relatively high? Formal education certainly goes on that list . . . Protection of health – everything promoting physical health, bodily vigour and longevity – is also undoubtedly on the list of values rated relatively high. This motive without question justifies any expenditure of time and money. Physical comfort and bodily cleanliness too, it may be alleged, rank relatively high in the American standard of living. "Americanisation", it is quite frankly said at times, means inculcation of our passion for hot water, large and numerous towels, soaps, baths and other cleansing agents. The physical comfort motive shows itself in the widespread systems of central heating, electric fans, refrigeration and easy chairs.'*

Hygiene, cleanliness and comfort are general, unspecific qualities with which no reasonable person, whether Lithuanian Jew or Japanese, could possibly disagree. So suitable have they proved that they have been seized upon avidly by all who wish to show that they are indeed Americans, creating in the process all sorts of curious effects – Americans pay more for white-shelled eggs than for brown, whereas the converse is true in Britain.

If hygiene and purity were important constituents of the idea of Americanness, so too was the belief in material prosperity and the abundance of commodities, which thus needed to be not only freely available, but also identifiably American. An industry based upon markets consisting of specific minority groups could be expected neither to achieve mass sales nor to promote the idea of prosperity with a specifically American basis. The problem, then, was to discover the characteristics that would make products identifiable as American. In this task, design was to provide some answers, one of which would appear to have been represented by the Lucky Strike packet.

Drawing upon the existing association between cleanliness and Americanness gave the Lucky Strike packet an American image, which ensured it a national market. A member of any ethnic group could identify Lucky Strike as an American cigarette by virtue of the pack's conspicuous cleanliness, and perhaps, by purchasing a packet, instantly feel part of American culture. Indeed, the packet was so recognisably American that, within a very short space of time, Lucky Strike became famous throughout the world as a symbol of the American way of life.

Unless we are to invent some fiction about the design being 'time-less' (a device much favoured by design historians for evading the problem of design's relation to society), we can suggest two distinct factors as lying behind the Lucky Strike packet's success within a particular society at a particular point in history. The ideas of cleanliness and Americanness signified by the design belonged in the minds of all Americans and cannot in any way be said to have been an invention of the designer. The other factor in the design's success was the way in which an association between the ideas of whiteness, cleanliness and America was set up by means of a single image. This image was the creation of the designer, and Loewy and his office certainly deserve credit for their skill in devising a form that conveyed the association so effectively.

No design works unless it embodies ideas that are held in common by the people for whom the object is intended. To represent design purely as the creative acts of individuals, as Nikolaus Pevsner did in *Pioneers of Modern Design*, temporarily enhances the importance of designers, but ultimately only degrades design by severing it from its part in the workings of society. This book has set out to show the ways in which design turns ideas about the world and social relations into the form of physical objects. Only by exploring this process and by shifting our attention away from the person of the designer can we properly comprehend what design is, and appreciate how important it has been in representing to us the ideas and beliefs through which we assimilate and adjust to the material facts of everyday life.

Bibliography

Adam, Robert & James *The Works in Architecture of Robert and James Adam*, 1778, vol.1.

Ames, K.L. 'Meaning in Artefacts: Hall Furnishings in Victorian America', *Journal of Interdisciplinary History*, vol.IX, no.1, 1978, pp.19-46.

Anderson, G. *Victorian Clerks*, Manchester, 1976.

Archer, L. Bruce 'Honest Styling' *Design*, no.108, 1957, pp.36-38.

Archer, L. Bruce 'Electric Food Mixers', *Design*, no.125, May 1959, pp.41-43.

Ariès, Philippe *Centuries of Childhood*, London, 1962.

Baines, E. *History of the Cotton Manufacture in Great Britain*, London, 1835.

Ballin, H.H. *The Organisation of Electricity Supply in Great Britain*, London, 1946.

Banham, Reyner 'Household Godjets' reprinted from *New Society* in *Arts in Society*, edited by P. Barker, London, 1977, pp.164-169.

Barker, Lady [M.A. Broome] *The Bedroom & the Boudoir*, London, 1878.

Barker, T.C. & Robbins, Michael *A History of London Transport*, vol.2, London, 1974.

Barman, Christian *The Man Who Built London Transport*, Newton Abbot, 1979.

Barman, Christian 'Frank Pick', Architectural Review, vol.XCI, 1942, pp.1-2.

Barnard, H. *School Architecture*, 5th edition, New York, 1854.

Barthes, Roland *Mythologies*, Paris, 1957; Englsh translation, London, 1972.

Bayley, Stephen *In Good Shape. Style in Industrial Products 1900 to 1960*, London, 1979.

Bell, Quentin *The Schools of Design*, London, 1963.

Belling, C.R. 'Electric Fires and Cookers', *Electrical Review*, vol.108, 19th June 1931, p.1048.

Benjamin, W. 'Paris – the Capital of the Nineteenth Century' in *Charles Baudelaire: a Lyric Poet in the Era of High Capitalism*, London, 1973, pp.155-176.

Best, R.D. *Design and be Damned* (unpublished typescript).

Bowley, A.L. & Stamp, J. *The National Income, 1924*, Oxford, 1927.

Branca, P. *Silent Sisterhood*, London, 1975.

Brandon, R. *Singer and the Sewing Machine, A Capitalist Romance*, London, 1977.

Braverman, H. *Labor and Monopoly Capital*, New York & London, 1974.

Briggs, A. *The Golden Age of Wireless*, London, 1965.

British Labour Statistics Historical Abstract, 1886-1968, Department of Employment, London, 1971.

Brown, Baldwin *Young Men and Maidens. A Pastoral for the Times*, London, 1871.

Bruyn Andrews, C. (ed.) *The Torrington Diaries*, 4 vols, London, 1934-1938.

Buck, A. 'The Dress of Domestic Servants in the Eighteenth Century' in *Strata of Society*, Proceedings of the Seventh Annual Conference of the Costume Society, London, 1974, pp.10-16.

Burdett, H.C. *Hospitals and Asylums of the World*, 4 vols, London, 1893.

Burgess, M.M. *Health*, London, 1914.

Burnett, J. (ed.) *Useful Toil*, London, 1974.

Butler, C.V. *Domestic Service, an Enquiry by the Women's Industrial Council*, London, 1916.

Calico Printers' Petition, Minutes of Evidence, *Parliamentary Papers*, 1806-07, vol.II.

Callen, Anthea *The Angel in the Studio*, London, 1979.

Census Reports, Great Britain, 1891 to 1931.

Chandler, Raymond *Farewell My Lovely*, Harmondsworth, 1949.

'Chats' about Electricity, Electrical Development Association pamphlet no.422, 1925.

Chew, V.K. *Talking Machines*, London, 1967.

Clapham, A.W. *English Romanesque Architecture after the Conquest*, Oxford, 1934.

Clegg, H.A. *Labour Relations in London Transport*, Oxford, 1950.

Cobbe, Frances Power 'The Final Cause of Woman' in *Woman's Work and Culture* edited by Josephine Butler, London, 1869.

Cook, C. *The House Beautiful, Essays on Beds and Tables, Stools and Candlesticks*, New York, 1878.

Cooper, Grace R. *The Sewing Machine, Its Invention and Development*, 2nd edition, Washington D.C., 1976.

Cooper, Nicholas *The Opulent Eye*, London, 1979.

Cooper, W.R. 'Domestic Electricity Supply (including Heating and Cooking) as Affected by Tariffs', *Journal of the Institution of Electrical Engineers*, vol.XLII, 1908-09, pp.26-48.

Corley, T.A.B. *Domestic Electrical Appliances*, London, 1966.

Coulson, Anthony J. *A Bibliography of Design in Britain 1851-1970*, London, 1979.

'Counsel to Designers of Woven Fabrics', *Journal of Design*, no.18, vol.III, August 1850, pp.179 ff.

Cowan, R. Schwartz 'The "Industrial Revolution" in the Home: Household Technology and Social Change in the Twentieth Century', *Technology and Culture*, vol.XVII, no.I, January 1976, pp.1-23.

Cowan, R. Schwartz 'Two washes in the morning and a bridge party at night: the American Housewife between the wars', *Women's Studies* vol.III, no.2, 1976, pp.147-172.

Crompton, R.E. 'The Cost of the Generation and Distribution of Electrical Energy', *Proceedings of the Institute of Civil Engineers*, vol.CVI, 1891, pp.2-28.

Crompton, R.E. 'President's Inaugural Address' *Journal of the Institution of Electrical Engineers*, vol.XXIV, 1895, pp.4-29.

Cunnington, C.W. & P. *Handbook of English Costume in the Nineteenth Century*, London, 1959.

Cunnington, P. *Costume of Household Servants*, London, 1974.

Curwen, A. 'Architectural Heating', *Electrical Review*, vol.114, 9th February 1934, pp.188 ff.

Daily Mail Ideal Home Book, 1955.

Davidoff, Leonore *The Best Circles*, London, 1973.

Davidoff, Leonore 'Mastered for Life: Servant and Wife in Victorian and Edwardian England', *Journal of Social History*, vol.7, no.4.

Davin, A. 'Imperialism and Motherhood' *History Workshop Journal*, no.5, Spring 1978, pp.9-65.

'Design Review, Braun', *Architectural Review*, vol.131, 1962.

Deslandres, Y. *Le costume, l'image de l'homme*, Paris, 1976.

De Wolfe, Elsie *The House in Good Taste*, New York, 1913.

Digest of United Kingdom Energy Statistics, United Kingdom Department of Energy, 1980.

Dodd, G. *The Textile Manufacturers of Great Britain*, London, 1844.

Douglas, Mary *Purity and Danger*, Harmondsworth, 1970.

Dreyfuss, Henry *Designing for People*, New York, 1955.

Duffy, F. & Cave, C. 'Bürolandschaft, an Appraisal' in *Planning Office Space*, edited by F. Duffy, C. Cave & J. Worthington, London, 1976.

Duffy, F. 'Bürolandschaft '58-'78', *Architectural Review* vol.CLXV, no.983, January 1979, pp.54-58.

Duffy, F. 'Office Building and Organisational Change', in *Buildings and Society*, edited by Anthony D. King, London, 1980.

Eastlake, Charles *Hints on Household Taste*, London, 1868.

Edis, Robert *Decoration and Furniture of Town Houses*, London, 1881.

Edis, Robert 'Internal Decoration' in *Our Homes and How to Make Them Healthy*, edited by S.F. Murphy, London, 1883, pp.309-364.

Edis, Robert 'Healthy Furniture and Decoration', *Health in the Dwelling*, vol.I of *International Health Exhibition Literature*, London, 1884, pp.287-365.

Edwards, H.R. *Competition and Monopoly in the British Soap Industry*, Oxford, 1962.

Ehrenreich, B. & English, D. *For Her Own Good, 150 Years of Advice to Women*, London, 1979.

Ellis, Mrs *The Daughters of England*, London, 1845.

Ellis, Mrs *The Mother's Mistake*, London, 1860, originally published in serial form in the *Family Friend*, new series, vol.III, 1854.

Evans, Joan *Monastic Life at Cluny 910-1157*, London, 1931.

Evans, Joan *The Romanesque Architecture of the Order of Cluny*, Cambridge, 1938.

Evans, R. *The Fabrication of Virtue*, Cambridge, 1982.

Ewing, E. *Dress and Undress*, London, 1978.

Farrer, K.E. (ed.) *The Letters of Josiah Wedgwood*, 2 vols, 1903.

Farrer, K.E. (ed.) *Correspondence of Josiah Wedgwood 1781-1794*, 1906.

'The Fashion of Furniture' *Cornhill Magazine*, vol.IX, March 1864, pp.337-349.

Ferranti, Dr S.Z., manuscript notebooks held by Ferranti Ltd, Holmwood, Lancs.

The Ferranti Fire publicity booklet, n.d.

Finer, A. & Savage, George (eds.) *The Selected Letters of Josiah Wedgwood*, London, 1965.

Floud, P. *English Printed Textiles 1720-1836*, Victoria & Albert Museum, London, 1960.

Flügel, J.C., *The Psychology of Clothes*, London, 1930.

Forty, Adrian 'Wireless Style: Symbolic Design and the English Radio Cabinet 1928-33' *Architectural Association Quarterly* vol.4., Spring 1972, pp.22-31.

Forty, Adrian 'The Electric Home', Unit 20 of Open University Course A305 *History of Architecture and Design 1890-1939*, Milton Keynes, 1975.

Forty, Adrian 'Lorenzo of the Underground', *London Journal*, vol.5, no.1, 1979, pp.113-119.

Forty, Adrian 'The Modern Hospital in England and France: the Social and Medical Uses of Architecture', in *Buildings and Society*, edited by Anthony D. King, London, 1980.

Frazer, Mrs J.G. [L. Grove] *First Aid to the Servantless*, Cambridge, 1913.

Frederick, Christine *Scientific Management in the Home: Household Engineering*, London, 1920.

Frederick, Christine 'How I Would Sell Vacuum Cleaners', *Electrician*, 30th September 1927, pp.396-397.

Freud, Sigmund *The Interpretation of Dreams*, 2 vols, Standard Edition of the Complete Works of Sigmund Freud, vols IV & V, London, 1955. First published, Vienna, 1900.

Freud, Sigmund & Breuer, Joseph *Studies in Hysteria*, Standard Edition of the Complete Works of Sigmund Freud, vol.II, London, 1955.

Galloway, L. *Office Management. Its Principles and Practice*, New York, 1919.

Galton, Francis *Inquiry into Human Faculty and its Development*, London, 1883.

Garrett, R.& A. *Suggestions for House Decoration*, London, 1879.

Gaskell, Elizabeth *Wives and Daughters*, London, 1866.

Gibbon, Edward *The History of the Decline and Fall of the Roman Empire*, 6 vols, London, 1776-1788.

Gibson, C.R. *Electricity as a Wizard*, London, 1929.

Giedion, Siegfried *Mechanization Takes Command*, New York, 1948.

Giedion, Siegfried 'Vacuum in the Home' *Technology Review*, January 1947, pp.157-160.

Gielgud, Val *British Radio Drama*, London, 1957.

Gilbert, C. *The Life and Work of Thomas Chippendale*, London, 1978.

Girouard, Mark *The Victorian Country House*, Oxford, 1971.

Girouard, Mark *Sweetness and Light*, Oxford, 1977.

Goldthorpe, J.H., Lockwood, D., Bechhofer, F., & Platt, J. *The Affluent Worker in the Class Structure*, Cambridge, 1969.

Gray, H. 'Electric Heating as Applied to Cooking Apparatus', *Journal of the Institution of Electrical Engineers*, vol.XLVII, 1911, pp.249-263.

Great Exhibition of 1851, Jury Reports, vol. IV, 'Supplementary Report on Design to Class XXX'.

Grossmith, George & Weedon *The Diary of a Nobody*, London, 1892.

Hamilton Ellis, C. *Railway Carriages in the British Isles from 1830 to 1914*,   London, 1965.

Handcock, H.W. & Dykes, A.H. 'The Present Aspect of Electric Lighting', *Journal of the Institution of Electrical Engineers*, vol.XLIV, 1909-10, pp.57-73.

Handlin, D.P. *The American Home*, Boston, 1979.

Hannah, L. *Electricity Before Nationalisation*, London, 1979.

'Happy Homes' in *Family Friend*, new series, vol.II, 1853.

Harmsworth's Household Encyclopaedia, vol.I, 1923.

Haweis, M.E. *The Art of Decoration*, London, 1881.

Heller, G. *"Propre en Ordre:" Habitation et vie domestique 1850-1930: l'exemple vaudois*, Lausanne, 1979.

Héricourt, Dr J. *L'Hygiène Moderne*, Paris, 1907.

The Home of Today, Daily Express Publications, London, n.d. [c.1935].

Honour, Hugh *Neo-Classicism*, Harmondsworth, 1968.

Hood, E. *Fighting Dirt, the World's Greatest Warfare. A Hygiene Reader*, London, 1916.

Hopkinson, James *Victorian Cabinet Maker*, edited by J.B. Goodman, London, 1968.

Houghton, W.E. *The Victorian Frame of Mind*, New Haven, 1957.

Jackson, Alan A. *Semi-Detached London*, London, 1973.

Jackson, Vincent E. *Modern Office Appliances*, London, 1936.

James, C.H. & Yerbury, F.R. *Modern English Houses & Interiors*, London, 1925.

John Flaxman R.A., catalogue of an exhibition at the Royal Academy of Arts, London, 1979.

Klingender, F.D. *Art and the Industrial Revolution*, revised edition, London, 1968.

Klingender, F.D. *The Conditions of Clerical Labour in Britain*, London, 1935.

Kron, J. & Slesin, S. *High Tech*, London, 1979.

Kusamitsu, T. 'Great Exhibitions before 1851', *History Workshop Journal*, no.9, Spring 1980, pp.70-89.

Kyrk, Hazel *Economic Problems of the Family*, New York, 1933.

Lancaster, Maud *Electric Cooking, Heating, Cleaning etc., being a Manual of Electricity in the Service of the Home*, London, 1914.

Landauer, W. 'Plastics', *Trend*, vol. 1, 1936, pp.75-91.

Le Corbusier *Towards a New Architecture*, trans. F. Etchells, London, 1927.

Lee, C.E. *Passenger Class Distinctions*, London, 1946.

Leffingwell, W.H. *The Office Appliance Manual*, 1926.

Leffingwell, W.H. *Office Management*, Chicago & New York, 1927.

Leffingwell, W.H. *Scientific Office Management*, Chicago, 1917.

Lockwood, D. *The Black Coated Worker*, London, 1958.

Loewy, Raymond *Industrial Design*, London and Boston, 1979.

Loewy, Raymond *Never Leave Well Enough Alone*, New York, 1951.

Loftie, W.J. *A Plea for Art in the Home*, London, 1879.

London Passenger Transport Board, *Fifth Annual Report*, London, 1938.

Loudon, J.C. *Encyclopaedia of Cottage, Farm and Villa Architecture*, London, 1833 and many later editions.

Mankowitz, Wolf *Wedgwood*, London, 1953.

Manser, J. 'New Thinking in Office Furniture', *Design*, no.236, 1968, pp.16-18.

Manual of Modern Business Equipment: Dictating Machines, 2nd edition, London, 1962.

Mark Rutherford's Deliverance [by William H. White], London, 1888 (first edition, 1885).

Marsh, C.W. *Recollections 1837-1910*, Chicago, 1910, quoted in Dewhurst, C.K., MacDowell, B., MacDowell, M. *Artists in Aprons*, New York, 1979.

Marx, Karl *Capital*, vol. I, Harmondsworth, 1976.

Maurice, F. 'National Health: A Soldier's Study', *Contemporary Review*, January 1903.

Mayes, L.J. *The History of Chairmaking in High Wycombe*, London, 1960.

Mayhew, Henry *London Labour and the London Poor*, 4 vols, London, 1860.

Mayhew, Henry 'Labour and the Poor, Letter LIX; Sawyers', *Morning Chronicle*, 4th July 1850, p.6.

Mayhew, Henry 'Fancy Cabinet Makers of London', *Morning Chronicle*, 8th August 1850.

Mayhew, Henry & Augustus, *The Greatest Plague in Life*, London, 1847.

Mayo, E. *The Human Problems of an Industrial Civilization*, New York, 1933.

McBride, T.M. *The Domestic Revolution*, London, 1976.

McKendrick, N., Brewer, J. and Plumb, J.H. *The Birth of Consumer Society. The Commercialization of Eighteenth Century England*, London, 1982.

McKendrick, N. 'Josiah Wedgwood: an Eighteenth Century Entrepreneur in Salesmanship and Marketing Techniques', *Economic History Review*, 2nd series, vol.XII, no.3, 1960, pp.408-433.

McKendrick, N. 'Josiah Wedgwood and Factory Discipline', *Historical Journal*, vol.IV, no.1, 1961, p.30-55.

McKendrick, N. 'Josiah Wedgwood and Thomas Bentley: an Inventor-Entrepreneur Partnership in the Industrial Revolution', *Transactions of the Royal Historical Society*, 5th series, vol.XIV, 1964, pp.1-34.

Meikle, Jeffrey *Twentieth Century Limited*, Philadelphia, 1979.

Merkle, Judith A. *Management and Ideology*, Berkeley, 1980.

Merrifield, Mrs *Dress as a Fine Art*, London, 1854.

Mitchell, B.R. & Jones, H.G. *Second Abstract of British Historical Statistics*, Cambridge, 1971.

Moll Weiss, Augusta *Les Ecoles Ménagères à L'Etranger et en France*, Paris, 1908.

Moll Weiss, Augusta *Le Livre du Foyer*, 2nd edition, Paris, 1912.

Morris, William, 'Art and its Producers', *Collected Works of William Morris*, vol.XXII, London, 1914.

Muggeridge, Malcolm *The Thirties*, London, 1940.

Mullin, S. 'Some Notes on an Activity', in *Planning Office Space*, edited by F. Duffy, C. Cave, & J. Worthington, London, 1976.

Murphy, S.F. (ed.) *Our Homes and How to Make Them Healthy*, 1883.

Nelson, J.E. quoted in discussion of W.A. Gillot, 'Domestic Load Building' *Journal of the Institution of Electrical Engineers*, vol.LXI, 1922-23, pp.197-213.

News of the World *Better Homes Book*, London, n.d. [c.1953].

Newton, S.M. *Health, Art and Reason*, London, 1974.

Nightingale, Florence *Notes on Hospitals*, London, 1859.

The Nursery Book, Heal & Co., n.d. [1914].

Oakley, A. *Housewife*, London, 1974.

Odham's Household Management Illustrated, n.d. [c.1950].

Olins, Wally *The Corporate Personality. An Inquiry into the Nature of Corporate Identity*, London, 1978.

Orrinsmith, Mrs *The Drawing Room*, London, 1978.

'Overseas Review', *Design*, no.104, August 1957, pp.43-46.

Packard, Vance *The Hidden Persuaders*, London, 1957.

Panton, J.E. *Suburban Residences and How to Circumvent Them*, London, 1896.

Papaneck, V. *Design for the Real World*, London, 1972.

Parker, Rozsika *The Subversive Stitch*, London, 1984.

Pattison, Mary S. *The Business of Home Management*, New York, 1915.

Pevsner, Nikolaus *An Enquiry into Industrial Art in England*, Cambridge, 1937.

Pevsner, Nikolaus *Pioneers of Modern Design*, Harmondsworth, 1960.

Pevsner, Nikolaus 'Patient Progress One: Frank Pick' in his *Studies in Art, Architecture and Design* vol.2, London, 1968, pp.190-209, (reprinted from *Architectural Review* vol.XCII, 1942.)

Phillips, R. Randal *The Servantless House*, London, 1920.

Pick, Frank 'Organisation of Transport with Special Reference to the London Passenger Transport Board', *Journal of the Royal Society of Arts*, vol.84, 1936.

Pile, J. (ed.) *Interiors Second Book of Offices*, New York, 1969.

Plumb, J.H. 'The New World of Children in Eighteenth Century England', *Past and Present*, no. 67, May 1975, pp.64-95.

Political and Economic Planning (PEP), *The Market for Household Appliances*, London, 1945.

Post, Emily *The Personality of a House*, New York, 1930.

Powell, Margaret *Below Stairs*, London, 1968.

Pringle, Sir John *Observations on Diseases of the Army in Camp and Garrison*, 2nd edition, London, 1753.

Ravenhill, A. 'Some Relations of Sanitary Science to Family Life and Individual Efficiency', *Household Administration*, edited by A. Ravenhill & C. Schiff, London, 1910.

Recreations of a Country Parson, London, 1861.

Reid, Margaret G. *Economics of Household Production*, New York, 1934.

Religious Worship in England and Wales, General Register Office, London, 1854.

'Report on the Domestic Servant Problem', Ministry of Reconstruction, Women's Advisory Committee, Cmd.67, *Parliamentary Papers*, 1919, vol.29.

'The Rise and Progress of Great Manufactories, by the Proprietors – Messrs. Hargreaves Calico Print Works at Broad Oak, Accrington', *Journal of Design*, no.13, vol.III, March 1850. pp.5-9.

Robson, E.R. *School Architecture* London, 1874.

Roethlisberger, F.J. & Dickson, W.J. *Management and the Worker*, Cambridge, Mass., 1943.

Routh, G. *Occupation and Pay in Great Britain 1906-60*, Cambridge, 1965.

Rowntree, Diana 'Desk and Chair: Basic Tools of Urban Life', *Design*, no.105, 1957, pp.16-21.

Royal Commission on Children's Employment, Second Report, *Parliamentary Papers*, 1864, vol.XXII.

Ruskin, John *Sesame and Lilies* (1865) in *Collected Works of John Ruskin*, edited by E.T. Cook & A. Wedderburn, vol.XVIII, London, 1905.

Ruskin, John 'The Awakening Conscience', letter to *The Times*, 25th May 1854, *Collected Works of John Ruskin*, edited by E.T. Cook & A. Wedderburn vol.XII, London, 1904, pp.333-335.

Russell, Gordon *Designer's Trade*, London, 1968.

Samuel, Raphael 'The Workshop of the World', *History Workshop Journal*, no.3, Spring 1977, pp.5-72.

Schaefer, Herwin *The Roots of Modern Design*, London, 1970.

School Board of London, City and Guilds of London Institute, and the Drapers' Committee, Joint Committee, 'Manual Training Classes: Theoretical Examination in Housewifery, 21 January 1893', SBL 1423, Greater London Council Records Office).

School Board for London, Final Report of the, 2nd edition, revised, London, 1904.

Schulze, J.W. *The American Office*, New York, 1913.

Scott, Walter D. *Increasing Human Efficiency in Business*, New York, 1911.

Select Committee on Arts and Manufactures, Minutes of Evidence, *Parliamentary Papers*, 1836, vol.IX.

Select Committee on the Copyright of Designs, Minutes of Evidence, *Parliamentary Papers*, 1840, vol.VI.

Select Committee on the Duties on Printed Cotton Goods, Minutes of Evidence, *Parliamentary Papers*, 1818, vol.III.

Senior, N.W. *et al. On the Improvement of Designs and Patterns, and Extension of Copyright*, London, 1841.

Sennett, R. *The Fall of Public Man*, Cambridge, 1977.

Sharp, D., Benton, T., & Cole, B.C. *PEL and Tubular Steel Furniture of the Thirties*, London, 1977.

Shephard, Jon M. *Automation and Alienation: A Study of Office and Factory Workers*, Cambridge, Mass., 1971.

Sherer, J. 'The Management of the Home', *Family Friend*, 5th series, vol.III, no.3, March 1867, pp.199-204.

Steadman, P. *The Evolution of Designs*, Cambridge, 1979.

Swenarton, M. 'Should We Stop Exhibiting Design?', *London Journal*, vol.6, no.1, 1980, pp.112-115.

Swenarton, M. 'Having a Bath', in *Leisure in the Twentieth Century*, Papers given at the Second Conference on Twentieth Century Design History, London, 1977, pp.92-99.

Tafuri, Manfredo *Architecture and Utopia*, Cambridge, Mass., 1979.

Tafuri, Manfredo 'Design and Technological Utopia' in *Italy, The New Domestic Landscape*, edited by E. Ambasz, New York, 1972, pp.388-404.

Tennent, J. Emerson *A Treatise on the Copyright of Designs for Printed Fabrics*, London, 1841.

Tenon, J.R. *Mémoires sur les Hôpitaux de Paris*, Paris, 1788.

Thirties, British Art and Design Before the War, Arts Council of Great Britain, catalogue of exhibition at the Hayward Gallery, London, 1979.

Thomas, J. *The Rise of the Staffordshire Potteries*, Bath, 1971.

Thompson, E.P. *The Making of the English Working Class*, Harmondsworth, 1968.

Thompson, E.P. & Yeo, E. (eds) *The Unknown Mayhew*, Harmondsworth, 1973.

Thompson, J.D. & Goldin, G. *The Hospital: a Social and Architectural History*, New Haven and London, 1975.

Tickner, L. 'Women and Trousers' in *Leisure in the Twentieth Century*, Papers at the Second Conference on Twentieth Century Design History, London, 1977, pp.56-68.

Tilley, E.Y. *Healthy Man Badge for Boy Scouts*, Glasgow, 1923.

Tooker, K.O. & Pierce, F.L. 'The Hoover One Fifty', *Modern Plastics*, vol.14, November 1936, pp.32-33.

The Torrington Diaries, edited by C. Bruyn Andrews, 4 vols, London, 1934-1938.

Towner, D. *Creamware*, London and Boston, 1978.

Turnbull, G. *A History of the Calico Printing Industry of Great Britain*, Altrincham, 1951.

Twentieth Century Cookery, Electrical Development Association publication no.297/1, c.1930.

Vanier, H. *La Mode et ses Métiers*, Paris, 1960.

Veblen, Thorstein *The Theory of the Leisure Class*, New York, 1899.

Wallis, G. 'Recent Progress in Design as Applied to Manufactures', *Journal of the Society of Arts*, no.173, vol.IV, 14th March 1856, pp.291-301.

Watkins, C., Harvey, W. & Senft, R. *Shelley Potteries*, London, 1980.

Watson, Rosamund Marriot *The Art of the House*, London, 1897.

Weatherill, L. *The Pottery Trade and North Staffordshire 1660-1760*, Manchester, 1971.

Whyte, A.G. *The All-Electric Age*, London, 1922.

Williams, Raymond *Marxism and Literature*, Oxford, 1977.

Wilmshurst, T.P. 'Commercial Aspects of Electric Cooking and Heating' *Journal of the Institution of Electrical Engineers* vol.LI, 1913, pp.180-194.

Wilson, Charles *The History of Unilever*, 2 vols, London, 1954.

Wilson, D.A. 'The Economic Development of the Electricity Supply Industry in Great Britain 1919-1939', Ph.D. thesis, University of Loughborough, 1976.

Wilson, G.B.L. 'Domestic Appliances' in *A History of Technology*, edited by T.I. Williams, vol.VII, part 2, chapter 47, Oxford, 1978.

Wilson, R.L. *Soap Through the Ages*, Port Sunlight, 1952.

Wilson, W. quoted in discussion of Parker Smith, 'The All Electric House', *Journal of the Institution of Electrical Engineers*, vol.LXIV, 1925-26.

Wolff, J. *The Social Production of Art*, London, 1981.

Woodforde, J. *The Diary of a Country Parson*, edited by J. Beresford, vol.V, London, 1931.

Wright, Gwendolyn *Building the Dream, A Social History of Housing in America*, New York, 1981.

Young, Arthur *A Six Months Tour through the North of England*, London, 1770.

Acknowledgements

Text quotations are acknowledged in margin notes throughout the book. Pictures are reproduced by courtesy of the following:

Architectural Press 103; 145 (photograph by Richard Bryant)
Army & Navy Stores 64a, 64b, 65a, 65b, 69b, 86b
B.T. Batsford Ltd 204a
Berec (Ever Ready) Ltd 206
Bodleian Library, Oxford (John Johnson Collection) 204c, 204d, 205a
Braun AG 219, 218b
British Library 33, 45, 122, 123a, 123b, 126, 127a, 127b, 129a, 129b, 129c, 129d, 130, 131a, 131b, 132b, 135b, 136b, 138a, 138b, 140, 153a, 156a, 158, 169, 177a, 178, 181, 186a, 186b, 187, 215
British Rail Western Region 164b, 165b
Bucks County Library (High Wycombe Museum) 89a, 89b, 90a, 90b
Cleveland Museum of Art, Gift of the John Huntingdon Art and Polytechnic Trust 15
Design Council 132a, 135c, 139, 148, 149, 151a, 151b, 153b, 154b, 211
Duffy, Eley, Giffone & Worthington, Architects 142, 146
From the EDA Archive, by permission of the Electricity Council 191, 195, 199b, 207
EMI Music Archives 136a
Ferranti Ltd 196c
Gladstone Museum, Stoke-on-Trent 35a, 35b
Greater London Council Photograph Library 161, 162
Ronald Goodearl 90a
Gordon Russell Ltd 152
The Guardian 141
Heal & Co. 201a, 201b
Hearst Magazines Inc. (from *Never Leave Well Enough Alone* by Raymond Loewy 242,243
Herman Miller Ltd 150
Hoover Ltd 180a, 180b
IBM Ltd 155a
Illustrated London News 95b
London Transport 224, 225a, 225b, 226a, 226b, 227, 228a, 228b, 229a, 229b, 230, 231, 232, 233, 234, 235, 236, 237
John Maltby Ltd 183b
Montgomery Ward & Co 62a, 62b, 124b
Museum of Childhood, Edinburgh 70b
National Monuments Record 101, 112, 113, 166
Norfolk County Library 145a
Olivetti Ltd 155b, 155c
Patent Office (BL Science Division) 92
Philips Electronic and Associated Industries Ltd 66a, 66b

Phoenix Assurance Co. 144
Public Records Office 80a, 80b, 81a, 81b
Pye Ltd 10
Royal Institute of British Architects Drawings Collection 22a
Science Museum, London – Crown Copyright 14, 77, 78, 79a, 79b, 95, 96b, 132d, 133, 134a, 134b, 153c, 154a, 183a, 188, 192, 200, 216
Sears, Roebuck and Co. 156b
Smithsonian Institution, Washington 96a, 98a, 98b, 98c
Southampton Art Gallery 164a, 165a
Stoke-on-Trent City Museum & Art Gallery 18, 31b
Sun Alliance & London Insurance Group 124a, 125
Tayler & Green Architects 119
Tate Gallery, London 67, 81c, 107
Thorn Domestic Appliances (Electrical) Ltd 218a, 218c
Twyfords Ltd 117, 167, 168
Ulster Folk and Transport Museum 99
University of London Library 170
Victoria & Albert Museum 19a, 19b, 30b, 40a, 46c, 48, 49, 50, 51a, 51b, 54, 75a, 75b, 76a, 76b, 97
Wandsworth Public Libraries 194
Trustees of the Wedgwood Museum, Josiah Wedgwood & Sons Ltd, Barlaston, Staffordshire 16a, 16b, 20a, 20b, 21, 22b, 24, 25a, 25b, 26a, 26b, 27a, 27b, 28a, 28b, 29, 30a, 30c, 31a, 32, 37, 38, 39
Duke of Westminster (Royal Academy photograph) 68

Index

Page numbers in italic refer to picture captions.